Quotation and Modern American Poetry

Quotation and Modern American Poetry

"'Imaginary Gardens with Real Toads'"

by *Elizabeth Gregory*

Rice University Press / Houston

Rice University Press
P.O. Box 1892
Houston, Texas 77251-1892

4 3 2 1

LIBRARY OF CONGRESS CATALOGING-IN-PUBLICATION DATA
Gregory, Elizabeth 1957–
Quotation and modern american poetry: imaginary gardens with real toads / Elizabeth Gregory. — 1st edition
p. cm.
Includes bibliographical references (p.) and index.
ISBN 0-89263-341-7
1. American poetry — 20th century — History and criticism. 2. Modernism (Literature) — United States. 3. Eliot, T. S. (Thomas Stearns), 1888–1965 — Knowledge — Literature. 4. Williams, William Carlos, 1883–1963 — Knowledge — Literature. 5. Moore, Marianne, 1887–1972 — Knowledge — Literature. 6. American poetry — European influences. 7. Influence (Literary, artistic, etc.). 8. Quotations in literature. I. Title.
PS310.M57G74 1995
811′ .5209 — dc20 95-32708
CIP

For my parents,
Jacqueline Theis Gregory
and John Charles Gregory, Jr.

Acknowledgments

It has been my privilege and pleasure to work with two excellent advisers, Guy Davenport and John Hollander, at the first and second stages of this project. In addition, Ayşe Agiş, Harriet Chessman, Ian Duncan, Romolo Gandolfo, Margaret Homans, Gudrun Klein, Mary Loeffelholz, Olga Malea, David Mikics, Sheila Murnaghan, Suzanne Raitt, Alison Rieke, Joel Sanders, Julia Saville, Jeanne Theis Whitaker, and Patricia C. Willis all offered important insights and encouragement. I thank them all.

For general support and necessary friendship during this project's process, I am happy to thank Mindy Gregory Boyer, Geneva Boyer, Patty Boyer, Susan Brind, Lydia Buechler, Jill Pollack Capuzzo, Gena Grant, Emilie Craven Gregory, W. Lawrence Hogue, Victoria Jones, Lydia Lehr, Sarah McCoubrey, Heloïse d'Ormesson, Jan Petrow, Carl Strehlke, and Patrick Peters. I am also grateful for the persistent helpfulness of the librarians at the Beinecke Rare Book and Manuscript Library and the Rosenbach Museum and Library. This book was completed with the assistance of generous grants from the National Endowment for the Humanities and the University of Houston Research Initiation Grant and Limited Grant in Aid of Research programs.

I am grateful to the National Poetry Foundation for permission to reprint the portion of chapter 4 that first appeared in *Marianne Moore: Woman and Poet*.

Grateful acknowledgment is given to New Directions Publishing Corporation for permission to quote from the following copyrighted works of William

Carlos Williams: *The Autobiography of William Carlos Williams.* Copyright © 1951 by William Carlos Williams. *The Collected Poems of William Carlos Williams: Volume I, 1909–1939.* Copyright 1938 by New Directions Publishing Corporation. Copyright © 1982, 1986 by William Eric Williams and Paul H. Williams. *Imaginations.* Copyright © 1970 by Florence H. Williams. *In the American Grain.* Copyright © 1933 by William Carlos Williams. *Paterson.* Copyright © 1946, 1948, 1949, 1951, 1958 by William Carlos Williams, 1963 by Florence Williams. Grateful acknowledgment is made to the Yale Collection of American Literature, Beinecke Rare Book and Manuscript Library, Yale University, for permission to quote from the manuscript of *Paterson.*

Excerpts from "Tradition and the Individual Talent" in *Selected Prose of T. S. Eliot*, copyright 1950 by Harcourt Brace & Company and renewed 1978 by Esme Valerie Eliot, are reprinted by permission of the publisher. Excerpts from *The Waste Land* and "Dans le Restaurant" in *Collected Poems, 1909–1962* by T. S. Eliot, copyright 1936 by Harcourt Brace & Company, copyright © 1964, 1963 by T. S. Eliot, are reprinted by permission of the publisher. Excerpt from "Philip Massinger" in *Selected Essays, 1917–1932* by T. S. Eliot, copyright 1950 by Harcourt Brace & Company and renewed 1978 by Esme Valerie Eliot, is reprinted by permission of the publisher. Grateful acknowledgment is also given to Faber and Faber Ltd. and to the Eliot Estate for permission to quote from these works.

Quotations from the poetry of Marianne Moore are reprinted with permission of Simon & Schuster, Inc. from *Collected Poems of Marianne Moore.* Copyright 1935 by Marianne Moore, renewed 1963 by Marianne Moore and T. S. Eliot. Quotations from *Selected Poems of Marianne Moore* are reprinted with permission of Simon & Schuster, Inc. Copyright 1935 by Marianne Moore, renewed 1963 by Marianne Moore and T. S. Eliot. Grateful acknowledgment is also made to Faber and Faber Ltd. for permission to quote from *The Complete Poems of Marianne Moore* and *Selected Poems by Marianne Moore.* Grateful acknowledgment is made to the Literary Estate of Marianne Moore for permission to quote from *Observations* and to both the Moore Estate and the Rosenbach Museum and Library for permission to quote from an unpublished draft of "Silence."

Table of Contents

Quotation and Modern American Poetry

Chapter One

Introduction

I sat upon the shore
Fishing, with the arid plain behind me
Shall I at least set my lands in order?
London Bridge is falling down falling down falling down
Poi s'ascose nel foco che gli affina
Quando fiam uti chelidon — O swallow swallow
Le Prince d'Aquitaine à la tour abolie
These fragments I have shored against my ruins
(T. S. Eliot, *The Waste Land*, lines 424–31)

Innumerable women, each like a flower.

But
only one man — like a city.

In regard to the poems I left with you; will you be so kind as to return them to me at my new address? And without bothering to comment upon them if you should find that embarrassing — for it was the human situation and not the literary one that motivated my phone call and visit. . . .

(William Carlos Williams, *Paterson* I, lines 39–45)

"Picking periwinkles from the cracks"
or killing prey with the concentric crushing rigor of the python,
it hovers forward "spider fashion
on its arms" misleadingly like lace;
its "ghostly pallor changing
to the green metallic tinge of an anemone-starred pool."
(Marianne Moore, "An Octopus," lines 9–14)

Up until the modernist moment, allusion was the preferred and time-honored mode of intertextual reference in poetry; quotations appeared only rarely. But as this chapter's epigraphs attest, quotation—exact repetition of words from pre-existent texts—proliferates in the work of American modernist poets. The passages cited above appropriate very different kinds of materials—T. S. Eliot imports a line each from a nursery rhyme, Dante's *Purgatorio*, an anonymous Latin poem, and a Nerval sonnet (the last three set in italics); William Carlos Williams includes part of a letter from a younger poet (set off in smaller type, as a block); and Marianne Moore borrows phrases from a Parks Commission handbook (set in quotation marks)[1]—and the poems differ greatly in argument and in affect. But their shared reliance on quotation suggests that they have as well a commonality of concerns—concerns that remain of interest in the postmodern world, where quotation, both poetic and nonpoetic, has become so common that it could serve as part of the definition of the postmodern. This book explores those common concerns and the range of responses to them, represented in the uses of quotation in the work of Eliot, Williams, and Moore.

The practice of poetic quotation came into vogue among the Americans writing in the early part of the twentieth century. Pound, Zukofsky, Williams, Moore, Eliot, Brown, and Crane all employ borrowed words meant to be recognized as such. This practice is striking because it seems initially to flout the expectation that poetry will make some gesture toward originality. Quotation as mode stands in opposition to the mode of allusive transformation that characterizes most poetry. Through reference to earlier works the allusive poet sets her or his work within the tradition of earlier poetry, but in altering what is borrowed suggests as well the possibility of reconstitution and redistribution of authority and some measure of originality among sequent generations. Refusal of quotation and of the submissiveness it suggests has long been a defining characteristic of the practice of poetry. But in spite of appearances, the decision to use the device does not signal any simple abandonment of claims to originality. American modernist quotation is instead the site of a complex of responses to a variety of related pressures: to find new means to express originality at a point when originality's familiar modes of expression were no longer adequate or appropriate; to represent the ambiguous cultural position these poets felt themselves in as Americans; and to define the sources of authority in the modernist world, in which traditional hierarchies of all kinds seemed to be disintegrating. Because changes in gender hierarchies, in themselves and as emblems of changes in wider hierarchic structures, were of particular concern to these poets, quotation use reflects a marked gender awareness. In negotiating their relation to authority, all three poets considered here return to the oedipal paradigm—attempting through their quotations either to reinforce the familiar hierarchial model of paternal authority (in Eliot's case), or to reimagine authority less hierarchically along lines specifically associated with the maternal (in the cases of Moore and to a lesser extent Williams).

The appeal of quotation to the American modernists was multiplex. In the first place, these poets seized upon quotation because its dialogic structure in itself raised the issues that engaged them. For instance, the use of old words in new works provided poets with a fitting forum for working through questions about the relation of the present to the past and of their American culture to that of the Old World. Secondly, in its parody of the more familiar poetic allusion, quotation raised questions about the possibility of originality, since it could be understood to embody specifically a failure of invention. At the same time, however, in its newness to poetry, quotation also represented in itself evidence of the very originality it questioned. In embodying at once both sides of a contradiction—investment in originality and a challenge to originality's value—quotation emblematizes the modernist position: a position which combines nostalgia with forward looking. Modernist quotation tropes the paradoxical historical situation of the poets who employ it.

A third structural attribute of quotation also made it attractive to the modernists. Quotation marks—or any means of suggesting that the words one utters are not one's own—can signal ironic intention as well as direct borrowing (and it can be argued that all quotations are in some measure ironic because the present speaker maintains a distance from the words she or he speaks). This attribute offers poets who quote the chance to represent their ambivalences toward the historical changes of their moment, allowing them to try on some positions without endorsing them definitely and to critique others indirectly (or even both at once).

Quotation's structural accommodations of modernist concerns are reinforced by historical factors of three kinds. The first of these is the history of quotation per se: the mode has a history of occurrences and effects in other, nonpoetic, texts, and these are alluded to and played upon when quotation enters poetry. The second is the historical context of modernism's development out of romanticism: quotation serves as a means of modernist response to romanticism both because it provides an apt forum for the exploration of issues of originality (romanticism's special province), and because poetic quotation did appear within romantic work, on a very limited scale, as an example of the unacceptable. The third of the historical factors is the simultaneous flourishing of quotation in art forms other than poetry during the modernist period, especially in collage art. Before moving on in the chapters that follow to explore quotation's operation in modernist poetry, we will look first at the historical background against which modernist quotation comes to significance. This account does not attempt a complete history of the ways in which quotation has been employed across time. Instead, it depicts those aspects of earlier quotation use in relation to which modernist uses of the device developed.[2]

Historical Background to Modernist Quotation as Mode

Though the borrowing of the words of others has a history that extends back at least as far as Plato, and no doubt an extensive prehistory as well, quotation was pivotally defined for modern use by Christian scriptural commentary and homily. The classical world turned to the sayings of wise men for advice in the form of sententiae or proverbs (for instance, Socrates' citations of Homer and Hesiod in *The Republic*),[3] and citations from the work of great poets provided examples in discussions of literary technique, but such uses were less weighty and less frequent than those of the Christians. In the Christian era, biblical quotations filled religious texts of all kinds, linking quotation and power in a new way. Like a fetish, each quoted biblical phrase was understood not as a fragment of the divine whole, but as a synecdochal manifestation of the unfragmentable Logos. "One can see thus," writes Antoine Compagnon, "the extraordinary value that Biblical citation would have in theological discourse, and how it would be radically different from the maxims of Aristotle or the sententiae of Quintilian. These latter had just the value of general expressions, of contingent judgments or of circumstantial propositions of which the appropriateness was established in each case by an epilogue. Biblical citations on the other hand were always offered as a necessary judgment, a universal proposition, an eternal truth."[4] Such citations create an intimate link between hierarchy and authority. The authority of Scripture is both differentiated from the lesser authority of the sermon and employed to enforce the authority of the priest and his sermon over that of his congregation and their views. Biblical quotations served so powerfully as guarantors of the authority of the texts they were cited within that even today quotations of all kinds inherit some of this association with indubitability.

At the same time that they embody authority through quotation, Christian religious texts of all kinds—sermons, commentaries, spiritual treatises, even the New Testament itself—demonstrate an attitude of submissiveness. They signal their authors' intention of internal, spiritual obedience through their refusal to exercise external, linguistic wilfulness.[5] This submissiveness complements the assertion of the authority of the sacred text. But reverence gives only part of the story. Some degree of irreverence inhabits every quotation, even the most apparently submissive, insofar as speech of any kind involves per se an assertion of the speaker's own authority. "The dream of the commentary or of the discourse of scriptural quotation," suggests Compagnon, "is always to be the first, to take the place of the first."[6] This aspect of quotation is most obvious in the frequent use of the device to signal irony or, more extremely, parody. Where authority represents both protection and threat, responses to it involve both reverence and rebelliousness, though in general one or the other receives greater emphasis. Quotation embodies this twofold response, both at a micro level within each individual quotation and at a macro level in the very different uses to which quotation is put.

Though it is with Christian commentary that quotation comes fully into its own, the device has a model in the Gospels themselves. The model demonstrates its irreverent aspect much more directly than its successors would be allowed to do, a difference called forth by the very different relation the Gospel writers have to the sacred text they inherit. The reverent and irreverent modes intersect in the books of the evangelists, who speak for a sharply disjunctive moment in which they radically alter the Judaic tradition even as they insist upon its continuance. Meaning both to set themselves within the tradition of the Old Testament (and so to borrow on its authority) and to deny that tradition through wholesale reinterpretation of its text, they quote and then reinterpret Old Testament sources. For instance, in the sermon on the mount, Jesus cites injunctions from the Old Testament and then reworks them:

> Ye have heard that it was said by them of old time, Thou shalt not kill; and whosoever shall kill shall be in danger of the judgment;
>
> But I say unto you, That whosoever is angry with his brother without a cause shall be in danger of the judgment . . .
>
> (Matthew, 5:21–22)[7]

In such instances, submissive form is combined with transformational effect.

The hybrid quality of these quotations is represented particularly clearly in the first line of the Gospel of John, which begins with a brief quotation that suggests submission to the original and certainly borrows on its authority ("In the beginning") and then moves quickly on to tell a very different story. (Where Genesis has "In the beginning God created the heaven and the earth," John has "In the beginning was the Word.")[8] At a literal level John's restatement corrects Genesis, arguing semantics, in such a way as to stress the textuality of the Old Testament (made of words) and thus to suggest its openness to (re-)interpretation such as his own. In its revision of the first phrase of Genesis, John's phrase "In the beginning was the Word" leaves us to infer "and the word was open to interpretation,"[9] and so gives license to his rereading of the Hebrew Bible. In borrowing this phrase about beginnings particularly, John suggests a new beginning in Christianity and so works to co-opt the authority of the Old Testament not only through quotation, which imports the world of the Old Testament into the world of the New Testament as a relic bearing its authority in its antiquity,[10] but also by co-opting the priority. In Genesis, the coincidence of the literal beginning of the Bible with the discussion of the beginning of the world suggests a naturalistic source to the book's claims to truth. It is counterintuitive that a writer who works to add himself to the *end* of this book should know more about the beginning than did his predecessors. John attempts to liberate the notion of priority from its naturalistic sense, and to make the last first a bit earlier than Jesus anticipated.[11]

The pattern upon which John the Evangelist's work depends, of building new work through revision of the work of a predecessor, John of Patmos goes on to forbid to Christians who might aim to succeed him ("And if any man shall add unto these things, God shall add unto him the plagues that are written in this book," Rev. 22:18). His closing of the Holy Book against succeeding prophets, as Michael closes the gates of Eden behind Adam and Eve, repeats explicitly the move implicit in the closing of the canon of the Hebrew Bible roughly two centuries before (150 BCE), a closing in protest against which the New Testament may be understood in part to have arisen. But if the New Testament did involve such a protest, it was not a protest made on the part of others as well: to those who follow him who would prophesy, those who would speak with an authority derived from the Christian God, John of Patmos leaves options even further limited than those that were left to John the Evangelist. While they would be Christians, those who follow him are left to the world of direct, submissive quotation and reaffirmative commentary.

And indeed, the Middle Ages were an era of quotation, wherein secular literature and with it allusion were suppressed, while sermons and religious treatises multiplied exuberantly, each one constructed around apposite scriptural citations.[12] The great commentators—Origen, Augustine, Jerome—quoted Scripture and in the process came themselves to have authority (*auctoritas*); they were even called authorities or, in a phrase that also tropes authorship, church fathers. Their commentaries explained away discrepancies between Old and New Testaments and filled in doctrinal gaps, and their word became law. As commentaries multiplied, instances of disagreement between authorities became frequent, opening the way to arguments for and against them, a process that eventually diminished the authority of commentary.[13] Patristic commentary came gradually to an end, but the explicatory model was not abandoned. It continued in sermons, though there the explications did not become law. And it continued in medieval studies of classical works.

The period from the time of Charlemagne to the late twelfth century saw a rise in interest in education and in the classics. Classical texts served as models for learning Latin, and familiarity bred enthusiasm for the texts in themselves. The medievals were not prepared, however, to admit un-Christian arguments, a refusal which led in the scholastic period (roughly the thirteenth and fourteenth centuries) to a medievalization of the ancients. What at first might seem un-Christian in ancient texts was read allegorically and revealed to have Christian purpose after all. And along with Christian methods of reading went Christian methods of quotation. The ancient texts (in their new, Christianized versions) were given the same sort of respect formerly accorded only to religious texts; scholarship retained the form of submission to outside authority while switching the source of that authority from the religious to the secular realm. In the medieval university, Aristotle became not the subject of or a guide to rational inquiry but an authority in himself, whose sayings were appealed to as law.

At the same time that reverent quotation flourished in both Christian and scholastic texts, parodic quotation also flourished, in opposition to the authoritative mode. Parodic quotation builds on the impulse to irreverence and undermines the same authority that reverent quotation means to invoke and continue; it equalizes where the other works hierarchize. Both effects are achieved through distanciation—an effect physically represented in the use of the quotation marks themselves, which set quoted words apart from others on the page. Importing words from elsewhere and stressing their foreignness creates a mood of awe in the religious context. In the parodic context the same methods are employed to create instead a critical distance: either the specific sayings or gestures of an individual or, more generally, a kind of discourse associated with a person or group of people is cited, marked as alien, and held up to ridicule. Though parody does not always involve quotation specifically, the genre as a whole can be understood as a form of quotation, carried out with varying degrees of literal-mindedness.

Without trying to account for the entire provenance of parodic quotation, we can note that a version of it did exist in classical work—Aristophanes' borrowings from Euripides in *The Frogs* give one famous example. Centos, patchwork poems made up of phrases taken from (generally well-known) pre-existent works, were one form of parody popular among both Christians and pagans of the premodern period of the Common Era. Centos of Virgil seem to have been fairly usual—both secular and sacred (one work, for instance, organizes phrases from Virgil into a description of events of the Old and New Testaments)[14]—as were biblical centos. Tertullian, in about 220 CE, says that all heresies are founded on scriptural centos, which set lines from the Bible in new contexts and make them mean differently (a clear representation of the dangers of interpretation).[15]

Extremely reverent and extremely parodic quotation, both characteristic of the Middle Ages, embody the two essential tendencies at work in quotation as we know it: the tendency to honor and invoke authority and the tendency to lay it low. Between them a broad spectrum of attitudes toward the speech of others stretches out, and it is in the more central range of the spectrum (that is, from positions that combine elements of reverence with elements of parody into a more ambiguous irony) that modernist work builds.

The arrival of the Renaissance, with its new emphasis on the secular and on literature, did not mean the disappearance of quotation. Renaissance scholarship built on scholasticism—continuing to quote, but in a new spirit that moved away from submission to the authority of earlier texts, away from glosses of their "true" meaning, toward active interpretation that sought no single or final reading, and toward parody of a subtle sort. But while Renaissance scholarship inquired much more into the reasoning behind classical arguments than had its predecessor, it also retained much of the submissive pattern of scholasticism, and this balance continues in modern scholars' use of quotation.

At the same time, the reverent purpose of scholastic quotation was parodied and reframed in the work of Montaigne, Erasmus, and others. Terence Cave demonstrates that, by arranging fragments of many texts within their own, without reference to the order in which they appeared originally or the relation that originally obtained between the texts, these writers got a very different effect from that achieved by scholarly or religious explication of an earlier text. Montaigne, who carried this rearrangement further than others, misquoting and disguising both quotes and sources, was the premier exemplar of this use. Instead of submitting the present work to the earlier one, the relation implicit in a gloss, Montaigne turned the technique of quotation on its head and stressed the role of the present author in the creation of the new whole. He thus emphasized the new over the old and suggested the possibility of modern originality (though of an attenuated sort). Drawing on the work of Compagnon, who similarly reads Renaissance quotation rhetoric as evidence of the transition navigated in this period between religious and secular structures of authority, Cave understands Montaigne to model for his readers the infinite possibilities for reinterpretation available at each reading of any text, without abandoning belief in the possibility of a single authoritative meaning inherent in each text (a belief congruent with the pious quotation operative in the religiously structured world from which they move away).[16] This kind of quotation shares qualities with allusion, but by maintaining its distinction from allusion Montaigne and his fellows emphasize the break in tradition that occurs at this point rather than suggesting a smooth continuity, as would allusion.[17]

It was during the Renaissance as well that quotation entered the field of "creative" work, via the development of the novel.[18] The gesture of including words borrowed from other sources was part of the novel from its inception, and this borrowing was frequently thematized. *Don Quixote*, for example, includes many borrowed lines, and these borrowings echo the novel's subject: a man so haunted by the books he has read that they take over his life; he becomes a kind of quotation of romance literature.[19] Bakhtin's characterization of the novel as a dialogue between genres or between the styles of speech of different classes can assist here. "Under conditions of the novel," he writes, "every direct word—epic, lyric, strictly dramatic—is to a greater or lesser degree made into an object, the word itself becomes a bounded image."[20] This same effect he describes also as "intonational quotation marks": the words are marked as borrowed—not from a specific earlier text but from the more general text of a particular kind of person's speech. The presence of several stylistic voices prohibits any one from having the last word; all are marked as relative, born of a specific place, time, and class. And no *one* in particular is endorsed; each is accorded its own authority. Importation of actual quotations into novels literalizes this figurative borrowing of kinds of speech. While the abundant quotations included in *Don Quixote*, and similarly in *Gargantua and Pantagruel*, work at the most obvious level as parodies of religious and scholarly quotation, they also bring to the surface the underlying dialogic dynamic.[21] And it is this principle of openness to multiple voices that continues to be represented when later novels not engaged in scholarly parody also quote freely.[22]

A third Renaissance development in the use of quotation came in the epigraph, which links novels and nonliterary texts alike with the medieval, Christian tradition of quotation. The habit of setting quotations in frontispieces arose in this period, combining medieval method with classical matter to new, peculiarly Renaissance effect. At the same time that it developed its own tradition, the epigraph led the way to another new genre developing simultaneously with the novel: that of advertisement. Although not quite literary in itself, this genre was closely linked to the world of books. Epigraphs were the first advertisements, born along with the printed book and part of the process of the commodification of literature. The epigraphs at the front of early books play on ideas of authority in two ways: they ask readers to submit to the authority of the text invoked and purchase the new book, which the old one is purported through the association to endorse, and they suggest that the new text will have the same value (and authority) that the old one is understood to have.

This model soon came to be widely applied: advertisements for products of all sorts used literary tags as endorsements. In a secular age literary texts were made to function as a reassuring link with old religious forms of authority. But instead of operating to guarantee the absolute stability of a social hierarchy, that authority was put to work endorsing an endless progression of "absolute" desires, for goods. The movement of the effects of religious quotation into this rather different realm has an effect almost of parody, but in this use parody is turned inside out in a way similar to that in which authority is turned inside out in ads. Certain of the effects of parody operate in advertisements—for instance, a democratizing effect is achieved in the equalization of all goods and all buyers. But the effect is not straightforward parody, since no real critical distance or attitude is desired. In the Renaissance, advertisement combined elements of reverent and parodic quotation to new effect.

The reliance of advertising on literary quotation grew with the industry. By the nineteenth century, writes Jennifer Wicke, literature had become "the primary thematic allusive system" used in American advertising. According to

Wicke, "[t]he literary spectrum from Mother Goose to Shakespeare formed a plenum along which advertisers plucked at will."[23] Literature developed an authority qua literature: Mother Goose could be invoked simply because she had an established place on the literary spectrum; the fact that hers was children's literature did not lessen its appeal. (In fact, Bella Landauer suggests that Mother Goose may have been popular precisely because advertisers think of consumers, particularly women consumers, as children.[24]) The voices of Shakespeare and Mother Goose might sit beside one another in separate ads on a single page, or they might conceivably be combined in a single ad. This kind of use of literary quotations literalized the bringing together of voices from all spheres that took place within the industrialized economy as a whole.

Although more recently advertisements have not drawn exclusively on literary authority to sell goods, the model has continued to be that of association with a quoted authority of some sort. Ads that "cite" famous paintings, for instance, are an obvious reiteration of the model. Sometimes the guises in which authority has appeared have looked quite different from the literary quotation model, but the principle remains. For instance, another kind of advertising endorsement, the testimonial from a satisfied customer, began to be prevalent early in the days of ads. These testimonials, like the classical tags, were written out and presented specifically as quotations, as they sometimes still are, though today they are more commonly "reenacted" on television. Sometimes the endorsing phrase, in quotation marks with a signature, is superimposed on the screen, making clear the connection to the old method of citation. In these ads the experience of ordinary citizens is offered as authority in place of that of some highly ranked source. This kind of valuation of ordinary experience works with the same mechanism as scriptural quotation, but it is here marked by changes introduced with the Reformation. In granting all souls the authority to interpret the Bible for themselves, the Reformation created those same souls as intimates of the Infinite, whose personal experience comes therefore into a new authority. Ads that draw on the experience of everyman tie into an authority just as hierarchically established as the ads that borrow the words of the well known, though that authority is routed through different channels.

From the Renaissance onward, quotation was part of the literary realm. It entered that realm directly via the novel and the epigraph and it operated in association with literature in advertisements that quoted literary texts. It did not, however, become acceptable in poetry during this period (the standard there still called for an imitation of the best features of your predecessors' work, but always with enough transformation of those models to mark the new work as your own and as authoritative therefore).[25] In fact, the prohibitions against quotation's appearance in poetry became much more explicit, especially around the period when novels and advertisements really began to proliferate, at the end of the eighteenth century in the romantic moment. When the modernists did eventually move to employ quotation in poetry, it was precisely its inadmissibility to poetry that they played upon, along with its associations with religion, with scholarship, with parody and irony, and with ads.

Quotation's Background in Romanticism

Modernist concern with issues of originality develops out of modernism's relation to romanticism, the romantics having invented the notion of originality as we know it. Thomas MacFarland suggests that in the face of the flood of equally valuable citizens engendered by the rise in democratic sympathies at the end of the eighteenth century, fictions of individual difference became necessary to prop up a diminishing sense of self-worth.[26] The romantic moment marks a point of rupture, represented most clearly by the French Revolution, a moment of breakdown of external hierarchies and a break with tradition and its society-bound structures of meaning. This change was experienced as both gain and loss. While the structural changes that resulted from this rupture relieved the too-great pressure of the constraints of tradition, they meant also a loss of stability and of authority structures and, as a consequence, a loss of the sense of stable meaning that proceeds therefrom. To fill this lack, the idea of the individual was reworked to include a new stability and authority of its own. Rather than deriving his or her identity through membership in a group with a clear place in the social order, the individual self was reconstituted as a "self"-contained version of the lost external hierarchy. The romantic self came to be understood to exist in an essential form that overruled all mitigating circumstances of nurture or accident. And the dominance of this creature was not restricted by the limits of any particular body. The claims of the abstract individual were superior in this schema to those of community and other competing interests. The stability of the structure of this new self could then allow for the production of a new sort of stable meaning, one fed with the authority of its own voice. For this new concept—of an authority emanating from within the individual—the new word "originality" was coined.[27] The word counters anxieties about temporal lateness—that is, great distance from the moment of origin and from the priority generally assumed to be necessary to claims to authority. Such anxieties, common to romanticism and other moments characterized by a deep awareness of history, were balanced by the assertion of an access to origins within each of us. Originality emerged as a preeminent value in the romantic period, coincident with and dependent upon the development of the modern notion of the individual self.

This romantic moment witnessed not an invention of the self per se, nor of originality, but a new privileging and recontextualizing of these concepts, which had long been present, in tension with socially defined roles and tradition, their counterparts.[28] The romantic moment seems to have differed from other moments in which originality had precedence over tradition (Augustan Rome and fifth-century Athens among them) in the extent to which it repressed awareness of the role of tradition.[29] Though the romantics did not invent originality in any absolute sense, the romantic version of the concept is the legacy with which the moderns struggled to come to terms.

While the development of the romantic concept of originality was an extremely attractive and successful handling of the problems of locating authority in a secular, democratic world, it created immediate problems for those who followed. When originality no longer seemed new, it had to go underground and find new forms. We can recognize such a rerouted originality in the moody nostalgic posture of much of Victorian art and culture, a swerve (the appropriately Bloomian term) from the prima facie, self-declaring originality of the romantics. This swerve maintained an investment in newness for the Victorians (recorded in their mourning of its loss), while not merely repeating the variety of newness associated with their impressive precursors. At the same time, it introduced a variation on the romantic model insofar as it embodied a movement away from the exclusive valuation of the new, since these self-admittedly belated poems claimed value for themslves in their very existence.

The modernists accomplished the same sort of swerve in rejecting the nostalgic attitude of the Victorians. As a consequence of its move away from familiar methods, the apparent unoriginality of modernist quotation represents in itself a kind of (attenuated) originality, and as such a continuation of the romantic idea. But the modern moment cannot be defined merely as a late romantic moment, in which a basic romantic pattern was reworked in a new fabric; during the interval the pattern changed. In the time between the two periods, the notion of the autonomous self was debilitated, on the one hand by the work of nineteenth-century science (led by Darwin and culminating with Freud), and on the other by the changed social context. This change replaced the environment of bourgeois liberalism, in which the individual could claim to produce his or her own desires, with one in which the individual is seen to be produced, along with his or her desires, by the machinery of consumer culture. Where the modern moment maintained some connection with the romantic moment, through an insistent if deluded myth of the continuation of the stable self as a bulwark against the encroaching dissolution of order, modernists had before them a great deal of evidence against the existence of such a self, and therefore against the possibilities of originality. While the side of the modernist awareness that remains linked to its romantic ancestry emerges in those aspects of the poetry that assert an originality, the side that breaks with that ancestry emerges when the poetry works to question or make moot the possibility of originality.[30] When modernist poets quote, the two sides emerge at once on the same site.

The site in which the partnership between originality and the romantic ego developed (and with which it continues to be associated) was precisely the romantic poem, in which an individual voice reflects upon himself (most paradigmatically) and, in other variations, upon the sense of that self's relation to the rest of the world. This pattern develops on the traditional understanding of the poem as the province of an individual, visionary speaker, and is defined more sharply in this period through contrast with the novel, which accommodates a variety of voices whose complex relation can mirror the complexity of the society at large.

The romantic hypervaluation of the individual can be read as an extension of the development of the concept of imagination in the sixteenth and seventeenth centuries. John Guillory charts the progress, from the Renaissance through the Protestant Reformation, of the demythization of poetic inspiration—the replacement of models of sacred vision, whose source is divine and external, with models of secular imagination, whose source is the poet's own mind. He locates in Spenser and especially in Milton a complex rejection of patterns of secular imagination then coming to prominence, a rejection which nonetheless draws strength from what it rejects: "The poetic fantasy [imagination] is under repression in Milton (to a lesser extent, in Spenser also) because it means usurpation to him, the intervention of the human into the divinely originated process of mediation. At the same time, however, this usurpation is very deeply desired, because it is the means by which every poet makes his origin, his place of beginning." To accommodate both needs, they redirect the act of usurpation, and usurp the usurpers of the sacred: "The authority both poets felt they had to displace was the *secular itself*, or the established authority of Renaissance literature. So Spenser displaced secular romance into sacred quest . . . and Milton displaced Shakespearean drama into dramatic narratives of Protestant eschatology."[31]

But within this complex dynamic, such displacement includes its reverse. Thus, while *Paradise Lost* reiterates a biblical story and so affirms the sacred, it also involves a secular takeover of the sacred story of origins—an authoritative maneuver in itself. Milton retells and expands on the Genesis story, almost entirely in his own words. Only very occasionally does he employ direct biblical quotations, and these borrowings consistently draw on biblical authority without bowing to it. The first such borrowing comes in line 9 of book 1, where Milton repeats the words "In the beginning." Milton cites the same line John does, and, like John, he transforms the line as he re-employs it. By setting his borrowing in line 9 rather than line 1, Milton at once acknowledges the importance of these words and gives priority to his own words (in lines 1 through 8).

A similar pattern operates in two borrowings in book 12, which are incorporated into the angel Michael's forecast of things to come after the expulsion from Eden. Of Nimrod Michael tells us "A mighty hunter thence he shall be styled / Before the Lord" (lines 33–35),[32] and Noah's curse on Ham's son Canaan is predicted: "witness the irreverent son / Of him who built the ark, who for the shame / Done to his father, heard this heavy curse, / *Servant of servants*, on his vicious race" (lines 101–104).[33] Both these quotations are made to anticipate their biblical antecedents. The borrowings operate less as direct conduits of sacred authority than as familiar phrases that suggest a seamless segue between the biblical source and Milton's poem.

In the creation scene, where the pressure of Scripture's specific formulations is perhaps most great, Milton generally takes pains to avoid quotation by altering a phrase just enough to make it his own. Thus we get "Again, God said, Let there be firmament / Amid the waters, and let it divide / The waters from the waters: and God made / The firmament, expanse of liquid, pure, / Transparent, elemental air, diffused, / In circuit to the uttermost convex / Of this great round" (lines 261–67)[34] and "Let us now make man in our image, man / In our similitude, and let them rule / Over the fish and fowl of sea and air, / Beast of the field, and over all the earth, / And every creeping thing that creeps the ground" (lines 519–23).[35] The pressure in this scene is given in to, however, and thus relieved, by one particularly straightforward borrowing. Even here Milton softens the rhythm of the phrase as he incorporates it, so that: "And

God said, Let there be light: and there was light" (Gen. 1:3) becomes "Let there be light, said God, and forthwith light / Ethereal, first of things, quintessence pure, / Sprung from the deep" (book 7, lines 243–45). The authoritative caesura of the biblical version is made much less imposing in Milton's version, and the change represents the assertion of Milton's authority on the biblical text that characterizes the poem as a whole.

The ratio of sacred to secular power, already under great stress in Milton's day, is reversed in the work of the romantics. Noting that Wordsworth experiences his own soul as other in much the same way that Milton experiences the mystery of the divine will as other, and that in both cases it is the very otherness that supplies authority, Guillory reads Wordsworth's valuation of the powers of his own mind as an introjection of sacred authority.[36] Milton and Wordsworth stand at opposing thresholds of a segment of time that lets out on Milton's side onto a precedent in which the sacred element had played the larger though diminishing part and on Wordsworth's side onto a succedent in which the secular element played the larger and enlarging role. Where Milton takes strength from the developing power of secular imagination to fuel his assertion of the power of sacred vision, Wordsworth takes strength from the waning power of sacred vision to fuel his assertion of the power of imagination. The transformation of sources of authority in Milton's day is marked in the coming to currency of the word *imagination*, where before *inspiration* alone had had value.[37] The transformation in the understanding of the source of authority that occurs between Milton and Wordsworth is marked by the emergence of the new word *originality*.

In the context of this understanding that romantic originality employs aspects of the sacred to effect its own takeover of the role of that same sacred, it makes sense that while there are almost no instances of romantic quotation (since as a mode of religious submission, quotation would seem to be originality's antithesis), a few do occur, and these are pivotal. We will consider here two such instances, from Coleridge's "The Nightingale" and from the Prospectus to Wordsworth's *The Excursion*, both of which refute the claims to superiority of earlier authority (either by directly denying the statement of the quotation or by indirectly impugning it), while betraying nonetheless a good deal of anxiety about this refutation. In both cases, that authority is represented in a line from Milton.

When a line from "Il Penseroso" enters Coleridge's poem, he speaks against it directly:

And hark! the Nightingale begins its song,
"Most musical, most melancholy" bird!
A melancholy bird? Oh! idle thought!
In Nature there is nothing melancholy.[38]
(lines 12–15)

The poem continues responding to Milton's "mischaracterization" of the nightingale for the next thirty-four lines, complaining first of the strong influence Milton continues to have on young poets and their readers. Obedient to Milton's wrong teaching, they continue to associate nightingales and, by analogy, all of nature with melancholy and so miss its real pleasures, both in their experiences of it and in their poetic descriptions. This poet, however, claims that he (along with both William and Dorothy Wordsworth) is free of that influence:

My Friend, and thou, our Sister! we have learnt
A different lore: we may not thus profane
Nature's sweet voices, always full of love
And joyance! 'Tis the merry Nightingale . . .
(lines 40–43)

Coleridge goes on to assert that he can turn the tide of Milton's strong influence and teach his son to love the nightingale's song so that "with the night / He may associate joy" (lines 108–9).[39] However, we know that the father still associates joy with day (and therefore melancholy with night, the nightingale, and nature), in spite of his claims to having overcome that understanding, when he describes the nightingales "Stirring the air with such a harmony, / That should you close your eyes, you might almost / Forget it was not day!" (lines 62–64).

Wordsworth's quotation of Milton is, importantly, not exact, but he sets his slightly altered phrase in quotation marks and follows it with pointed reference to *Paradise Lost:*

I sing: —"fit audience let me find though few!"
So prayed, more gaining than he asked, the Bard—
In holiest mood. Urania, I shall need
Thy guidance, or a greater Muse, if such
Descend to earth or dwell in highest heaven![40]
(lines 23–27)

For Wordsworth, the quotation represents a challenge to his own assertion of authority, which he then goes on to claim to be sure about meeting and even exceeding, though the fact of needing to make the claim puts that sureness immediately in question.

For both Coleridge and Wordsworth, the anxiety over this presumption of authority has (at least) two sources. One of these sources is specifically poetic (and Milton's line stands in here both for earlier poets in general and for his own poetry in particular). This anxiety brings the terms of the romantic revision of the notion of originality to bear on their own readings of their predecessors, who it is feared may prove more "original," in the new, romantic sense, retroactively. Milton's poetry is especially likely to demonstrate such an anachronistic power. If he did not accomplish the positing of secular originality achieved by Coleridge and Wordsworth, Milton at least was part of the beginning of the process, and so lies closer to the origin of romantic originality per se.

A second and related source of the anxiety betrayed in these quotations springs from the affront to the notion of the sacred that the doctrine of romantic originality involves. The quotation itself in its formal aspect, apart from such particularities as its author and its statement, alludes to the earlier sacred context in which quotations are the norm and so is present in the poem as a kind of icon, almost a religious object. The transformation of the quotation that then occurs refutes not just the statement of the quotation, but its range of sacred associations as well. In Coleridge's poem, just as the denials in the explicit argument do not cover the underlying misgivings completely, so the argument promulgated through the treatment of the quotation runs into difficulty. The presence of the line from Milton speaking so clearly of and for itself, in spite of the refutation that follows, works to undermine Coleridge's argument against the sacred mode (the mode in which quotation is appropriate) and for the mode of secular originality. Wordsworth suggests the same process of transformation more successfully in the Prospectus by conflating the two steps, using the quotation marks but altering the line he sets within them.[41]

If the English romantics worked against historical evidence to assert their own priority, their American contemporaries added to this historical burden the additional one of cultural secondariness. As was to be the case with their modernist progeny, the American transcendentalists were brought, by the undeniable fact of their country's remove from direct contact with the sources of Western authority, to try to come to terms with their lack of primacy and to recuperate it as value in itself, rather than attempt (merely) to repress it.

In his essay "Quotation and Originality" (1835), Emerson, who quotes extensively throughout his prose work, reflects upon the relation and importance of the two modes in his title. Incorporating the romantic internalization of authority into his own schema, Emerson accepts originality as value. In his work, quotation operates not so much as a challenge to originality's authority (though his frequent borrowings from Herbert suggest that for him the mode still retains strong associations with the religious). Instead, it represents the position of American culture, which knew itself as a kind of decontextualized quotation of the earlier society, and serves him as a mode of self-examination.

Defining quotation much more loosely than I have (including under that rubric not just word-for-word borrowings but recycled ideas set in new phrases as well), Emerson remarks on the world's scarcity of new thoughts and concludes that quotation is inevitable: "Our debt to tradition through reading and conversation is so massive, our protest or private addition so rare and insignificant, — and this commonly on the ground of other reading or hearing, — that, in a large sense, one would say there is no pure originality. All minds quote. . . . By necessity, by proclivity, and by delight, we all quote."[42] Deemphasizing the particular virulence of American indebtedness by stressing the extent to which all cultures are indebted, Emerson then goes on (in an early version of Eliot's argument in "Tradition and the Individual Talent") to insist that quotation and originality are not mutually exclusive, that the genius for arrangement of inherited materials is all that has ever been the stuff of originality:

> But there remains the indefeasible persistency of the individual to be himself. . . . He must draw the elements into him for food, and, if they be granite and silex, will prefer them cooked by sun and rain, by time and art, to his hand. But, however received, these elements pass into the substance of his constitution, will be assimilated, and tend always to form, not a partisan, but a possessor of truth. To all that can be said of the preponderance of the Past, the single word Genius is a sufficient reply. The divine resides in the new. The divine never quotes, but is, and creates. (191)

Emerson gives "quote" here a sense different from that which he gives it in the passage cited just above. Building on the argument that one cannot help but quote (that is, borrow words or ideas), he goes on to hold that one may still refrain from "quoting" (that is, writing work indebted entirely to earlier work).

The argument implicit here for an identity of quotation and originality (one may quote and yet be original) is literalized and expanded upon in the poetry of Emerson's modernist progeny. Where Emerson deals with a sense of cultural secondariness, his modernist heirs cope with a still further increased sense of secondariness, both cultural and temporal. In the eyes of the American making the comparison, the European past, modeling originality as value, implies the secondariness of American modernist work on both counts—its Americanness and its modernity. Primary place in this model goes to the more original work (closer, that is, to the point of origin).[43] While all moderns deal with a sense of secondariness, American moderns, aware of the dependence of their culture on other (particularly European) cultures, deal with a doubled portion. Given this, the familiar reading of modernists as belated romantics might be inverted so that romantics are read as modernists manqué—without the full awareness of their secondariness, though such secondariness is implicit in the romantic position.[44]

The sense of temporal secondariness that sprang from comparison of the modernists' own position with that of the romantics was furthered by the perception common in that era that it was a period of transition from a hierarchically structured world of clearly apportioned values toward a less hierarchic world, where values were relative rather than absolute. This perception arose in response to a coincident set of broad changes that included such diverse shifts in the status quo as the beginnings of the breakdown of the colonial system, the collapse of morale attendant on World War I, the advances of both workers' and women's movements, the psychoanalytic attenuation of the notion of the autonomous self, and the threat to distinctions between "high" and "low" art introduced by the widespread reproduction of images of both sorts. Such changes taken together, though apparently not directly related, reinforced the impression of increasing relativism that each alone suggested. Loss of hierarchies was associated with loss of authority, since hierarchy was the structure within which authority in its familiar forms functioned. And loss of authority—with its connotations of access to an empowering source or author—was linked also to loss of originality. Those who perceived such changes as loss (Spengler, for instance, read the network of relativizations as the sure sign of the West's decline) took them as further signs of the secondariness of the modern moment and longed nostalgically for a return to what were perceived as more value-filled and orderly systems. Those who stood to gain by the changes tended, conversely, to welcome the new possibilities offered in the apparently less strictly structured present.

These disparate reactions are reflected in the work of the American modernists, who responded to their sense of secondariness along two lines: some by reaffirming hierarchy but denying any basis for *their* being ranked secondary; others by denying the relevance of the hierarchies and reinterpreting the secondary as valuable. Such reinterpretation works within a relativist scheme that values alterity per se rather than condemning it. This variation in response is reflected among American modernist poets in the manner in which they employ quotation. In their variety, Eliot, Williams, and Moore represent a spectrum of American modernist positions.[45] While other modernists also employed quotation, the range is charted in these three. This range expresses a conflict at the heart of much twentieth-century work, which tends to endorse relative values and at the same time to draw back from them.

Gender plays a complex part in this dynamic. On the one hand, the gender of individuals seems to have affected their positions on hierarchy—with women having an interest in its upset and men having an interest in maintaining the status quo.[46] We will see this split exemplified in the cases of Moore and Eliot: she steadily questions the impositions of hierarchy, while he at once insists on hierarchy's necessity and denies the basis for his work's being ranked secondary (that basis being, its Americanness—and this view carries into Eliot's personal life, most visibly in his renunciation of American citizenship).[47] On the other hand, gender alone did not determine one's position on hierarchy absolutely. The (secondary) American position was linked via analogy with the (secondary) feminine position. As a consequence, embrace of the American and challenge of the hierarchy in which it was rated low made adoption of a "feminine" position attractive for some males as well as for females. And, likewise, women found some aspects of the orderly structure of hierarchy attractively reassuring. In the work of Williams, for instance, gender ambivalence combines with a similar ambivalence about hierarchy. While this ambivalence occurs to some degree in the work of Eliot and Moore, Williams's work embodies it with particular insistence. All three poets employ quotation to scrutinize the gendering of authority, a process that involves two of them in attempts at reworking received models of gender relations within families. I will draw on the work of Jessica Benjamin in exploring these attempts.

The contradictions within and between the texts reveal and confirm their direct relation to a specific moment *in history*, always and necessarily a situation of flux, of movement from one configuration of powers to another. These poets' use of quotation is one of the principal means by which they engage their moment. In the chapters that follow, I will explore the complexities of the confluent streams of meaning navigated by modernist poetic quotation.

Quotation in the Modernist Milieu

Quotation's popularity with the modernist poets was reinforced by the fact that modernist painters and novelists found it attractive too. Modernist collage constitutes a kind of quotation, of the mass-produced materials Picasso pasted onto his canvases or of the objects and printed material Kurt Schwitters organized in his constructions. And while, as we saw earlier, quotation had been part of the novel's domain from its start, Joyce's last two books particularly emphasize that aspect of the genre, full as they are of phrases borrowed from popular song, from advertisements, and from literature. Jorge Luis Borges also played with an insistent version of quotation when he had his Pierre Menard reconstruct *Don Quixote* (a novel that, as we have seen, was itself full of quotations) verbatim.[48] But while poetic quotation has sources related to those of quotation in prose and in painting and learns from the use of the device in these arts (Williams, for instance, refers pointedly to collage in *Paterson*), the resonance of the method within the context of each art form varies, since in each it plays against a specific and peculiar history.

For instance, following through on the examples introduced above, the impetus to collage springs from a fascination with the mass production of images, and it challenges the purist claims of earlier aesthetic movements.[49] The collagists explored the effects of the new wide reproducibility of art (for example, as posters), which had formerly derived an important measure of its authority, as Walter Benjamin has famously argued, from the physical uniqueness of each work.[50] And they addressed ironically both traditional assumptions that high art and popular art are distinct and more recent claims, made most emphatically by the symbolists, for an essential separation between high art and mass culture.[51]

Quotation's role in modernist novels relates to this issue of expanded mechanical reproduction via the collage effect of the newspaper format. Marshall McLuhan notes that both Picasso and Joyce learned their collage techniques from the newspaper, which sets disparate stories side by side, and then sets these by ads and recipes.[52] Picasso's frequent inclusions of news clippings—and particularly of segments of the word *Journal*—in his collages bear witness to this genealogy, as does the Aeolus chapter in *Ulysses*, set in a newsroom. But quotation's valence in prose differs from its valences in both poetry and painting in that it does not play in prose against the same expectation of great originality. While readers may expect the framing concept of a novel to be "original," the gesture of including borrowed words is as old as the genre. We can return here to Bakhtin's characterization of the novel as a dialogue between styles of speech that the author "quotes." Since quotation from other texts sets up a similar kind of dialogue in the paintings and poems in which it is employed, we may read the movement of quotation into the realms of painting and poetry as, in Bakhtin's terms, the "novelization" of those forms—their transformation into dialogic texts from forms in which a single, monologic voice speaks.[53]

Quotation's valence in poetry, like that in collage, plays on a tension with the expectation that poetry will attempt to be original. But unlike the situation with collage, quotation in poetry is not a new possibility. Though it has always been a possibility in poetry, it has been so consistently rejected that before the modernist moment its rejection was implicit in the definition of the poetic. Modernist poets engage this history when they decide to break with it.

Chapter Two

T. S. Eliot's *The Waste Land*

In the work of all three of the modernists considered in this study, quotation is linked to issues of poetic filiation and through that to questions of nationality and gender. In *The Waste Land* the three are tied together through a set of narratives about the poem's own genesis conducted via borrowed phrases. Eliot fills his poem with such phrases—direct quotations, emphatic allusions (phrasings clearly based on priorly existent phrasings and clearly meant to be recognized as such), and appropriations. And in case one were to miss the heavy reliance on the phrases of others, the notes put the point home. The notes do not, however, account for all the borrowings—indeed they coyly misdirect readers at several points. After years of following through on their vague references, critics have come to recognize the notes as a basket of red herrings, part of the poem rather than guides to it.[1] Instead of the tarot pack and the Holy Grail, the poem's concerns are with its parentage, its own claims to authority, and its capacity to claim an originality in spite of the counterintuitiveness of making such a claim at so late a date.

Such critics as Gregory S. Jay and Perry Meisel have explicated *The Waste Land* along Bloomian lines, though with different emphases, and this study builds on that work, also with different emphasis. (As Jay points out, not only is the poem the paradigmatic Bloomian text, but it is itself a progenitor of the Bloomian argument.) Such readings take the view that *The Waste Land* portrays a literary oedipal struggle, figured at the level of the explicit plot (or what passes for such in this obscure poem) in the relation of the castrated or murdered fisher king to the quester.[2] As does the Bloomian model they work with, such readings omit mention of the relation between mothers and sons in the dynamic of poetic relations. But both an initial identification with and a subsequent silencing of mothers—and of the feminine more generally—are important parts of the story of the poem's genesis. They too are related within the poem, and linked to the repression of the American.

In extending the analysis of the poem's handling of issues of its own genesis and authority to the level of the quotations and allusions (both those acknowledged in the notes and those not acknowledged), I will not attempt to account for each borrowed phrase. Instead I will trace the pattern of borrowing and look at the provenance and contextual penumbra of a selection of examples, to illustrate the kinds of concerns to which these borrowings speak. I will assume readers' familiarity with the poem, and deal specifically with the "plot" only as it is expressed in the quotations.

The notes direct our attention to nineteen direct quotations and twenty overt allusions (a category that includes both near-quotations and much less direct ones, which would go unrecognized were they not brought by the fact of their attribution in the note much closer to the realm of quotation than they would otherwise have come).[3] These thirty-nine borrowings fill all or part of 77 of the poem proper's 444 lines.[4] As we will see, a much larger proportion of the lines than those marked in the notes relies on earlier texts. Some of these lines many readers may recognize without assistance, while others are likely to be recognized only when commentators point them out. Altogether, these borrowings do several jobs in the course of a reader's experience of the poem. Initially they support the general atmosphere of loss suggested by the poem's invocation of the fisher king/grail story. Their presence serves as evidence of the unfruitfulness of the land and seconds the despairing rhetoric by suggesting a running down of modern poetic ability to transform the inspiring work of preceding poets into new and independent works. The quotations themselves—from poems whose authors wrote their own words and did not feel the need to take over those of others—work as witnesses to a more meaningful, earlier world, now lost, for which the poem is nostalgic.

This first role of quotation in the poem is only one of several that surface as the poem proceeds (and as the reader's familiarity with the poem increases), and it participates in the first of the poem's narratives of origin. This narrative I call the poem's quotation plot, because it is associated with the use of quotation, as well as with quotation's close cousin, emphatic allusion. This narrative presents a set of anxieties about secondariness—in relation to the poem's romantic predecessors, its national identity, and its gendering—and then works to deny those anxieties. In the course of this first narrative, Eliot claims a set of poetic fathers via the notes and the quotes. As various critics have noted, these fathers serve as a cover for the poem's "true" father, Walt Whitman, whom Eliot does not acknowledge directly. Whitman appears, however, in a second narrative, which gives voice to the poem's "unconscious," operating through allusion and echo rather than quotation.[5] A third narrative is conducted via borrowings from conversations with three women. These quotations, unrecognizable without note, are not marked off or noted in the poem, but Eliot later acknowledged the presence of two and the third has been widely assumed. The repression of this third narrative turns out to be linked to the repression of the Whitman connection. Eliot's apparent lack of anxiety about these appropriations—quite different from the moods surrounding the other borrowings—contributes to a tale of women's nonparticipation in the generation of poetry on which the other two narratives, which concern themselves specifically with relations between poetic fathers and sons, depend.

In *The Waste Land* Eliot employs quotation in ways that draw on several of its antecedent forms. His "scholarly" notes reinforce the sense that the poem's quotations operate in the scholarly mode, but at the same time the quotations (and the notes) work within the tradition of parodic quotation. Their large effect is one of mockery of those who take seriously the poem's early claims to poetic incapacity, which the scholarly apparatus is employed, in part, to support. The deepest connection of the poem's quotations lies, however, in their ties to biblical quotation. Actual borrowings from the Old Testament occur only in the second verse paragraph, but links to the New Testament story of Christ's resurrection (an analogue to the process of quotation, in which the old reappears unchanged in the new) carry throughout the poem the story of the later text's takeover of the authority of the earlier one, without sacrifice of the notion of authority per se.

Eliot's quotation plot tells through exaggeration the story of its poetic power struggles. This story is then seconded within the poem's lower depths through the narratives of allusion and appropriation, two related but more subtle forms of borrowing. Together these borrowings reassert a hierarchic structure within which Eliot can claim authority and originality, even granted certain acknowledgments of the attenuated nature of such claims. In making these claims, Eliot must deny those aspects of his situation that make traditional hierarchies problematic for those who desire authority. In Eliot's case that means denying his Americanness along with his modernity and any aspects of himself that might be read as feminine.

The quotation plot opens with the poem: Eliot introduces his poem's engagement with quotation in its first words. The title itself he borrows from Jessie Weston's *From Ritual to Romance,* as Eliot informs us in a note. This borrowing is seconded in the epigraphs, which are marked clearly as quotations by quotation marks and italics and by their foreignness.[6]

> 'Nam Sibyllam quidem Cumis ego ipse oculis meis vidi in ampulla pendere, et cum illi pueri dicerent: *Σίβυλλα τί θέλεις*; respondebat illa: *ἀποθανεῖν θέλω*.'
>
> For Ezra Pound
>
> *il miglior fabbro.*[7]

Since epigraphs are usually quotations, these appear particularly noteworthy only when we recognize them as metaquotations, quotations that themselves involve quotation, and which comment on the indebtedness they portray.

Only the second of the two epigraphs, the dedication to Pound (added in 1925), speaks directly of a debt. In setting Dante's characterization of the Provençal poet Arnaut Daniel ("the better maker") as appositive to the dedication, Eliot manages at once to pay a general tribute to Pound (a particular fan of Provençal poetry) and to suggest this poem's particular debt to the man whose skill at making informs it so unusually directly. For Dante demonstrates the extent of his admiration for Arnaut in the *Purgatorio* by following up this friendly judgment with the clearest tribute he could offer: he allows Arnaut, alone among all the other speakers of *The Divine Comedy,* to speak his own words in his own language rather than in Dante's Italian.[8] In alluding to this opening of one poet's work to the language of another poet, Eliot transforms Dante's line into a statement of Pound's similar relation to *The Waste Land,*[9] though Pound's editing of the poem involved principally cuts, not additions.[10]

Eliot chooses the line from Petronius's *Satyricon* for the first epigraph most obviously because the sibyl's despair over her position in time, linked by her association with sand to images of dryness, leads smoothly to the larger poem's concerns with those same issues and images. In addition, both epigraphs involve reference to a contrast of earlier and more recent languages (contemporary with their moment of composition) that suggests a decline from an earlier and better world: from the Greek-speaking world of the sibyl's youth to the Latinized world of her great age and from the better *(miglior)* world of Provençal poetry to the diminished world in which Dante writes in Tuscan. In his use of the quotation from the *Purgatorio,* Eliot remakes Dante's Provençal/Italian comparison in terms contemporary to *his* readers by juxtaposing a line in English with the line in Dante's Italian, suggesting even a further decline from Dante's time to our own.[11] In beginning *The Waste Land* with two quotations that either include or allude to other quotations, Eliot shows his technical hand up front. These borrowed lines involving borrowed words signal from the start that borrowing will be a major concern in *The Waste Land*.

Having been alerted by the epigraphs to the poem's concern with belatedness and indebtedness, we recognize similar concerns in the poem proper. The first section title, "The Burial of the Dead," comes directly (though without note) from the Church of England's burial service, and continues the lugubrious mood. The stanza that follows suggests a world near death, in which all meaning is located in the past. The poem's first lines are not a quotation, however, but an overtly allusive transformation of the first lines of the General Prologue to Chaucer's *Canterbury Tales:*

> April is the cruellest month, breeding
> Lilacs out of the dead land, mixing
> Memory and desire, stirring
> Dull roots with spring rain.

Though he begins *The Waste Land* with a clear assertion of misery, the larger statement of Eliot's first few lines is indirect, depending on their readers' recognition of their allusion to Chaucer's lines:

> Whan that Aprill with his shoures soote
> The droghte of March hath perced to the roote,
> And bathed every veyne in swich licour
> Of which vertue engendred is the flour . . .[12]

The insistent allusion calls for comparison of the two texts. The comparison informs reading so that we recognize that the revision of the feeling of April from sweetness to cruelty comes from the intrusion of temporal distance, articulated as memory. The season and its effects are unchanged, rain falls and flowers tremble into life in both poems; only the awareness of the intervention of many Aprils between Chaucer's and Eliot's own differentiates them. But the difference, we can infer, mars all.

The intervening years have introduced a difficulty, which goes unnamed but is demonstrated in the fact of the overt allusion. We can deduce the logic of the argument implicit in this first stanza thus: where Chaucer could celebrate the creativity of spring as a parallel to his own creativity, this later poet hates spring for the lack of parallel it points out to him, since he is able only to write poetry that sounds very much like that of his predecessors. Chaucer of course might dispute the understanding that he was unanxious, given both his extensive borrowings from Boccaccio, whom he mentioned only once, and his fabrication of a (pseudo)source whom he called Lollius and in whose debt he claimed to be. Eliot's point here is not historical correctness, however, but the construction of an image of Chaucer's garden as a paradise with which to contrast the modern poetic "waste land."

The allusion to the beginning of Chaucer's poem refers us analogically to several issues having to do with beginnings. Chaucer's status as first poet of the tradition of poetry in English in which Eliot works puts him in a relation to Eliot parallel to that of the Old Testament to John. And again, as with John, in rewriting Chaucer's story of the coming of spring, the beginning of the natural cycle, Eliot revises a predecessor's version of a creation story.

What follows in the rest of the verse paragraph continues the mood of decline established in the first lines:

> Winter kept us warm, covering
> Earth in forgetful snow, feeding
> A little life with dried tubers.
> Summer surprised us, coming over the Starnbergersee
> With a shower of rain; we stopped in the colonnade,
> And went on in sunlight, into the Hofgarten,
> And drank coffee, and talked for an hour.
> Bin gar keine Russin, stamm' aus Litauen, echt deutsch.
> And when we were children, staying at the arch-duke's,
> My cousin's, he took me out on a sled,
> And I was frightened. He said, Marie,
> Marie, hold on tight. And down we went.
> In the mountains, there you feel free.
> I read, much of the night, and go south in the winter.

While the description of the coffee in the sunlight after brief rain seems at first to suggest value and pleasure in it, the talk goes on only for an hour. Fleeting value in the terms of this poem is barely value at all, and at any rate it has now passed. The next line, "Bin gar keine Russin, stamm' aus Litauen, echt deutsch," continues the treatment of lack of originality (the speaker from Lithuania is *echt deutsch* only in a pointedly complicated way). The heteroglossic effect introduced by this foreign phrase supports a general effect of fragmentation and disorder, and the description of childhood at the archduke's in the next line associates earlier times with order and clear hierarchy that no longer obtain.

The stanza's final line, "I read, much of the night, and go south in the winter," transforms Chaucer's description of happy birds in springtime:

> And smale foweles maken melodye,
> That slepen al the nyght with open eye—
> (lines 9–10)

Eliot's version suggests a loss of peace and a confusion of the natural order of things in adulthood, associated both with the specific fall from meaning that occurs in the movement from childhood to adulthood, and with the fall across the larger temporal span from Chaucer to Eliot that gives rise to the loss of power in the contemporary exercise of poetic skill for which the poem argues.

This section also involves allusions to several works of small renown that are also not mentioned in the notes. These allusions, not caught by most readers but available to some, are on a par in terms of familiarity with many of the minor literary texts mentioned in the notes. They differ in being more recent. The notes and particularly their odd, incomplete character have put readers on the scent of further sources. At the same time, through their example, they have authorized readings of the relations between Eliot's poem and newly discovered source texts as in some respect part of the poem. The three such borrowings in the first verse paragraph continue the mood of diminished value, both in their specific statements and in comparison to the borrowing from Chaucer. They come from Charles-Louis Phillippe's novel *Bubu de Montparnasse* ("For our flesh has retained all our memories, and we mingle them with our desires"),[13] James Thomson's poem "To Our Ladies of Death" ("Our Mother feedeth thus our little life, / That we in turn may feed her with our death"),[14] and the memoires of a displaced White Russian called Marie Larisch (Eliot alludes not to specific phrases but to the circumstances Larish recalls, along with her first name).[15] On the scale of traditional literary value, these works sit at a substantial remove from the General Prologue, and their presence in this poem can be read as a sign of its decline from Chaucer's height.

In addition, these allusions support the general mood of decline through reference to the specific contexts from which they are taken. All three works—novel, poem, and memoire—describe worlds of diminished value. *Bubu* is the story of a Parisian whore, one of the world of "the inarticulate and underfed, those who are too depressed to be rebellious," as Eliot put it in his preface to an English translation of the novel.[16] Larisch's story is chiefly an account of the manifestations of congenital insanity in, and the erotic misbehaviors of, Austrian royalty, told by a woman who begins as her aunt the Empress Elizabeth's go-between and ends as the facilitator of the illicit romance that concluded in the suicide-murder of her cousin the Crown Prince Rudolph and his mistress at Meyerling. The invocation of such evidence of the fall of the mighty in this context thickens the mood of loss of value.

The suggestions of diminished value imported with the borrowings from "To Our Ladies of Death" are of a more complex sort. The poem is a prayer to and for Oblivion (the third and final lady of death), manifested either as rest that leads to new vigor or, if that is not granted, as death. Similar in theme to Eliot's section 1, Thomson's poem is also of interest for certain structural similarities to *The Waste Land*. It opens with an epigraph, from Shakespeare ("Tired with all these, for restful death I cry," from Sonnet 66), very like Eliot's own epigraph from Petronius, and a footnote to the title stresses the derivativeness of the governing image ("The Three Ladies suggested by the sublime sisterhood of Our Ladies of Sorrow, in the 'Suspiria de Profundis' of De Quincey")[17] in a manner quite like that of Eliot's admissions of influence in his notes.

Critics generally consider Thomson's poetry derivative, in the usual, negative sense this word has. "That Thomson's later poetry occasionally reflects the matter and manner of Browning has often been asserted," writes William Peterson, speaking for the consensus, ". . . [and it] is well known that his work bore traces of Shelley, Leopardi, and Blake, among others; doubtless his very inability to assimilate these influences smoothly into the texture of his verse is the identifying mark of a second-rate poet."[18] It is this usual judgment of the second-rate quality of poetry that does not absorb the voices of its predecessors that Eliot plays against in *The Waste Land*, aiming to incur this judgment in the early section of the poem (not finally for his own work, but for this stage in the poem's fiction) in order to reverse it by later transcending it.

Thomson epitomizes the extreme sense of loss of poetic vigor among Victorian poets, the sense of great weariness and languor infused by an awareness of the large influence that the work of their romantic antecedents had upon their own. His derivativeness extends even to his name. Because James Thomson, the eighteenth-century poet of "The Seasons," had prior claim to the name, most of the poems the later Thomson published in his lifetime appeared over the signature "B. V.," for Bysshe Vanolis (the first for Shelley, the second a scrambled version of Novalis).[19] This device manifests particularly effectively the sense common among Victorian poets of having no individual vision to assert.

Eliot's clear allusion to Thomson's "To Our Ladies of Death" has led critics to recognize similarities as well between *The Waste Land* and Thomson's most famous poem, "The City of Dreadful Night," a tale of loss of hope, faith, and love in an urban limbo that includes desert imagery and a narrator who sits "forlornly by the river-side" (section 6, line 1).[20] But it is not for the cluster of shared associations that this poem interests us here; rather, it is significant as part of the context invoked by the borrowing from the earlier Thomson poem. Attention to "The City of Dreadful Night" educates our reading of Eliot's use of "To Our Ladies of Death."

Of particular interest are the facts that "The City of Dreadful Night" begins with a compound epigraph, which joins a line from Dante with two verses from Leopardi, both very mournful, and that the poem includes a direct quotation in the first two lines:

> Lo, thus, as prostrate, "In the dust I write
> My heart's deep languor and my soul's sad tears."
> Yet why evoke the spectres of black night
> To blot the sunshine of exultant years?
> Why disinter dead faith from mouldering hidden?
> Why break the seals of mute despair unbidden,
> And wail life's discords into careless ears?
> (Proem, lines 1–7)

The lines from Shakespeare's *Titus Andronicus* (3.01.13) constitute a depressing literary spectre in Thomson's poem in the same way that Eliot's allusion to Chaucer's General Prologue invokes the earlier work in order to complain of its influence, commenting on the diminished vigor of the modern poet in relation to the early one.

Death in Thomson's schema offers not merely the relief of forgetting (and of being forgotten, a meaning equally present in the word *oblivion*). Where "To Our Ladies of Death" begins with a suggestion in the epigraph and footnote (clarified with reference to the beginning of "The City of Dreadful Night") of the misery of poetic lateness, the poem's close, from which Eliot borrows in section 1 of *The Waste Land,* looks forward to an acquisition of powers of influence on future generations similar to those the dead poets have exercised over him.

> Our Mother feedeth thus our little life,
> That we in turn may feed her with our death: . . .
> One part of me shall feed a little worm,
> And it a bird on which a man may feed;
> One lime the mould, one nourish insect-sperm;
> One thrill sweet grass, one pulse in bitter weed;
> This swell a fruit, and that evolve in air;
> Another trickle to a springlet's lair,
> Another paint a daisy on the mead:
>
> With cosmic interchange of parts for all,
> Through all the modes of being numberless
> Of every element, as may befall.
> And if earth's general soul hath consciousness,
> Their new life must with strange new joy be thrilled,
> Of perfect law all perfectly fulfilled;
> No sin, no fear, no failure, no excess.
> ("To Our Ladies of Death," lines 197–98; 204–17)

This passage suggests an awareness that the indebtedness he discovers in his own poetry is common to all poetries, an awareness that affords a bit of relief from the misery the poem describes to this point. This awareness does not evolve, however, to the full consciousness and control that might enable him to overcome entirely the earlier despair. The two lines of this passage that Eliot borrows on, read in this self-reflexive light, describe the very process enacted in the incorporation of this passage into Eliot's poem.[21]

Where Thomson uses his melancholy over his poetic situation as an enabling device in itself, Eliot works to transcend his melancholy by adding an element of ironizing parody, even as the epigraph from Petronius adumbrates. Thomson's poem includes only one explicit, self-dramatizing quotation, which represents the heavy allusiveness of his work generally and which leaves him still the victim (though a complicitous victim, since his victimization is the stuff of his poetry) of the belatedness he describes. Eliot's extensive—even excessive—quotation, on the other hand, figures a similar heavily allusive quality in his poetry, but allows him to claim to control his indebtedness, by making a point of it. In borrowing images from B. V., Eliot acknowledges *his* debt to B. V.'s earlier and peculiarly Victorian explication of the nature of poetic debt.

The Waste Land' s next stanza continues the mood of loss, beginning with more images of an unfruitful world:

> What are the roots that clutch, what branches grow
> Out of this stony rubbish? Son of man,
> You cannot say, or guess, for you know only
> A heap of broken images, where the sun beats,
> And the dead tree gives no shelter, the cricket no relief,
> And the dry stone no sound of water. Only
> There is shadow under this red rock,
> (Come in under the shadow of this red rock),
> And I will show you something different from either
> Your shadow at morning striding behind you
> Or your shadow at evening rising to meet you;
> I will show you fear in a handful of dust.

This section includes the first quotation in the poem proper. The notes tell us that lines 20 and 23 depend on Ezekiel and Ecclesiastes in some measure. In fact, these notes work as signposts for a general biblical indebtedness in this section. The first twelve lines of this verse paragraph jam together transformations of biblical warnings of evil days to come for those who forsake the words of God. Lines 19–20 rework Job 8:16–17 ("He is green before the sun, and his branch shooteth forth in his garden. His roots are wrapped about the heap, and seeth the place of stones"). In the address to the "Son of man" we meet the first direct quotation in the text; the first of the notes to section I guides us to a source in Ezekiel 2:1. This is the title by which the voice of the Lord addresses the prophet, the first of several instances of its use. In Ezekiel 2:1, the spirit enters Ezekiel and commissions him to warn transgressors. The final verses of the chapter instruct Ezekiel to eat the roll of a book on which the Lord's warnings are transcribed. The text that Ezekiel eats he is then supposed to recite to the Israelites—a clear image of quotation as ingestion of prior texts, and a nice figure for what goes on in *The Waste Land* as well. In lines 21–22, Ezekiel's warning "Your altars shall be desolate, and your images shall be broken" (6:4) enters the present. The evil days of Ecclesiastes 12:5 ("and the almond tree shall flourish, and the grasshopper shall be a burden, and desire shall fail") are joined with God's admonition in Isaiah 56:3 ("neither let the eunuch say, Behold, I am a dry tree") in line 23. The only hopeful moment, in line 25, redoes Isaiah 32:2 ("And a man shall be as an hiding place from the wind, and a covert from the tempest; as rivers of water in a dry place, as the shadow of a great rock in a weary land"). Whether or not one is aware of the particular sources of these lines, the reference to the language of the prophets is clear, as is the suggestion that the old prophecies have been fulfilled in the diminished present.

This flourish of biblical borrowing within a poem full of literary borrowing works as a reminder of religious quotation's status as antecedent of secular quotation, and so of the parallels between religious quotation and all the quotation of other poems that goes on here. Just as the mode of religious quotation involves submission to the authority of the Lord and His book, so *The Waste Land* points to its own submissiveness to the greater originality and authority of the works cited in it. But religious quotation also involves an attempt to win some of the authority of its source for the new speaker, and that same effort goes on here. From the start Eliot builds into *The Waste Land* simultaneous narratives of submission and self-assertion. In addition, Eliot's borrowing from biblical prophets here moves the tale of poetic origins back to a point much before Chaucer and works as a clarification of what the dream of contact with origins—of true originality—involves. The truly original poet not only is creative but has contact with the ultimate Creator. The truly original poet is a prophet. Those who assert that Eliot's purpose in building this poem around references to religious rituals is to find a way to a self-abnegating transcendence seem to forget the arrogance involved in prophecy and poetry both.[22] And by referring us to chapter 2 of Ezekiel, and the command that the prophet eat and then regurgitate the words of the Lord, Eliot reminds us that even those most privileged of speakers spoke with borrowed words, that prophecy is quotation. In so doing he elides the distinction between his quotation-filled poetry and prophecy. The parallel with Eliot's own methods at first would seem to mock the present text, but as the poem proceeds the mockery begins to unravel, which opens the way to Eliot's claiming some of the authority of prophecy for his poem.

From another angle, within the poem's insistently emphasized struggle with its poetic ancestors, the biblical allusions operate as references to Milton and particularly to his manner of moving into the realm of secular poetry, which maintained a measure of prophetic power for himself but left little for those who came after him. Eliot attempts to return to the paradise of poetic authority by assuming the position of deference that Milton refused. That refusal carried Milton out of the garden of pure authority, but he who has known paradise carries some of it with him into exile. His progeny retain no similarly glorious memories and, as Eliot's critical diatribes against Milton's bad influence on poetry testify, they do not always appreciate the loss.

Immediately after the borrowings from the prophets, the stanza continues with another borrowed passage and then goes on in the last lines to suggest yet another loss of Eden:

> *Frisch weht der Wind*
> *Der Heimat zu*
> *Mein Irisch Kind,*
> *Wo weilest du?*
> 'You gave me hyacinths first a year ago;
> 'They called me the hyacinth girl.'
> —Yet when we came back, late, from the hyacinth garden,
> Your arms full, and your hair wet, I could not
> Speak, and my eyes failed, I was neither
> Living nor dead, and I knew nothing,
> Looking into the heart of light, the silence.
> *Oed' und leer das Meer.*

The poem's second and third quotes, in lines 31–34 and 42, both come from Wagner's *Tristan und Isolde,* we are told in notes. The opera's story of failed love feeds the mood of sterility and loss, and Wagner's relation with his patron, King Ludwig, picks up on the earlier mention of the Starnbergersee, the lake in which the mad king drowned himself. Since both quotes are given in German, their foreignness to this text is evident, and again the heteroglossia furthers the sense of poetic disorder.

The lack of creativity suggested in the first stanzas is suggested as well in the rest of section 1. Further quotations appear, from Shakespeare ("Those are pearls that were his eyes" [line 48]) and Baudelaire ("'You! hypocrite lecteur!—mon semblable,—mon frère!'" [line 76]), as well as transformations of phrases from Dante, Webster, and Baudelaire, all of them noted. All import associations with death and decay to assist the general mood. These quotations, interpreted in synchrony with the effects of the rest of the poetry around them, evoke a world lost and suggest a nostalgia for an antique, meaningful order. While they are chosen in particular for their mesh with the poem's explicit concerns (the Parsifal story, the perversion of sexuality, and so on), and while the specific associations they carry contribute to the poem's advance, their borrowedness is itself of interest as well. They function, at this structural level at least, as exhibits for the poem's self-reflexive argument, claiming repeatedly to demonstrate a modern loss of poetic power. These fragments are themselves referred to within the poem through the figure of the broken images (line 22), gathered into this poetic heap to function as structural evidence of the decline the poem speaks of. Reference to them appears also in the reappearing corpse (the corpus) buried in the garden at the end of section 1 and in the poem's title.

So far I have discussed Eliot's quotations and his allusions without distinguishing between them, but they do differ and at this point we need to consider both *how* they differ and what their relation is. In using the term *allusion* I refer to overt allusions: phrasings clearly based on priorly existent phrasings, and clearly meant to be recognized as such. Transformations as extensive as that of Chaucer's General Prologue in the first four lines and as minimal as the substitution of "Dog" for "Wolf" and "friend" for "foe" in Webster's couplet in lines 74–75 are included under this rubric.

In terms of the model of poetic progress within a tradition (that is, movement forward, not necessarily improvement), even a small transformation suggests that some progress is possible (though consistent minuscule change might suggest that things had stalled), whereas no transformation suggests failure of progress emphatically. But while the allusions may be understood to contradict the quotations by offering evidence of the poem's transformative strength, they may also, alongside the quotes and in such number in the poem, be read as representing the last stage before the total decline that quotation represents, as with the heavily emphasized allusion to Chaucer in the first stanza. In addition, Eliot's provision of notes to sources for some of his allusions, by hanging out notice of the poet's indebtedness, brings them closer to the realm of quotation than they would normally come. In this view, the large number of quotes and overt allusions together make the point of the advancing breakdown of the transformative process. And the need for notes, insofar as it suggests readers' inability to recognize the works quoted, may in itself be taken as a sign of the general decline, though the assumption that earlier readers would have recognized more of the obscurer lines and more readily seems dubious.

Where the allusions give at once evidence of strength and of decline, the quotations too work both to make the point of decline and, subversively, to indicate strength. At the same time that Eliot employs quotation to convey the sense of decline the poem insists on through the first sections, he uses it also to construct a structural counterargument. Without the kind of support by analogy with the explicit argument of decline that the first structural argument has, this second argument builds more gradually. As poetic method, quotation (at least of this sustained sort) is new, an innovation. Eliot employs it to specific effect—to fill out the larger argument—and not because he is any less able than his predecessors to invent or to control the substance of his work (a failure that could fairly be read as a sign of real degeneration of poetic power). Awareness of Eliot's facility in handling the quotations grows gradually in the reader, making the case for the poet's skill. Part of the poem's strength, the adequacy of its response to the call for a transformation of the tradition that (Eliot among others has taught us) is the process of poetic development, comes from the claim to weakness, the claim to inadequacy that the quotations imply but do not fulfill. In this respect the quotations, in addition to representing the loss of poetic strength and originality that the poem mourns, are aspects as well of the "subversive posture of *ironic* modesty" that John Guillory remarks in Eliot generally.[23] Quotation, in concert with overt allusion, represents both the loss and the victory over that loss, the problem and its resolution.

These two linked modes are importantly distinguished, however, from echoes, which work less hard at being linked immediately to their sources and, as John Hollander defines them, "[make] new metaphors rather than learned gestures."[24] Of these echoes there also are many, but they operate at another level in the poem, outside the realm of the argument (in which the quotations and overt allusions participate) about the situation of the modern poet in relation to the tradition. The echoes make up the second narrative the poem offers about its own genesis, pointing to inspiring texts much closer to home.

The distinction between allusion and echo is bound to blur at points. The presence or absence of a note sometimes signals the difference. The notes function in the realm of overt reference, avoiding acknowledgment of poetic affiliations less under the control of the poem's superstructure. As Hollander has noted, "[t]he mode of acknowledgment in the notes . . . is most evasive, in itself. Not only is accreditation peculiarly supplied. . . . It is almost as if a kind of suppression were at work in the texture of recognition and avowal, a nod to allusion but not to echo."[25] The notes suppress echo to divert attention from the actual *process* of poetic influence and transformation that goes on within the poem and toward the *description of the process* of poetic influence that is, from this perspective, the poem's plot, the first of the genesis narratives, expressed through the quotations and allusions.

Eliot's use of allusion in *The Waste Land* differs markedly from his use of the device in other poems. He alludes extensively in his other work as well: William Arrowsmith suggests the depth of Eliot's classical allusiveness in his forty-seven-page source essay on the thirty-one-line poem "Dans le Restaurant."[26] And references to poets of the modern era, early and late, also fill Eliot's work: Webster, Shakespeare, Tennyson, Donne, and on and on. Peter Ackroyd explains the technique as the product of Eliot's way of feeling: "His feelings cluster around literary cadences; the images and themes of *The Waste Land* are both his own and not his own, a continual oscillation between what is remembered and what is introduced, the movement of other poets' words just beneath the surface of his own."[27] But while *The Waste Land* carries on the earlier habit of allusiveness, it makes changes in it as well. The technique of direct lifting that Eliot employs in *The Waste Land* represents a departure from his usual poetic procedures. In his other work Eliot transforms his borrowings in a manner that keeps it within the bounds of what we recognize as originality—he alters the phrases that motivate his own at least slightly upon absorbing them into his poem.

In *The Waste Land* Eliot brings his allusive network much closer to the surface, mixing direct quotations with quotations that have gone through transformations of varying thoroughness, effectively anatomizing his own poetic method, and, beyond that, suggesting that his is the method of all poets. The technique Eliot employs in *The Waste Land* follows the principles for poetic borrowing that he laid out famously in an essay on the Elizabethan poet Philip Massinger. The essay serves Eliot as an opportunity for further working out of his version of the theory of poetic influence (given its most complete expression in his earlier "Tradition and the Individual Talent").

> One of the surest of tests [of poetic merit] is the way in which a poet borrows. Immature poets imitate; mature poets steal; bad poets deface what they take; and good poets make it into something better, or at least something different. The good poet welds his theft into a whole of feeling which is unique, utterly different from that from which it was torn; the bad poet throws it into something which has no cohesion.[28]

The borrowing that Eliot describes in the Massinger essay seems to be of the allusive sort (not necessarily insistently allusive in the emphatic way of the overt allusions in *The Waste Land*, but more than echoic), a phrase or an idea stolen and then transformed into something different. But when set beside *The Waste Land*, the description can be seen to apply to the borrowing-as-quotation that goes on there as well (Eliot wrote both in the same year). *The Waste Land* fulfills the theft criterion for mature poetry so literally that it can be read as a skit on the essay's point.

Even without reference to the theory, the quotations in *The Waste Land* can be seen to remark on the process of poetic transformation of earlier works, especially in concert with the notes. They work as cartoon allusions, parodying the allusions of the earlier poems and of all poems, but at the same time, as do all parodies, they point up some essential characteristics of that which they mock. By setting direct quotations alongside near-quotations and then allusions in advancing stages of metamorphosis, Eliot points up the basis in borrowing of all poems.

The Waste Land offers demonstrations of at least three stages in the process by which earlier works are incorporated into a new poem. The first stage is the untransformed quotations. The second is evidenced in the slightly transformed overt allusions. For example, the variations on lines from Marvell's "To His Coy Mistress": "But at my back I alwaies hear / Times winged Charriot hurrying near" gets reworked into "But at my back in a cold blast I hear / The rattle of the bones, and chuckle spread from ear to ear" (lines 185–86, without note) and then "But at my back from time to time I hear / The sound of horns and motors" (lines 196–97, noted). The third stage is inevitably a little harder to locate, but it is there as well, in, for example, the line "HURRY UP PLEASE ITS TIME" (line 141 and elsewhere) that the bartender repeats five times in the latter part of section 2. This quotation from the parlance of bartenders all over the United Kingdom refers to Marvell's poem here only to demonstrate the third step in the process of absorbing the work of a predecessor, and so it resonates with Marvell's poem only in light of the other more explicitly mimetic allusions in *The Waste Land*. As signs of the process of absorption of earlier works into later, the quotations remark not just on Eliot's situation, but on the essential attenuation of all poetry. The poem's extensive concern with metamorphosis—both in the specific cases of Philomel's and Tiresias's changes and in the general case of the vegetative cycle of death and rebirth that is referred to in so many forms throughout the poem—is echoed in the varying degrees of transformation that we see enacted upon the quotations and allusions incorporated into *The Waste Land*. In their incorporation we witness the transformation of the past into the present, of one poem into another.

The Waste Land's demonstration lesson on the relation of all poetic texts to their precursors, distinguished from Harold Bloom's model by the benevolence with which it characterizes the dealings of poetic fathers and sons, directly contradicts and means to debunk the romantic fiction of poetic originality by taking as given that all poets borrow. Which is not to suggest that Eliot or his poem is content with this assertion of attenuation. For in so redefining as mystification the romantic concept of originality, Eliot, of course, lays claim to a (byzantine) originality of his own (and the need to offer the contradiction, and so to lay claim to his own "original" view, affirms the vital relation between Eliot's text and the romantic precursors he denies). It is an originality brought into question by its own product, but of sufficient artfulness to empower its poet.

The examples of the poetic process on the surface of the poem are not those that directly influence this particular poem, however. In suggesting that they may be, Eliot reiterates the obfuscational work he does in his critical essays, where he writes off the work of the poets who influence him most intimately and values instead a set of minor writers. Eliot challenges the fiction of originality by outlining the process of poetic indebtedness, but he disguises the specifics of his own debts, directing us to benign providers of material rather than the threatening providers of inspiration. Where overt allusions and quotations are part of the poem's portrait of the process of poetic influence, echoes are the signs of the process of influence that gives rise to this particular poem.

The echoes of the works with which Eliot contends for primacy of place happen at a less overt level in the poem, in the second genesis narrative. And they are echoes of poets much closer to him than the greats whose lines he borrows here and whom he praises in his essays. Reading behind Eliot's claims to benign correspondences between his work and that of all the poets he names as his principal teachers, Bloom finds that "Eliot's true and always unnamed precursor was not Dante or Donne or Jules Laforgue or Baudelaire, but an uneasy composite of Tennyson and Whitman, with Whitman being the main figure."[29] Gregory S. Jay, tracing the genealogy of Eliot's use of the elegaic form, points to Milton, Shelley, and Whitman as the pivotal precursors.[30] Of this set of four influential figures, echoes of Whitman appear most consistently across *The Waste Land*. The fact of Whitman's Americanness makes him both particularly relevant to Eliot and particularly dangerous, since it is through rejection of his Americanness that Eliot attempts to define himself and his work.

In *To Criticize the Critic*, Eliot summarizes Whitman quickly and antithetically as a "landmark" American poet whose great influence on modern poetry has probably been exaggerated, too much given to imitating his own innovative style and "disguising from himself that he has nothing to say."[31] In spite of this judgment, Eliot's choice of *The Waste Land* as title, especially in tandem with the images of dry grass singing in section 5, responds to Whitman's title *Leaves of Grass*. Several critics have noticed that the sequence of images throughout the poem follows that of Whitman's "When Lilacs Last in the Dooryard Bloom'd." As clearly as it alludes to the start of the General Prologue, *The Waste Land*'s first stanza echoes the first lines of Whitman's great elegy:

> When lilacs last in the dooryard bloom'd,
> And the great star early droop'd in the western sky in the night,
> I mourn'd, and yet shall mourn with ever-returning spring.
>
> Ever-returning spring, trinity sure to me you bring,
> Lilac blooming perennial and drooping star in the west,
> And thought of him I love.
> (lines 1–6)

The difference between allusion and echo here is not so much a matter of the extent of transformation—similarities and pointed contrasts of both imagery and theme are clear between Eliot's lines and Chaucer's and between Eliot's and Whitman's. And neither Chaucer nor Whitman is mentioned in the notes. The Chaucer borrowing is entirely in line, however, with the set of works that *are* mentioned in those notes—a partner to the Shakespeare and the Spenser. And it is a single reference, played upon and then moved on from. The Whitman, on the other hand, does not fit with the highly specialized, European canon the poem goes to great lengths to establish in the notes. And Eliot returns to the Whitman over and over as the poem proceeds, suggesting a very different and intimate kind of engagement.[32]

Eliot's carefully cultivated "European" poetry deliberately revises but does not evade the legacy of the earlier poet, the self-proclaimed barbarian, sensually and self-confidently American. It is Whitman's knowledge that Eliot's transforms. *The Waste Land*'s demonstration of poetic entwinedness across generations builds on Whitman's knowledge that awareness of death is necessary to song, that cycles of deaths of earlier poets have led to his own moment,[33] and that his death will lead to the songs of others.

> I bequeath myself to the dirt to grow from the grass I love,
> If you want me again look for me under your boot-soles.

You will hardly know who I am or what I mean,
But I shall be good health to you nevertheless,
And filter and fibre your blood.

Failing to fetch me at first keep encouraged,
Missing me one place search another,
I stop somewhere waiting for you.[34]
("Song of Myself," lines 1339–46)

Whitman predicts his own appearance in Eliot's poem.

The network of references, which works as further evidence for the argument that the work of all poets is intertwined with that of their predecessors, expands here when we notice that both Whitman's knowledge and his imagery of recycling nature are behind the passage from the close of Thomson's "To Our Ladies of Death" that Eliot transforms in the first stanza. Reading the three passages together, we can hear that Eliot's overt allusion to Thomson, an early Whitman fan, filters the echo of Whitman in Thomson's line.[35] The Whitman in Thomson emerges through the sympathetic resonance with the echoes of "When Lilacs Last in the Dooryard Bloom'd" that surround it.

Eliot's use of quotation to signal lack of originality itself echoes Coleridge, who in "The Nightingale" used the device as a sign both of anxiety over originality and of the overcoming of that anxiety, and Wordsworth, who similarly used the device in the Prospectus to *The Excursion*.[36] Along with these specific antecedents, Eliot's concern with originality, itself a romantic legacy, also places his work in intimate dialogue with romanticism. The echoes of Whitman and the romantics are part of the *process* of influence actually at work in this poem rather than part of the *description of the process* that the poem gives in the quotations and overt allusions.

The positions of Milton and the Victorians fit less easily into one or the other camp. John Guillory has pointed out that Eliot's insistent reaction against Milton seems exaggerated, given the big gap in time between them.[37] Eliot's choice of Milton as confessed principal adversary ("Milton's poetry could *only* be an influence for the worse, upon any poet whatever. . . . it is an influence against which we still have to struggle")[38] may be read to signal his identification with and real anxiety over those for whom Milton was an immediate obstacle, for whom "life to him would be death," to borrow the phrase that echoes throughout Eliot's two essays on Milton (and even appears, at a remove, as a quotation within a quotation in "Milton II"). These poets—the English romantics and their American counterparts—were doubly concerned with issues of originality in their combined temporal and national distances from the origins of Western culture. But Milton is of real concern to Eliot also, insofar as Eliot qua modern wrestles with the same sorts of difficulties as did his romantic predecessors.

A similar doubleness characterizes Eliot's relation to the Victorians. The clear likeness between their situation and his own makes them at once more and less threatening than the differently situated romantics and Whitman. These latter poets claim an originality that Eliot labors here to disprove, and while the difference is complicated by Eliot's desire to overcome it (recognizedly impossible), that difference is nonetheless fairly clear. The situations of the Victorians and the moderns are, however, alike in their lateness. They are distinguished from one another by the ironic approach to their situation with which the moderns attempt to control the by now even greater belatedness they inherit.[39] The presences of both Milton and the Victorians in *The Waste Land* inhabit both the realm of the process and the realm of the description of the process of influence, the realms of echo and quotation.

The presence, for instance, of direct quotations from Tennyson (unnoted but clear in line 30 and arguably present in line 378) suggests that his influence was less problematic for Eliot than that of the romantics or Whitman, whose words are transformed. But there are echoes of Tennyson as well (along with echoes of Shelley and Milton and Whitman), particularly in the drowning of Phlebas (which was much more directly a transformation of Tennyson's "Ulysses" in the earlier version of section 4). Of all the poets *The Waste Land* quotes directly, Tennyson stands in the most direct temporal and linguistic line of influence on Eliot. But while he has some directly inspiring influence, Tennyson serves also as a mediating figure for Eliot, providing a safer, British substitute for the more dangerous influence of his near contemporary Whitman.

As with the poets he pointedly refrains from quoting, Eliot's relation to the poets he does quote and allude to is not what he says it is. When understood to represent a standard of poetic excellence and creativity against which the "failure" in the present is judged, the collection of names is peculiar (for simplicity's sake I include here only those named in the notes and the two others not named there but firmly identifiable as quotations, indicated with asterisks): Petronius,* Dante, Ezekiel, Ecclesiastes, Wagner, Shakespeare, Baudelaire, Webster, Middleton, Virgil, Milton, Ovid, Spenser, Marvell, Day, an Australian ballad, Verlaine, Sappho, Goldsmith, Saint Augustine, Buddha, the

Upanishads, a nursery rhyme,* the poet of the *Pervigilium Veneris,* Nerval, and Kyd.[40]

With the exception of the ballad and the nursery rhyme, which support the general mood of decline by falling into the realm of "low" art, the citations and allusions come from the body of writing we recognize as important literature; that is, texts that receive or at one point received critical attention, and are preserved in libraries and at least an occasional new edition. They do not all come from any standard canon of great works, however. Instead, works from several canons are combined with some obscure titles to achieve a generally off-balance effect for the set as a whole. We get a mixed bag of religious texts, a sprinkling of antique texts, some of the standard canon of English literature, a heavy dose of obscure Elizabethans, three French decadents, and one German composer.

Eliot's purpose in assembling this mixed group seconds that served in his critical essays, where he argues against acceptance of the standard canon of English literature. In those essays he builds an alternative canon, made up of "minor" English poets and a mixture of great and minor poets from non-English traditions. Eliot wrote essays in praise of four of those whose words appear in *The Waste Land* (Dante, Middleton, Baudelaire, and Marvell),[41] and Webster was included in his defense of Elizabethan dramatists. His essays on Shakespeare and Milton, on the other hand, work with opposite purpose, to teach us to see the problems inherent in the acknowledged greatness of their subjects.

In his criticism Eliot constructed an English canon in which membership was based on minority status—a tricky kind of minority, since Eliot redefines majority status as badness, in spite of greatness. "Many people will agree that a man may be a great artist, and yet have a bad influence," he writes. "There is more of Milton's influence in the badness of the bad verse of the eighteenth century than of anybody's else."[42] Eliot sees minority status as most good: "It is more important, in some vital respects to be a *good* poet than to be a *great* poet."[43] The greatness of foreign poets does not seem to have been the same kind of issue for Eliot, and while those that he singles out for praise no doubt deserve it, the decision to move outside the English language and far backward in time repeats the gesture inherent in Eliot's decision to leave America behind. Both involve Eliot's feeling not so much an attraction for what he moves toward as a will to deny immediate influence.

Many readers have noticed the defensive action at work behind Eliot's stellification of these minor and foreign poets. His creation of this alternative canon provided a means by which he could backhandedly elevate himself to (a new kind of) greatness (after greatness in the old sense is redefined as smallness) by tacking himself on (modestly) at the end of the new canon. "Few writers of our century," writes Guillory, "seem more oppressed than Eliot by the feeling that the canon is by its very nature closed and that it can be reopened only by the most elaborate and even covert of strategies."[44] The argument suggested by Eliot's selection of quotations and overt allusions in *The Waste Land* is exactly such a covert strategy for introducing himself into the canonic hierarchy. By mixing together lines taken from works of the standard canon with (a larger proportion of) lines taken from works of his alternative canon within the context of the explicit argument about contemporary poetic decline from a prior world of poetic fecundity, Eliot can suggest a parity between the canons. Association with the lines from the standard canon implies that the quotations from the alternative canon share their value. And this opens the way for the inclusion of Eliot himself, another "minor" poet writing in English, among the ranks of the highly valued.[45]

Eliot's arguments for an alternative canon and his lessons on the absorption of prior works into new ones are implicit in each instance of borrowing and in the interactions between the borrowings; they accrete gradually in the reader's awareness, through examples rather than through a direct narrative. These indirect narratives support and are supported by the quotation plot, which develops across the poem via the changing pattern of quotation use.

I find seven quotations of and thirteen overt allusions to earlier work in section 1, filling 29 of the 77 lines (including the title), and others might find more.[46] In section 2, "A Game of Chess," the proportion tapers off a bit, the point of decline having been made strongly at the outset. The eight noted or recognizable allusions and four noted or recognizable quotations, from Middleton, Shakespeare *(Antony and Cleopatra),* Virgil, Milton, Webster, Shakespeare *(The Tempest),* and Shakespeare again *(Hamlet),* fill 14.5 of the 97 lines.[47] In section 3, "The Fire Sermon," the proportion increases again: twenty-six noted or recognizable quotations and overt allusions fill 35 of the 140 lines.[48]

The pattern of quotations introduced in the first section, continued in the second, and emphasized in the third corresponds to the progress of the more explicit fisher king/quest narrative, through its accretion of images signifying loss of both value and meaning. And just as it represents a change of direction in the quest narrative, the fourth section also represents a change in the pattern of quotations. It is much shorter than the other sections, and it consists entirely of a slightly reworked ten-line passage, in translation, which mixes direct quotation from one work—Eliot's own early French poem "Dans le Restaurant" (published in 1920)[49]—with new phrases to fit the new context. Here follow the last stanza of "Dans le Restaurant," a direct translation of that last stanza, and finally the version that is "Death by Water":

> Phlébas, le Phénicien, pendant quinze jours noyé,
> Oubliait les cris des mouettes et la houle de Cornouaille,
> Et les profits et les pertes, et la cargaison d'étain:
> Un courant de sous-mer l'emporta très loin,
> Le repassant aux étapes de sa vie antérieure.
> Figurez-vous donc, c'était un sort pénible;
> Cependant, ce fut jadis un bel homme, de haute taille.[50]

[Phlebas the Phoenician, drowned a fortnight past, / forgot the cries of the gulls, and the Cornish swell, / And the profits and the losses, and the cargo of tin: / A current undersea carried him far away, / And made him pass through the stages of his former life again. / You can imagine, it was a painful fate; / And yet, he was once a handsome man, and tall of stature."][51]

> Phlebas the Phoenician, a fortnight dead,
> Forgot the cry of gulls, and the deep sea swell
> And the profit and loss.
>   A current under sea
> Picked his bones in whispers. As he rose and fell
> He passed the stages of his age and youth
> Entering the whirlpool.
>   Gentile or Jew
> O you who turn the wheel and look to windward,
> Consider Phlebas, who was once handsome and tall as you.

The Cornish swell, the cargo of tin, and the painful fate are gone; the invocation of the reader in lines 319–20 is added; and the current behaves a bit differently, but the relation of "Death by Water" to the last stanza of "Dans le Restaurant" is unmistakable.

In setting his own poem here, at this pivotal point, Eliot literally adds his name to the list of "great [minor] works" he has obliquely canonized.[52] This reading may at first seem to reduce the poem to an elaborately set-up joke, with a punch line hardly worth the effort. A joking undercurrent does play in here, another instance of the tongue-in-cheek defensiveness about its own impossible aspirations to actual priority that runs throughout the poem. But as with all Eliot's jokes, it has serious intent and works as part of the poem's larger consideration. The issue here is not merely one of Eliot's adding his own name glibly to the canon, a list people work hard to be included on, but a response to the question raised in the first three sections of the poem: whether the state of the poetic world is not so much in decline that no one can ever be added again. In adding his own name here, Eliot claims that there is hope both for the world and for himself in it.

"Death by Water" carries out the sea change anticipated in the quotations from *The Tempest* (Ariel's song and Ferdinand's remarks just before the song), reiterated in earlier sections (lines 48, 125, 191–92, and 257). This change is part of the story line at the same time that it occurs at a structural level. The consideration of the position of the poet in history—which had been taking place at a structural level up to this point—surfaces in the story line here, though still heavily clothed in metaphor. When Phlebas is read as an analogue for the poet whose case the poem has considered covertly so far, his death figures the death the would-be poet welcomes, though not without some remorse: the killing of the merely human self in creation of the greater self, whose song never ends though the singer is no more—the poet of reputation.

The echo of *The Tempest* informs reading here, teaching us to view Phlebas's death by analogy with Alonso's as a short-term ill that serves a larger good. And the analogy with Alonso, who after all is not truly dead (though the mistaken belief that he is leads to the happy ending), gives us leave to entertain the possibility that this death is perhaps not so definite as at first it seems. Though the Phoenician has died, his is a welcome death, leading to new life.

This reading of Phlebas as poet figure gains support from a coincidence in the images and phrasings of "Death by Water" and "Tradition and the Individual Talent," the essay written five years earlier (1917) in which Eliot most famously sets out his theory of poetic development. The points of overlap of "Death by Water" and the essay clarify the logic of the place of section 4 in *The Waste Land*'s structural argument, the quotation plot I have been outlining here. And these overlaps occur within the phrases added or changed when Eliot revised "Dans le Restaurant" into "Death by Water," suggesting that the earlier poem has been reworked specifically to include the concerns of the essay.

The first of these changes is contextual. In *The Waste Land* the "Death by Water" section is led into at the end of "The Fire Sermon" section by a joining of lines from Saint Augustine with allusions to Buddha's Fire Sermon, both specifically identified in the notes. These lines begin as a lament of a too-great immersion in sensuality, figured as fire, and then begin to suggest, in lines 309–10, its overcoming:

> To Carthage then I came
>
> Burning burning burning burning
> O Lord Thou pluckest me out
> O Lord Thou pluckest
> burning[53]

The movement into water from this threatening fire is clearly ameliorative, though the good effect seems to be overdone when the extinguishing of fire becomes drowning. But the self that drowns in "Death by Water" seems, in this context, to be the very sensuality (the sensual self, as opposed to the spiritual more-than-self) that threatened in the first place, and the drowning ceases to seem (such) an ill. At the level of the explicit plot, this movement describes a religious transformation. At the level of the structural discussion, the positioning of Phlebas's drowning just after the ascetic crescendo at the end of "The Fire Sermon" (which suggests what is not clear in section 4 on its own—that Phlebas's death is a self-sacrifice) describes a poetic transformation analogous to the famous anti-romantic doctrine of poetic impersonality of "Tradition and the Individual Talent."[54] Rather than a Song of Myself, we get here a Song of the Denial of Myself.

When read as part of the discussion of the relation of the modern poet to the tradition, "Death by Water" offers a new view of this relation to replace the one that has been operative in the poem to this point. Previously the poet was assumed to be at a loss, the sterile scion of a very old line, because unable to transform the words of his predecessors into something uniquely his own. Here, however, in the character of Phlebas, he learns that he has all along been mistaken in his enterprise. Rather than seeking to impose his personality on the tradition, he must seek to lose himself in it. Phlebas's drowning is the lesson learned, the "continual surrender of himself as he is at the moment to something which is more valuable. . . . [the] continual self-sacrifice"[55] that is the progress of the true artist, according to Eliot the critic. Viewed from this perspective, quotation would be entirely appropriate to poetry.

Essay and poem overlap further in the similar actions of mind and sea. The essay describes the role of the mind of the truly traditional poet, which both "digest[s] and transmute[s] the passions which are its material," and is a "receptacle for seizing and storing up numberless feelings,[56] phrases, images," which then go on to form new compounds (poems). This characterization reappears in the figure of the sea and its currents, which similarly digest and transform the body of the sailor.[57] In "Dans le Restaurant," Phlebas's body underwent no changes.

In entering the whirlpool where both "the stages of his age and youth" are present, the sailor achieves the historical sense essential to a true grasp of the tradition, the historical sense which

> involves a perception, not only of the pastness of the past, but of its presence; [which] compels a man to write not merely with his own generation in his bones, but with a feeling that the whole of the literature of Europe from Homer and within it the whole of the literature of his own country has a simultaneous existence and composes a simultaneous order.[58]

The sense of the simultaneous presence of past and present is not part of the version of the story in "Dans le Restaurant," where the sailor seems to move backward through time.

When we combine notice of the overlap of the "current under sea [that] / Picked his bones in whispers" with the bones in this last paragraph and with the "main current [of the tradition], which does not at all flow invariably through the most distinguished reputations," of which "the poet must be very conscious" (the current but not the bones were present in the earlier poem), it becomes clear that the currents picking Phlebas's bones figure the action of the tradition to which he has submitted, cutting away the worthless individuality (figured as flesh) of his work and revealing the conformity to past (the skeleton here, the bones with more than one generation in them) that makes it truly valuable.[59] "Whispers" works here as a synonym for "echoes," describing quite effectively the presence of earlier works within the lines of a new poem, speaking still, but softly.

In general, insofar as the borrowing from "Dans le Restaurant" refers us to the poem in its entirety, we are reminded of that poem's success at weaving together a wide network of allusions, encompassing Greek, Roman, and medieval texts.[60] Such an ability to absorb the classics demonstrates successful submission to the current of tradition, which clearly does flow through it. It also works as further evidence of the transformation of the poet that takes place in "Death by Water," both insofar as he is understood to be the poet character whose development is charted in the structural plot, and insofar as he is identified with Eliot.

The stanza from "Dans le Restaurant" serves this moment well also through its allusion to a specific context. As William Arrowsmith explains, the Phlebas of this section derives principally from the *Philebus*, Plato's dialogue on the nature of pleasure. The final line of the stanza in both the French and English versions is, if not a direct quotation (in translation) of Plato's Greek, certainly an overt allusion, though an allusion that would be very little recognized without the (oblique) direction to Plato in the sailor's name. The line borrowed comes in a discussion of the nature of the ridiculous, which is determined to derive from a failure of self-knowledge: "There are [many] people who think themselves taller and more handsome and physically finer . . . than they really and truly are."[61] Where the young man Philebos takes pleasure as his good, Phlebas, as Arrowsmith elegantly reads him, is a Philebos who has transcended mere subjective concerns, a Ph(i)lebos without the "I."[62]

The allusions within "Dans le Restaurant" do not merely repeat themselves in *The Waste Land*, however. They take on new resonances in the new context. Eliot's absorption of Plato in *The Waste Land*, specifically of a phrase addressing the need to overcome pride of self, offers a particularly good example of an ability to absorb and transform to fit new context. The stanza serves as evidence, though any number of poems would have served as well on this score, of Eliot's skill at transforming allusions and in fact accomplishing the poetic work that his quotations and overt allusions in the first three sections of *The Waste Land* argue he cannot, as a modern poet, accomplish.

Arrowsmith notes a muted suggestion of rebirth in the Phoenician/phoenix pun in "Dans le Restaurant," though the emphasis there is much more on death's finality. In the second version this suggestion is brought much more to the fore than in the first, specifically through interaction with the lines from *The Tempest* in earlier sections, as well as generally by the shape of the poem's larger argument.[63] The stanza from "Dans le Restaurant" is, effectively, transformed into a tale of transformation in the course of moving into the new poem. It functions as an explication of the effect of relocation of all quotations from earlier works into new poetic locales and as an implicit retroactive recuperation of the loss of poetic power represented within the poem's fiction by quotations and overt allusions in the first three sections of the poem.

Over the course of the poem so far we have had demonstrated for us that, in spite of the suggestions to the contrary (the ironic element of which is by now at least recognizable), they are not merely repetitions of old meanings. They mean quite differently in their new context, in the hands of their new poet. This emphatically transformational quotation in "Death by Water" presses the lesson home. The implicit structural logic suggests that the earlier quotations also are, or have been reconstituted as, (cultured) pearls, though they had seemed the flotsam of a shipwrecked tradition.

But in spite of all this evidence for the appropriateness of this material to this moment in the poem, the fact that the representative moment of self-erasure (even in pursuit of an eventual redefinition of self) is figured through a self-quotation undercuts the argument's effect not a little. The essential contradiction of concerns reveals the complexity of Eliot's relation to his own argument. The assertion of self that surfaces in this action belies the anti-romantic argument of the text. Eliot holds that the only way to ensure poetic immortality is to kill your own presence in your poetry. That he makes this claim within a context of self-quotation demonstrates the paradoxical circumstance of the postromantic poet who finds the means to originality, to making it new, in deconstruction of the whole notion of originality; who finds the means to self-vaunting in self-suppression.

This kind of contradictory dynamic in which loss becomes gain inheres in elegy—the form in which the passing of another provides the occasion for the advance of the poet who mourns that passing. "Death by Water" tells the story of a drowning, resonant with echoes of "Lycidas" and "Adonais" that second the elegaic resonance imported to the poem as a whole by the many echoes of "When Lilacs Last in the Dooryard Bloom'd."[64] Within this tradition Eliot effects his own peculiar version of such a transformation of mourning into opportunity, taking on both the role of the dead poet (insofar as Phlebas figures the poet of "Tradition and the Individual Talent") and that of the surviving singer. While purporting to tell the story of the necessity of the "death" of the individual in pursuit of a depersonalized immortality as part of the greater poetic community, Eliot effectively promotes his own individual poetic immortality.[65] In addition, the poem as a whole is constructed as an elegy for poetry, the dismembered limbs of which, thrown up on the shores of the waste land, are figured in the borrowed lines. And there too, what begins as sign of loss proves as the poem proceeds to demonstrate exactly the opposite.

But it is not elegy alone that accomplishes this kind of transformation of loss into gain. The same effect is achieved in quest poetry, where loss of what must then be sought gives rise to the poems that record the process, and in love poetry, where the absence of the beloved instigates the song. Eliot insists on our noticing his poem's quest structure,[66] and the case might be made as well for reading *The Waste Land* as a love poem—one that mourns not a specific absent love but the absence of love in the more general scope. In all these forms, a sense of the burden of history—of a better world lost—provokes a nostalgic desire for a return to origins. The desire provides the motive force to get such poems under way, but in the course of their proceeding many of these poems demonstrate an awareness that if they were to achieve their object there would be nothing left to write, and so reread failure as success. This position, full of contradiction and conflict, makes a virtue of those conflicts rather than denying them or their inevitability, and turns anxiety into the model of progress and even, paradoxically, of pleasure.

While the self-acceptance that his self-quotation involves points to Eliot's investment in the romantic creed of originality and self-assertion in general, the section's most intimate engagement is again with Whitman, the American version of the romantic individualist. Whitman's "Sea-Drift" poems specifically are invoked here. The first of these, "Out of the Cradle Endlessly Rocking," tells the tale of a death beside the sea (whose "fitful risings and fallings I heard," "Out of the Cradle," line 9) that gives rise to this song, which perpetuates the voices of generations past. The quotation from Plato's *Philebus* is also an echo of Whitman's "young steersman steering with care" ("Aboard at a Ship's Helm," lines 1–2), who so far has managed to avoid drowning. And the drowning of Phlebas specifically revises Whitman's "Song for All Seas, All Ships," which celebrates seamen of all sorts: "Of the few, very choice, taciturn, whom fate can never surprise nor death dismay, / Pick'd sparingly without noise by thee old ocean, chosen by thee" (lines 8–9). Eliot's similar "a current under sea / Picked his bones in whispers" plays on an alternate definition of the word *picked,* again contradicting a statement of self-confidence and self-assertion. If self-assertion is the romantic creed, then America is the romantic nation—the nation that holds that creed most dear. Eliot's very Americanness would seem then to be the motor behind his decision to declare his individuality, his difference from other Americans, by declaring himself an Englishman. His investment in self-assertion provides the prompt for his doctrine of self-erasure. These differences constitute his distinct reworking of Whitman's American self-laud.

"Death by Water" accomplishes, then, two transitions for Eliot's poem within the frame of reference of the quotation plot. At one level it offers a new interpretation of the role of the poet toward tradition, substituting a doctrine of immersion in tradition for the understanding that a poet ought to be original. In sections 1 through 3 of the poem, this understanding functions as a standard of judgment against which this poem full of quotations is measured, within its own fiction, and found wanting. At a deeper level, "Death by Water" reinterprets its own reinterpretation, and, by means of the self-quotation, informs us that the doctrine of poetic impersonality and submission to tradition is itself the means by which this poet intends to establish his own originality, redefined as attenuation.

The transition through self-quotation in "Death by Water" leads to a radical transformation of the poem's pattern of quotation in "What the Thunder Said." The first seventy-nine lines of section 5 are remarkable for including *no* quotations. The notes include several fairly spurious background explanations for various passages within this long stretch,[67] but no sources for phrases or directions to the originals of allusions. A victory over the creative drought that the heavy use of quotation signalled in the first three sections has been effected,[68] though the landscape described in this fifth section is precisely one of drought.

The first quotation comes in lines 401–2: "Da / *Datta*." The note to line 402 supplies some details on this and the sequent thunderclaps: "'Datta, dayadhvam, damyata' (Give, sympathise, control). The fable of the meaning of the Thunder is found in the *Brihadaranyaka—Upanishad,* 5, 1. A translation is found in Deussen's *Sechzig Upanishads des Veda,* p. 489." Line 408, the notes tell us, gives an overt allusion (another of the sort that would hardly qualify as such without the note), a transformation of a line from Webster.[69] The next quotation comes in lines 411–12: "Da / *Dayadhvam*," followed immediately by a transformation of a phrase from Dante.[70] The third quote, and final saying of the thunder, comes in lines 418–19: "Da / *Damyata*." After a gap of six more lines, the poem ends in a rush of quotations, introduced by an overt allusion and broken by one unattenuated line:

> Shall I at least set my lands in order?
> London Bridge is falling down falling down falling down
> *Poi s'ascose nel foco che gli affina*
> *Quando fiam uti chelidon*—O swallow swallow
> *Le Prince d'Aquitaine à la tour abolie*
> These fragments I have shored against my ruins
> Why then Ile fit you. Hieronymo's mad againe.
> Datta. Dayadhvam. Damyata.
> Shantih shantih shantih

Line 426, a transformation of Isaiah 38:1 ("Thus saith the Lord, Set thine house in order: for thou shalt die, and not live"), comes without note. The nursery rhyme in line 427 we would all presumably know. Sources are given in the notes for lines 428 (*Purgatorio*, XXVI, 148), the first half (in Latin) of 429 (*Pervigilium Veneris* [the anonymous *Vigil of Venus*]), 430 (Gérard de Nerval, Sonnet *El Desdichado*), 432 (Kyd's *The Spanish Tragedy*), and 434 ("Repeated as here, a formal ending to an Upanishad"), all of which most readers could be expected not to recognize. The English words in line 429, from Tennyson's *The Princess*, are not accounted for. Line 431, which comments on the surround of quotations, is not borrowed.

At the level of the quotation plot, the great change introduced in section 4 comes into full force in section 5. Though at the level of the overt plot the mood remains one of loss for at least the first few stanzas, at the level of the quotation plot the burden of the past, exhibited in the quotations that filled the earlier sections, seems to have been transcended. Having demonstrated control of his relation to the past by adding himself on to the list of great poets in section 4, Eliot-the-poet-as-character claims now to be able to write his own verse without trouble. That Eliot later spoke of the twenty-nine lines of the water-dripping song, included in this stretch, as his favorite makes sense in this light.[71] That echoes of Whitman fill this section more than any other also deserves notice.

Within the grail quest/religious search, the "DA"'s are offered as linguistic demonstration of a divine transcendence of the human. Calvin Bedient names this transcendence the "Silence":

> Reached for, as it were, across continents, the Sanskrit words are the most flagrant instance of the heteroglossic restiveness of the poem. On the other hand, they promulgate a beatific condition that theoretically transcends language (tapping into what is prior to it, a preformal fluent fullness). The protagonist can evoke it for us, and meditate on it, only if he uses language. . . . The thunder is the authoritative "word" of what is in the last analysis, and beyond analysis, Silence, but because of its very authenticity (one allowed by a devout fiction), the human mind cannot understand it except through an inspired act of interpretation. It would seem to spawn heteroglossia anew, except that it *will* be understood by those earnest for instruction, leading to "shantih" or the peace that passes understanding.[72]

Bedient argues that the heteroglossic elements introduced through the unknown sounds and the mixing together of Hindu and Christian elements, along with the Buddhist references introduced at the end of section 3, are transcended in the poem's insistence that there is a right reading that overrides the fragmentariness of language and meaning, of which the poem has given so much evidence. But he reads the poem's desire, and only one of the poem's desires, when he reads the poem thus. For insofar as Eliot is the maker of this (or any) poem, his desire for transcendence springs from a nostalgia for a world in which he is the first poet, not for a world in which there are no poets. And insofar as he cannot achieve that end he is not nostalgic only, but practically present-minded as well. While nostalgia, transformed into a religious riddle, remains his subject, the means by which he can render it in poetry constitutes part of his subject as well. The relationship between these two concerns creates the dynamic of the poem.

Within the quotation plot, the three "DA"'s and their interpretations give a lesson in the great effect that context has on meaning. The three identical utterances with completely different meanings demonstrate that use of the same words need not signal decline. The crowd of quotations at the end, in light of this lesson, bespeaks even a further transcendence of the poet's belated situation than that of the quotationless lines at the start of section 5. Where in section 1 the fragments served as evidence of loss, we are told in line 431 that they offset ruin here, shored up in defense against it. The lesson of the three "DA"'s allows the poet to employ quotations with new ease because he has learned that they need not only burden, but it also continues the lesson of the "Death by Water" section, demonstrating that the quotations that filled the early sections of the poem need no longer be read as signs of loss. They become here signs of the skill demonstrated in weaving them so complexly into this new context.

But how can the concluding set of quotations be read as a claim for the poet's victory over the dreadful weight of history when the statements made by the fragments themselves are so ambiguous? They neither clearly celebrate nor clearly mourn. The bit of nursery rhyme speaks of collapse and itself represents decline, in its low literary value, but it is also rather playful. Dante's description of Arnaut's plunge back into the purgatorial fire does fairly definitely suggest a movement toward improvement, though certainly through a good deal of suffering. The phrase from the *Pervigilium Veneris* speaks of a transformation to come in the future, if ever. The mood of the phrase from Tennyson is ambiguous. The line from Nerval speaks of ruin, though the line that follows seems to speak of the prevention of ruin (or at least the attempt at prevention). The quotation from Kyd speaks positively, but of madness, another ambiguous moment. The final lines seem to speak of transcendence, but after all the ominous ambiguity this transcendence seems as much a refusal to face difficulty as a victory over it.

While their mournful ambiguity is pointedly played upon, however, the lines that seem to speak of loss turn out in their original contexts to speak of loss that leads to gain, and in several of the instances of loss that leads to specifically literary gain.

For example, the borrowing from Dante speaks directly to issues of poetic influence. In the *Commedia* Dante presents a benign model of the relation between poetic generations: earlier poets (for instance, Virgil) look fondly upon their successors and new poets have no trouble establishing their own authority within the tradition. All of the poets the character Dante meets, with one exception, are made to speak in Dante's language and thus to conform to his vision. The exception, as we saw above in the discussion of the epigraphal tribute to Pound, is Arnaut Daniel, and this exception proves the rule by demonstrating how the rule works. At the literal level, the level of the story, Arnaut's punishment is assigned to cleanse him of the stain of lust. At the literary level, however, the encounter of Dante's text and Arnaut's language figures the process through which precedent poetry is absorbed into that of a later poet.

Arnaut speaks a collage of remarks in Provençal.

"Tan m'abellis vostre cortes deman,
qu'ieu no me puesc ni voill a vos cobrire.
Ieu sui Arnaut, que plor e vau cantan;
consiros vei la passada folor,
e vei jausen lo joi qu'esper, denan.
Ara vos prec, per acquella valor
que vos guida al som de l'escalina,
sovenha vos a temps de ma dolor!"
Poi s'ascose nel foco che li affina.

"So does your courteous request please me—
I neither could nor would conceal myself
from you. I am Arnaut, who, going, weep
and sing; with grief, I see my former folly;
with joy, I see the hoped-for day draw near.
Now, by the Power that conducts you to
the summit of the stairway, I pray you:
remember, at time opportune, my pain!"
Then, in the fire that refines, he hid.[73]

Of these, the last three Provençal lines, along with the line that follows in Italian, are quoted in the notes to *The Waste Land*. The note on the Arnaut passage in Allen Mandelbaum's edition of the *Purgatorio* tells us that "[the] speech contains several turns of phrase reminiscent of lines from extant Provençal poems by Arnaut and others. Above all, his Provençal '*Ieu sui Arnaut*,'

'I am Arnaut,' is a direct quotation from one of his poems."[74] While the insistently individual direct quotation *("Ieu sui Arnaut")* is yet unchanged, the context is one of transformation of Provençal texts to fit Dante's poem. And the line that follows Arnaut's speech is the image of the absorption accomplished as Arnaut, who had stood apart, a better maker (though this description does not, importantly, compare Arnaut with Dante but with another Provençal poet), enters Dante's language and is hidden there: "Poi s'ascose nel foco che li affina."

In setting this line here at the end of his poem, Eliot suggests a similar absorption into his own text but of a different order, since in fact his use of Dante here is an unabsorbed quotation which figures a metaphorical absorption rather than representing in itself a literal absorption. Dante's failure to absorb Arnaut would have meant poetic failure in the terms of poetic succession that rule in the *Commedia* (the example would have made in fact no sense with any other result, since it is given as an explanatory demonstration of the process that operates in the rest of the poem). Eliot's failure to absorb Dante means success in the reversed terms of *The Waste Land*, where success is achieved through (original) subversion of the notion of originality. In setting the phrase "il miglior fabbro," the first mention of Arnaut Daniel in the *Purgatorio*, at the start of *The Waste Land* in 1925, balancing the presence at the end of *The Waste Land* of his last mention in the *Purgatorio*, Eliot creates a context in which we can read the poem that comes between the two framing quotes as a parallel to Dante's exemplary model of poetic absorption.

The quotation from the anonymous *Pervigilium Veneris*, which follows the Dante in *The Waste Land*, seems at first to suggest that no change has occurred in the poem's attitude toward its own use of quotation, especially when the context from which this phrase comes is considered. The world of this late Latin poem is exactly the world *The Waste Land* has claimed not to be, in both its explicit and implicit arguments: a vernal world full of rain, song, and fecundity.[75] But though the god of poets is at the festival of Venus described here, the singers are birds, and the speaker at the end claims to be unable himself to sing:

> Iam loquaces ore rauco stagna cycni perstrepunt:
> Adsonat Terei puella subter umbram populi,
> Ut putes motus amoris ore dici musicos,
> Et neges queri sororem de marito barbaro.

Illa cantat, nos tacemus: quando ver venit meum?
Quando fiam uti chelidon ut tacere desinam?
Perdidi musam tacendo, nec me Apollo respicit:
Sic Amyclas, cum tacerent, perdidit silentium.

Cras amet qui nunquam amavit quique amavit cras amet.
(lines 85–93, Clementi, 201)

[Now the swans with their raucous beaks chant loudly over the pools. The maiden of Tereus strikes up under the shade of the poplar, so that you might imagine that musical strains of love were uttered from her beak, and would not say that it is a sister complaining about a barbarous husband.

She sings. We are silent. When is my spring coming? When shall I be like a swallow, so that I may cease to be silent? I have lost the Muse through being silent, nor does Apollo throw me a glance. Thus it was that silence destroyed Amyclae, because it was silent.

Tomorrow let him love who has never loved, and let him who has loved love tomorrow.]
(Penguin, 79)

He has been silenced by too much listening.[76] And not, we can reason, to real birds.

This poem, full of echoes of Virgil, as well as of Ovid, Statius, and many others,[77] discovers itself at its close to be a consideration of the same poetic dilemma Eliot faces. Too much awed attention to earlier poets (imaged as Procne) who have succeeded in transforming their pain into song makes this poet unable to do the same with his. (In this respect this fragment reinforces the point of the Dante fragment, as in both temporary pain leads to an eternal, or at least long-lived, reward.) The story of his own muteness—source of *his* pain—provides the means of the resolution of this poet's problem. When love and song are linked, as they are throughout the poem, the forward-looking refrain can be read as a pointedly anti-retrospective defense against the burden of the past. But this gesture is of course exactly the one that Virgil employs against Homer in the *Aeneid,* sending his heroes onward into history instead of back to Ithaca. The story of this anonymous poet's burden is (almost) the same story that his predecessors had to tell. And not only the story is similar: specific lines of the poetry too are transformed over generations, as the echoes of Virgil, like Virgil's echoes of Homer, attest.

In employing this line here Eliot again refers not only to the particular lament, but to its context. In invoking this poem about the ways of poetic succession, Eliot points to his own method. The fact that he quotes rather than, standardly, echoing is the sign he offers of his own transformation of the story. And where in this context in *The Waste Land* the line from the *Pervigilium Veneris* seems at first to argue against the understanding that any progress has been made over the course of the poem, and for the understanding that in speaking the words of others the poet of the present poem continues voiceless, it proves upon closer consideration to be argument for the very change it seems to belie.

The same double awareness characterizes the second half of line 429—"O swallow swallow"—though Eliot's choice of this phrase in particular is also motivated by its resonance with the Procne and Philomel motif that has played across the poem. The phrase comes from a song in Tennyson's *The Princess*, a tale of an attempt by a group of feminists to establish a university and a way of life that allows women the same chances of education and adventure that society traditionally grants men. This song is sung by the Prince, come disguised as a woman to win the Princess back. He offers "O Swallow, Swallow" after "Tears, idle tears" (sung by a young woman) has been condemned by the Princess for its nostalgia:

> "Know you no song of your own land," she said,
> "Not such as moans about the retrospect,
> But deals with the other distance and the hues
> Of promise; not a death's-head at the wine?"
> Then I remember'd one myself had made,
> What time I watch'd the swallow winging south
>
> From mine own land, part made long since, and part
> Now while I sang, and maiden-like as far
> As I could ape their treble did I sing.
> (*The Princess*, 4, lines 66–74)[78]

Though the Prince's song lacks the specifically nostalgic subject of the first song, the Princess recognizes the implicitly nostalgic character of its love lyric and condemns it as well,[79] on grounds that love per se constitutes a form of slavery for women.

Like the Prince who speaks the poem, the Princess also figures the poet. In her demands for an un- or anti-nostalgic poetry, she represents that part of the poet who would be original, abrogating all ties to old ways. But her effort fails, in large part due to her own betrayal of her ends. She reveals herself as being as much tied to the old ways as the men who contest her desire to break with those ways. Like the Princess, and *The Princess* itself, all songs in Tennyson's poem work out to be nostalgic in some degree. Desire for originality loses out to ties to the past, which may be read on similar grounds as the stuff of either loyalty or oppression. But it does not lose out entirely; we get signs of the poem's discontent with its resolution when the Prince and Princess plan a more equal future for themselves, and when the audience for the story of these two, included in a framing tale, wishes the end had been otherwise.

Tennyson's play with the role of his own lack of originality—his nostalgia—becomes quite complicated, here and throughout his work. Like Thomson, Tennyson makes both his nostalgia and his dissatisfaction over his belatedness work as a kind of originality in themselves. The melancholic stance provides these Victorians with a strategy for moving out of the enervating shadow of romanticism. Paradoxically, real enervation is overcome via masqueraded enervation. In Tennyson's work a tendency to large-scale allusiveness bordering on plagiarism supports this pose. Only after they had thoroughly documented the extent of his borrowing did Tennyson's critics determine that he does not in fact cross the border into plagiarism.[80] Tennyson's borrowing is a less self-consciously articulated sibling to Whitman's outline of the system of poetic relations and indebtedness. Both of these anatomies of influence come into being under pressure of the need to respond to romanticism. While Tennyson's melancholy at belatedness has similarities to that of the *Pervigilium* poet, it displays much more self-consciousness about its lack of originality. The post-Victorian Eliot revises the melancholic stance of his predecessors by working out his own even more self-conscious version, both in his stance of lament (bordering on parody) and in his anatomy of poetic influence.

The line from Nerval continues the mood of nostalgic melancholy. In "El Desdichado" the widowed prince with the ruined tower asks for the return of a paradisal past ("Rends-moi le Pausilippe et la mer d'Italie, / La *fleur* qui plaisait tant à mon coeur désoleé / Et la treille où le pampre à la rose s'allie" [Give me back Posilipo and the Italian sea, the *flower* which pleased my grief-stricken heart so much, and the arbour where the vine joins with the rose]).[81] But in the later stanzas the mood of failure is brought into question when the prince goes on to speak of himself as an Orpheus figure. While the point of the analogy seems initially to be the joint failure of El Desdichado and Orpheus to revive their wives, the poem closes in celebration of the prince's poetic successes:

Suis-je Amour ou Phébus? . . . Lusignan ou Biron?
Mon front est rouge encor du baiser de la reine;
J'ai rêvé dans la grotte où nage la syrène. . . .

Et j'ai deux fois vainqueur traversé l'Achéron:
Modulant tour à tour sur la lyre d'Orphée
Les soupirs de la sainte et les cris de la fée.

[Am I Love or Phoebus? . . . Lusignan or Biron? My brow is still red from the queen's kiss; I have dreamed in the cave where the siren swims. . . .

And I have twice crossed Acheron victoriously: tuning in turn on Orpheus's lyre the sighs of the saint and the fairy's cries.][82]

The choice between roles, Amour or Phébus, love or music, is clearly made in the last stanza; the real pain of the start is forgotten and the song that commemorates it is itself celebrated.

But the poem need not be read even *so* literally—no actual woman need be understood here, no personal loss as food for song, when the lost wife is read as a figure for the muse, who functions as such only when out of reach. The poet seeks exile because the fascination of the muse's presence makes composition impossible.[83] The siren in the poem figures this aspect of the muse, and her singing links her not only to an abstract muse but to earlier, inspiring poets as well.

"El Desdichado" echoes the argument of the *Pervigilium Veneris* and *The Princess*. As with the *Pervigilium*, the poet refers to a mythic story of actual loss that gives rise to song (Procne's sorrow over Philomel's rape and Orpheus's loss of Eurydice), but his own story of inspiration turns on loss of the ability to make poetry, which he mourns and which itself provides the subject of his song. The lament recuperates in itself what is lamented. (*The Princess* works less overtly as the lament of a poet, but the implicit argument echoes that of the other poems with which Eliot links it.) And, again, the parallel with *The Waste Land* is clear. The line absorbed into *The Waste Land* plays strongly upon the despairing mood at the start of Nerval's poem, but again, as with the *Pervigilium Veneris,* that despair is itself revealed to be the motor of its own dispelling.

The next quotation, from *The Spanish Tragedy*, "Why then Ile fit you," speaks in its first context of Hieronymo's (adequate but horrible) response to the world's disorder. When the two princes who have killed his son ask

Hieronymo to prepare an entertainment for them, he responds with this line, planning a play in which the princes will be killed in fact as well as in fiction. As Hieronymo turns his enemies' purpose to his own, Eliot does as well, transforming the fragmentariness of a world he objects to into the instrument of his own original transcendence of that fragmentariness.

In addition, Kyd's play is invoked here for the double remark it makes on processes of poetic transformation. The scene Eliot invokes here combines the play-that-tells-the-truth and the false-fight-that-turns-out-to-be-too-true that Shakespeare separates into distinct moments in *Hamlet*. With reference to *Hamlet*, then, *The Spanish Tragedy* embodies the first half of a process of absorption of an earlier work into a later. And at the same time, it emphasizes specifically its own transformation of earlier texts. Kyd fills his play with reworkings into English of scenes from classical sources, and he brings attention to these reworkings by including as well frequent outbreaks into Latin and Italian phrases that mix outright quotations with lines of Kyd's own composition. Kyd's use of these phrases seems at once to suggest ties between this work and the models from which he borrows and, by the jarring quality of their sudden appearances for no clear purpose of the plot, to effectively point up both the great distance between this work and its classical precursors and the author's confusion over what relation the classical world has to the world he describes here.[84] In this respect, Eliot's use of *The Spanish Tragedy* again points to the difference in the meaning of the same words introduced by new context.

The second half of line 432 comes from *The Spanish Tragedy* as well, though from a subtitle added to the 1615 quarto rather than from the play proper. With this phrase Hieronymo becomes a name for the poet of this poem, and his madness *his* response (adequate but horrible in his eyes, for in repairing the disorder he objected to he creates a new kind of disorder) to the disorder of his world.

The three interpretations of the Upanishad are then repeated once more, and the poem ends with the thrice repeated "shantih." This word is another, like "DA" before, that means differently when repeated: "Shantih. Repeated as here, a formal ending to an Upanishad" (note to line 434). Quotation blurs into ritualistic repetition here. But though the "as here" suggests that it might, the phrase's meaning does not remain unchanged when transferred from the end of the Upanishad to the end of *The Waste Land*. While it cannot turn Eliot's poem into a prophecy, it can express the will to a return to an empowering, if mythic, origin through contact with a deity, or failing that through an assertion of a structuring hierarchy.

The effect of quotation has been transformed at the poem's close, reflecting the poem's reevaluation of its own situation within the tradition. At the start, indebtedness and attenuation, signaled through the presence of so many quotations and overt allusions, and measured against a romantic standard of originality, were the source of great sorrow. By poem's end, the standard has been reinterpreted and judged false. Attenuation is discovered to be the condition of all poetry, and this poem's recognition of that condition is claimed as an originality in itself, though of a qualified sort given its understanding that no true origin ever existed. (And we do see the sources of this recognition in the poetry Eliot quotes; his difference from his sources lies in his putting the case so emphatically by means of his quotations.) Eliot's poem reaffirms the oedipal lesson that authority is transferrable from father to son, even at this late date.

Though it has been accomplished at the expense of an admission that no poetry has ever been fully original or unburdened with awareness of forerunners, the transformation affirms the possibility of a return to a kind of origin—that is, the attenuated originality that the quotations within the poem demonstrate to be necessary to authority. And the poem's argument for its own authority and for the possibility of authority in general—even at this late date—is supported at a structural level through its modeling of hierarchies, which contradict the poem's lamenting claims that such orders have fled the modern scene with the nymphs of section 3. Authoritative positions within these hierarchies are figured as desirable and attainable. For instance, the interaction of the poem proper and the notes constitutes a hierarchy of the poem's readers, who are inducted into the poem's ranking system via the notes. These notes at first make readers feel ignorant (and low therefore), working as evidence for the poem's portrait of a world in decline. But in providing the information that they at first seemed to mock readers for lacking, the notes go on to offer readers the sense that their ignorance, and with it the attenuation of the modern world, can be repaired with a course of directed reading. It is precisely the poem's offer of the possibility of mastery and so of a variety of kinds of authority—over the text, over one's earlier and less informed self, and over others less learned—that has appealed to masses of budding English majors, and the process of grappling with the poem has served them as a rite of passage.[85]

Another example of the poem's structural rankings lies in its literary hierarchy. We have seen already how Eliot rearranges familiar hierarchies of major and minor poets in his essays, and the blurring of familiar boundaries is continued in the poem, where the work of little-remembered artists like Day is set beside that of Marvell and Milton in a maneuver to bolster Eliot's own claims to majority. The apparent destruction of hierarchy in the initial leveling gesture then comes to reinforce hierarchy (and Eliot's place in it) in the long run. A hierarchy of *kinds* of influence also operates here. While most of the quotations are poetic, occasional nonpoetic borrowings are featured. The technique of quoting from "low" literature—for instance, the borrowings from the ballad of Mrs. Porter and her daughter and the "Shakespeherian Rag" line from the Follies show (line 128)—moves out of the realm of poetry and into those of rude songs and parodies of "high" literature. The ballad is noted, and the genre of the Follies line is recognizable even without the information that it is a quotation.[86] Aside from the evidence of cultural decline that they give, these quotations demonstrate the great difference between themselves and the poem in which they are included. Their very lowness works to prove by contrast the highness of Eliot's work. The greatness of the dichotomy defuses their threat to this text and offers a certain excitement in the same way that any foray out of the safety of a privileged environment into an unlike world provides a thrill, always assuming that a swift return is ensured. In one gesture, these borrowings suggest and deny the possibility of an influence of low literature on high.[87]

All these hierarchies reiterate the prototypical Freudian hierarchy, of masculine over feminine, inculcated in the moment of the male child's oedipal identification with the father. As Freud outlined it, this process requires the repression of feminine identification as prerequisite to the boy's eventual assumption of masculine authority, even as it requires that the superior power of father over son be acknowledged as well. The son takes up the passive position in the short term in exchange for reassurance that in the long term he need not be linked to the secondary, feminine role. In Eliot's schema, this repressive hierarchization of the child's paternal and maternal identifications is the backdrop against which not just general authority but poetic authority in particular passes, from older to younger poets. And to anchor the poem's other hierarchies, a specifically gendered hierarchy operates at the level of the poem's structure as well. A hierarchy of textual media is established through inclusion of three borrowings from speech, not even formally constituted as texts. The fact that all three have female sources reinforces the particularly unauthoritative position of these utterances in this text. These borrowings make up the third strand in the poem's narrative of its genesis, the narrative of appropriation. In the notes to the facsimile edition, Valerie Eliot, Eliot's second wife and the editor of the facsimile, reports that the Lil and Albert passage in section 3 (lines 139–72) came from the conversation of a servant named Ellen Kellond.[88] The extent to which the borrowing from Kellond quotes directly cannot be judged, though it can be clearly recognized as the speech of another, lower class than that sounded through the rest of the poem, both in its diction and in its subject matter.

A second, related source is taken for granted in accounts of *The Waste Land*'s background, but gets no mention in the notes to either the poem or the facsimile edition. The speech of Eliot's first wife, Vivien, seems to have been the source of that of the nervous woman in section 2, "A Game of Chess" (lines 111–38).[89] Again, the extent to which this section involves direct quotation cannot be gauged, but it apparently functioned for readers who knew the Eliots as at least an overt allusion.

A third such source has already been mentioned, although in a different context. That is Marie Larisch, whose memoires inform the poem's first verse paragraph. The poem's reliance on Larisch's text was pointed out in a 1954 essay by one G. L. K. Morris. Another note to the facsimile edition explains that Eliot had not read the book but had met Larisch (the circumstances of this meeting are not given), and that he quoted her conversation exactly in his poem.[90] This explanation may seem plausible—though the poem's reproduction of the shape of the story of Larisch's childhood trip to visit King Ludwig seems rather precise to have sprung from a social conversation, and the inspecificity of data on the meeting introduces further doubt. But Eliot's insistence that this borrowing has no printed source is particularly impressive. (Because no further explanation is provided, we can only assume that the notes record Valerie Eliot's discussions with the poet.) As we have seen, the poem claims in the first and second narratives of its genesis that it is primarily concerned with the work of other poets, and particularly the work of male poets—fathers struggled with in the poem's literary oedipal narrative. Unwritten status represents a demotion in this poem. In contrast to the first two, the third set of texts represents the maternal sphere, which is here linked with the nonliterary, via the association with speech, and repressed.

The offhand, apparently spoken, manner in which they are acknowledged (in the notes by Eliot's second wife) seems to mean to suggest that because they are speech (and, via the overlap, because their sources are female), they are open to appropriation without the anxiety attendant on borrowings from prior written texts marked in the notes and wrestled with in the quotation plot. But the poem's concerns with sexual confusions and the particular dwelling in the unedited version of the poem on the inevitable bad results when women turn to poetry[91] suggest that this field is anxiety-filled as well.

The connection of women's production with speech (a specifically physical phenomenon) rather than with written texts ties feminine creativity to the physical and, implicitly, to women's capacity to give birth. A familiar myth of a special feminine (physical) originality is called upon here, in contrast to which the masculine is linked to recognition of the impossibility of returns to (poetic) origins. Though this contrast, in aligning women with the full presence associated with the body and men with the absence requisite to writing, may seem at first to privilege the feminine position over the masculine, the deep effect is to deny women the position of writing and to link them to a (mythical) world of full presence: a world of nature. This model requires both that women be refused admission to the ranks of poetry and that sources outside the strictly poetic (lower, then, in the hierarchy of voices and markable thus as "feminine") not be understood to contribute to the process of poetic inspiration.

The buried story of female creativity has a twofold role then in the poem. It operates initially as site of a pre-oedipal identification with the mother (and envy of her capacity to bear), which in the oedipal process must be denied and repressed, only to reemerge, refunctioned for mature use, as linguistic or (when further developed) poetic creativity. In the process of this refunctioning, the linguistic (or conceptual) variety of creativity is associated with the masculine, both in contrast to the apparently feminine realm of physical creativity and through the (related) link of fathers to the world of symbolic thought.[92] Out of this gendering comes the second role of feminine creativity. Redefined as less valuable than literary, masculine creativity, feminine creativity can then provide the lower element in an initial or "original" hierarchy. This hierarchy of gender and of kinds of creativity in itself supports the possibility of ranked authority and this poem's aspirations to it, and in so doing provides the premise upon which the poem builds. The hierarchy at the poem's "origin" is here demonstrated to be based in the appropriation of the (spoken) words of women. The appropriation tale is thus part of the poem's oedipal genesis story, which requires not just the acknowledgment of fathers, but the demotion of mothers as well. By the oedipal logic, the appropriation narrative constitutes a necessary theft, which appropriates and in the same gesture claims not to do so. The claim rests on the understanding both that there can be no theft where there are no rights accruing to the source, and that the feminine is of too little consequence to make a real contribution to the poem anyway. But only because the voice has already been appropriated can such a claim be made.

The story of masculine appropriation of female creativity is complicated by the fact that little girls, like their brothers, also are inducted into the world of symbolic thought and utterance, and like their brothers they may become poets—an inconvenient fact that undoes neat gender hierarchies when allowed expression. While for many centuries the order of things was such that women generally remained in the world of literal creativity, by the modern period that order had changed. Sandra M. Gilbert and Susan Gubar have documented the anxiety that feminine transgressions of traditional gender orders caused among moderns.[93] For Eliot the overturning of familiar hierarchies had a particular resonance. Not only his female peers were given to poetic expression, but his mother, Charlotte Champe Stearns Eliot, had poetic aspirations as well. Eliot's biographer Peter Ackroyd discusses her career:

> Although her testimonials on leaving school described her as possessing "unusual brilliancy," she did not go to university and was obliged to earn her living as a teacher, moving from school to school until she met and married Henry Ware Eliot in St Louis in 1868. She had wanted desperately to attend college, she once told her son, and in the absence of such opportunities she considered herself to be a "dead failure." She was a poet or, rather, she wrote poems—most of them to friends or as contributions to newspapers. She pasted them into scrapbooks like so many pressed flowers. But she received no early recognition, and her own frustration with her literary gifts was channelled into ambition for those of her son.[94]

Eliot's experience seems then not to have imitated the oedipal model. He followed his mother's lead into poetry, a process involving an identification with a variety of the feminine not accounted for in Freud's story, or in Lacan's specifically linguistic version thereof. Any number of reasons might be adduced for Eliot's imposition of the oedipal model on the story of his poetic genesis, not least of them the example of Mrs. Eliot's lack of success in finding a means to move beyond aspiration to authority to the thing itself. The oedipal pattern provides Eliot with a time-tested route. Just as his repression of Americanness served his desire to reassert a clear hierarchy and his own primary position within it, so did he actively repress his maternal, or feminine, identification.

The Waste Land's genesis narratives thus represent concerns both peculiar to their author and of general moment to his peers.

It will be remarked that there are other, written texts by women cited in *The Waste Land*—most prominently Jessie Weston's book on the grail. But this reference, to a scholarly text, does not participate in the poem's portrait of influence patterns. Though it does supply the title, the reference to Weston is the lead red herring. It offers readers the promise of a scholarly map to the poem, but it then goes on to mock them for relying upon this map (in yet another implicit hierarchy of ironic reading over trust in simple statement, which figures yet again the impossibility of any return to an origin, or indeed of the existence of any origin in the first place). The headnote in which Eliot asserts his debts to Weston and to *The Golden Bough* constitutes part of the quotation plot's early claim of incapacity to invent.

> Not only the title, but the plan and a good deal of the incidental symbolism of the poem were suggested by Miss Jessie L. Weston's book on the Grail legend: *From Ritual to Romance* (Cambridge). Indeed, so deeply am I indebted, Miss Weston's book will elucidate the difficulties of the poem much better than my notes can do; and I recommend it (apart from the great interest of the book itself) to any who think such elucidation worth the trouble.[95]

This claim to integral dependence, on a nonpoetic source no less, contributes to the initial establishment of a sense of diminished present, which is then denied in the show of strength at the poem's end. Weston's femininity (stressed in the double use of "Miss") then becomes part of the joke—as if so masculine a poem could have depended on the work of a woman.

The only woman poet mentioned in the notes or in the poem's borrowings is Sappho, to whose line on the dusk of evening that "[brings] home all that bright morning scattered" Eliot's lines 220–21 ("At the violet hour, the evening that strives / Homeward, and brings the sailor home from the sea") claim a relation. The note in which Eliot compares his line to hers differs, however, from the notes to other texts, in including neither mention nor citation of the source. It reads simply: "221. This may not appear as exact as Sappho's lines, but I had in mind the 'longshore' or 'dory' fisherman, who returns at nightfall." Sappho, the most distant of the precursors cited, seems to have been included for her honored part in the tradition of poetic revision of earlier works, which Eliot points to throughout as evidence for the acceptability of his dependency on prior poems. "To take from Sappho what one can use for one's poems," writes Hugh Kenner with reference to Pound's various borrowings from her, "was a tradition understood by Catullus and practiced by English poets ever since, in the 19th century, there were accessible collections of her work to take from."[96] It seems also not accidental that she is a lesbian, a woman whose sexuality involves (or would seem to) a rejection of physical creativity. Her rejection seconds in a roundabout way the standard gendered division of physical and literary creativies that Eliot endorses. It is this that allows her to be the exception that proves an otherwise stable rule.

The three strands of narrative that make up *The Waste Land*'s tale of its own genesis variously substitute for and interact with one another. The most overt of these narratives, the poem's quotation plot, tells the story of the young poet's wrestling with paternal precursors, but suppresses the names of those of particular concern. The allusive narrative of the poem's descent from Whitman has special importance in the poem for its double repression: on the one hand for Whitman's formative effect on Eliot—shared with Shelley, Tennyson, and even Milton—and on the other for its Americanness, a quality Eliot finds particularly problematic. The secondariness of the American within the hierarchies Eliot asserts can lead us to understand the concern with Whitman to cover an earlier concern with the similarly secondary *maternal* precursor (and Whitman's frequent feminine representation may be understood also to refer to this earlier influence). While the three women whose words are appropriated supply specific material to Eliot's poem, they represent not so much examples of specific deep and early influences on Eliot's work as a class of precursors whose words and position served a formative role in his induction into poetry. The very fact of these women's lack of poetic renown, major or minor, represents the role accorded them within patriarchy, a role against which women were working as Eliot wrote and to which his poem restricts them, in order to make possible his own assumption of a position of primacy. The appropriation narrative fills out the tale begun in the quotation plot and continued in the allusions to Whitman. No one narrative tells the poem's genesis story alone: the three operate as a familial triad—son, father, and mother—and only in their relation is the full story of any one of them expressed.[97] At the same time, the poem opens up possibilities of other readings of the feminine because by default it witnesses both the inescapability of and the value of attenuation to poetry. And attentuation may, through its secondary position in the model that values the unattenuated most highly, be read as an analogy for the feminine.

Though only with the publication of the facsimile has the third narrative become visible to readers, its generative function has been at work all along. The three strands of the poem's genesis narrative employ quotation to portray Eliot's story of the oedipal rite of passage more complexly than has generally been recognized. His articulation of the dynamic of repression of the feminine seems to have been triggered by an anxiety about identification with the feminine, heightened by the linkage with the secondary that accrues to the American modern. Eliot's reassertion of that repression and the hierarchies the repression makes possible expresses, as we will see in the chapters that follow, just one aspect of the American modernist response to this anxiety. For those to whom denials of nationality and/or femininity are not attractive or possible, the oedipal model does not serve, and for them quotation works in very different ways, to different effects.

Chapter Three

William Carlos Williams's *Paterson*

Where for Eliot quotation serves as a means to affirm standard hierarchies, for Williams it contributes to an exploration of the virtues of dehierarchization and relativism. In suggesting this, I only partially join the recent trend in Williams studies (among deconstructors, proponents of alternative canons, ethicists, and some gender theorists) toward crediting Williams with a thoroughgoing enlightened relativism.[1] Like these critics, I understand Williams's work to involve a challenge to centered authority, but I will qualify the case in two ways, holding that Williams's relativism is both interested and ambivalent.

Williams's interest in overturning hierarchies grew out of his position as a post-romantic, an American, and a modern. The romantic principle of originality includes an implicit hierarchy, by which those things not considered original are rated secondary. So prevalent is the romantic paradigm in our culture that the term "secondary" does not merely describe, it also involves a negative judgment, as does the term "derivative" in common parlance. One way to overcome the judgment of secondariness is to reinvent the terms upon which originality is judged. As we have seen, the romantics themselves did a version of this, inventing the notion of artistic "originality," based on a claim of access to an origin within each individual, to displace their own sense of temporal secondariness. But once invented, this notion went on to create a new hierarchy in which those with whom originality was not original ranked lower than their predecessors. A relativist reworking of the romantic model, by denying the relevance of the hierarchies in which they might be ranked secondary, offers post-romantics a way out of this judgment. Such a model might lead to an aesthetic of pointed unoriginality, like that demonstrated in the extensive use of direct quotation. Though the overall effects for which they employed quotation differed widely, with this device those moderns who quote were alike provided with means both to depart from the romantic model of originality and to claim success within its terms (since such pointed unoriginality was original with them). Both stances enabled them to disclaim a secondary position, by at once claiming a primary place within the romantic hierarchy (in demonstrating originality after all) and denying the relevance of that hierarchy (via quotation, which suggests that all poetry has sources outside itself and so is unoriginal, and thus that all work is at least potentially of equal value).

As was suggested in the introduction, a related dynamic characterizes the terms "modern" and "American," both of which involve similar and implicit contradictions and hierarchies. While the word *modern* suggests a welcome of the present and of the new, it embeds within the very insistency of that welcome a contradictory anxiety about derivativeness. It suggests not just a break with outdated ways but a break with sustaining traditions as well, and so creates a two-sided dynamic of loss and gain. Similarly, the descendants of American immigrants have experienced double allegiances, to the Old World *and* to the New. In both cases, as with the case of romanticism, the old has tended to rank higher in comparisons of culture. This would seem to be because hierarchies work by being reassuring, and old hierarchies are more reassuring than new ones because they can claim a more natural authority on the tradition-equals-nature model. Though the American self-image embraces the new and speaks a rhetoric of inclusiveness, included in *that* is an element, à la James, of anxiety about derivativeness.

Where Eliot responds to this haunting sense of cultural secondariness by reaffirming hierarchy but denying his low position within it, obscuring his work's New World origins (particularly emphatically in the notes to *The Waste Land*) and renouncing his American citizenship, Williams attempts to exorcise this sense by denying the relevance of the hierarchies through which such rankings are made. In *Paterson* Williams extends the critique of hierarchy implicit in quotation's (ostensible) rejection of originality to challenge the notion of hierarchy per se, asserting instead a democratic value that obviates rank and working with a relativist scheme that reinterprets the secondary into value. This kind of valuation does not rename the secondary as primary, since that would defeat the point. Thus America cannot replace Europe in a new Williamsian hierarchy. Moreover, the European and the American are mutually informative, not so distinct as old/new parallels suggest. So, while Williams does feature the American most prominently in his work, European influences past and current are honored as well (as, for instance, in his borrowings from the surrealists).

The linked set of related hierarchic structures brought into question in *Paterson* includes the notion of canon, nostalgic hypervaluation of past over present, the relation between genders, the division between art and the mundane, and the romantic privileging of originality over attenuation—in short, any and all structures that assign value on exclusionary principles. At a structural level in *Paterson*, the challenge is implicit in the juxtapositions of prose and poetry. And Williams's lifelong search for a new measure suited especially to his "new" poetry works as a fine analogy for his concomitant effort to develop a new scale to measure the value of poetry so that his own need not (or at least need not inevitably) come up short. The variable foot stands in well for the principle of relative judgment inherent in the effort to undo hierarchy.

But Williams's attitude is not entirely consistent, for the task he sets himself is enormous. Bringing the notion of hierarchy into question threatens all that is familiar along with that which offends, and the burden of such a challenge to the known weighs heavy on him. A nostalgic desire for a more reassuringly ordered world, kept in check on some fronts, reappears, virulent, on others. Williams's work, like that of Eliot, exhibits the double allegiance of the American modernist poet toward both the European literary past (and the hierarchies it represents) and the American literary present. But where for Eliot one half of the doubleness is repressed along the pattern of the oedipal model, for Williams both sides flourish. As a consequence, the poem's take on standard hierarchies fluctuates. In particular the poem's ambivalence is apparent in its treatment of gender and, relatedly, of filiation. These concerns are both literal and metaphoric, representing a specific preoccupation with gender structures as well as a wider interest in the reworking of all hierarchies.

In *Paterson*, quite differently from Eliot in *The Waste Land*, Williams works in some measure to unrepress the feminine. Because his attempt is only half-hearted, he does not succeed entirely; but he does articulate the process of repression implicit in the maintenance of the oedipal structure and of all hierarchies, while enacting that process. In *Paterson*, the feminine surfaces and is acknowledged in the poem (in the letters from Cress, in Mme Curie, and in the quotation of Sappho) at the same time that it is being beaten down (also in the Cress letters as well as in letters from others and in the image of the "beautiful thing"). Where in *The Waste Land* the repression of the feminine is a fait accompli in the plot, recognizable to readers only after some digging, Williams represents the process of the repression within his poem, and so denaturalizes it.

As Brian Bremen has demonstrated, the work of Jessica Benjamin can assist elucidation of the alternative to the oedipal pattern modeled in *Paterson*.[2] Working from the understanding that the oedipal structure is one of domination and hierarchy and that all such structures are historically and culturally determined and so open to change,[3] Benjamin argues that it should be possible to revise the pattern of development so that neither role—that traditionally associated with the mother or that traditionally associated with the father—need be gendered. She argues that fathers and mothers may each model both nurturance and agency and that boy and girl children can identify usefully with both parents equally, without being confused about their gender identities. This equalizing of territory should lead, by her model, to an end to hierarchization of the attributes tied to the two roles. Given that this hierarchization may be understood to be the template from which other social hierarchies are patterned, it is at least arguable that such equalization would lead to a breakdown of hierarchies at other levels of society as well. While Bremen concludes that Williams departs fully from the oedipal model into the Benjaminian, I do not find that the poem surrenders its investment in hierarchies entirely. Instead, I hope to show that Williams's work enacts a stage in the process of revision of the model, while representing in itself a profound ambivalence over the changes it assists.

Williams began actively writing *Paterson* in 1942, twenty years after the publication of *The Waste Land* (1922) and twenty-five years after the publication of the first *Cantos* (1917). The long interval notwithstanding, *Paterson* is Williams's response to these earlier poems and to the statement he understood their poets to have made in emigrating (place of residence and poetry being intimately connected in Williams's view). Williams considered their move a retreat into the comforts of nostalgia from the difficult challenge of developing new positionalities for American poetry. Instead of wrestling as Williams did to develop a new system of valuation to replace the hierarchic structure that rated American modernists secondary, Eliot and Pound, in Williams's view, attempted to deny their Americanness and to claim a secure position within the standard hierarchy.

Like the poem as a whole, Williams's use of quotation in *Paterson* responds to Eliot and Pound, challenging their quotations' hierarchic mode. Williams's quotations have primarily American rather than European sources and come from historical texts and from letters to Williams rather than from "great" literature. In this last respect, Williams's method does learn something from Pound, for whom he always maintained some sympathy (the two were college friends). Williams's use of historical texts learns from Pound's "poem including history." But where Pound mixes his borrowings from canonic literature with episodes from the lives of well-known charismatic figures (offered as exemplars) and "luminous details" of history, Williams uses ordinary characters whose stories are chosen for their messiness, another refusal of hierarchy.

Williams's use of quotation in *Paterson* develops on his use of it in his book of essays titled *In the American Grain* (1925), an early response to *The Waste Land*. *In the American Grain* included citations from the journals and papers of the New World figures Williams described, along with his own prose.[4] In *Paterson* Williams expands the range of effects he achieves with quotation in the earlier text. Using historical quotations of the sort he used in *In the American Grain*, as well as collage technique, letters from contemporaries (including lesser-known contemporary poets), and even a few borrowings from the works of established poets (though he reacts against Pound and Eliot's use of such borrowings), Williams works to develop an antihierarchic, unnostalgic poetry adequate to the expression of his concept of a confidently American experience. But in the process he discovers that abandonment of familiar structures of meaning does not come easily and that his poetic constitution includes a nostalgic element along with the antinostalgic element stressed in the earlier work. *Paterson* as a whole offers a portrait of Williams's ambivalence about the desirability of hierarchy, and his uses of quotation in the poem express this ambivalence.[5] To understand the roles quotation plays in *Paterson*, we will look first at the background against which they developed and then go on to consider the ways in which Williams employs the device in the poem.

Williams's antipathy both for Pound's and Eliot's abandonment of the U.S. for Europe and for the poetry that followed their departure is well known. In *Kora in Hell* (1918) Williams directly speaks his opinion of his good friend Pound:

> E. P. is the best enemy United States verse has. He is interested, passionately interested—even if he doesn't know what he is talking about. But of course he does know what he is talking about. He does not, however, know everything, not by more than half. The accordances of which Americans have the parts and the colors but not the

> completions before them pass beyond the attempts of his thought. It is a middle-aging blight of the imagination.
>
> I praise those who have the wit and courage, and the conventionality, to go direct toward their vision of perfection in an objective world where the signposts are clearly marked, viz., to London. But confine them in hell for their paretic assumption that there is no alternative but their own groove.[6]

The image of stable conventionality attributed to Pound here evokes through opposition Williams's vision of a poetry of struggle. But if in 1918 Pound was Williams's enemy, in 1922 *The Waste Land* made Eliot his principal target. In his *Autobiography* (1951), Williams records his response to the poem's publication:

> Then out of the blue *The Dial* brought out *The Waste Land* and all our hilarity ended. It wiped out our world as if an atom bomb had been dropped upon it and our brave sallies into the unknown were turned to dust. . . .
>
> Critically Eliot returned us to the classroom just at the moment when I felt that we were on the point of an escape to matters much closer to the essence of a new art form itself—rooted in the locality which should give it fruit. . . .
>
> If with his skill he could have been kept here to be employed by our slowly shaping drive, what strides might we not have taken! . . . By his walking out on us we were stopped, for the moment, cold. It was a bad moment.[7]

Eliot's reliance on European source texts and his move back to the continent directly contradicted Williams's view of the American poet's task. A much-cited passage from *In the American Grain* suggests Williams's sense of his project:

> Americans have never recognized themselves. How can they? It is impossible until someone invent the ORIGINAL terms. As long as we are content to be called by somebody else's terms, we are incapable of being anything but our own dupes.[8]

Eliot's quotations, which Williams characterized as plagiarism in one review, as well as his alignment of himself with the tradition of European literature, seemed to Williams pointedly to refuse such an attempt at invention. But while Williams's antipathy was strongly felt, and for all the assistance a loyal Eliot and Pound might have afforded him in forging a new poetic, their leaving contributed significantly to the making of *Paterson* by providing a thesis to react energetically against.[9]

In *Paterson* Williams's polemic surfaces first in the preface, which asks readers from the start to consider the poem in oppositional relation to the work of those American poets who had left for Europe:

> just another dog
> among a lot of dogs. What
> else is there? And to do?
> The rest have run out—
> after the rabbits.
> Only the lame stands—on
> three legs.[10]

The play on "run out" taints the image of the other dogs' vigor with suggestions of cowardice and prepares the way for a similar reversal of associations to the lameness of the one who remains behind. And indeed, in the lines that follow Williams goes on to claim as an advantage the lameness that he attributes to himself and to *Paterson*: the "rest" turn out to have headed backward in moving back to the Old World, leaving this poet to recognize that "there is / no return" (*P*, 3) only forward movement into the future.[11] Further references to both Eliot and Pound occur as the poem continues.[12] The force of the contrast he sets up between his work and what he constitutes as their nostalgic poetries is used by Williams as a jumping off place to explore the modes of truly local American poetry in *Paterson*.

In both *In the American Grain* and *Paterson*, Williams responds to Pound and Eliot's nostalgia for Europe and "the clarity[,] . . . / loveliness and / authority" of its hierarchies (*P*, 36) by stressing the American and bringing the relevance of hierarchies into question. For instance, the set of Americans featured in *In the American Grain* differs greatly from those featured in the canons of American literature propounded by such writers as Van Wyck Brooks and Waldo Frank in the same period. As Vera Kutzinski has suggested, the Amerocentrism that flowered in the twenties among Williams's peers is revealed in *In the American Grain* to be a deluded repetition of the structures of Old World hierarchy within the context of the New World, paradoxically but effectively continuing the subordination of the American to the European that it claims to subvert.[13] The canon of nineteenth-century American writers that Frank and the others vaunt imitates the European canon both in the fact of its canonicity and in its selection of only those works that relate to the earlier canon. Williams's collection, on the other hand, is defined by its pointed lack of hierarchy—its openness to all voices, its "conceptual disorder that evolves into a literary method."[14] Like Williams himself, Kutzinski defines Williams's method in contrast with that of Eliot: "[In Eliot's texts] disorder is but a surface phenomenon. It is the result of desperate, yet frustrated, attempts to recover the myth of Literature and to transcend chaos and fragmentation through romantic visions of cosmic totality."[15] Williams's method or principle of disorder seems to Kutzinski to be "the beginning of a new era (and a new method) of writing."[16]

But the new writing Kutzinski sees Williams inaugurating in *In the American Grain* is not fulfilled in the poet's own later work.[17] Though the fame of *Paterson* brought *In the American Grain* into the critical limelight as an earlier working out of the issues and methods developed in *Paterson*, the later work is much more orderly than the method of New World writing operative in *In the American Grain* might lead us to expect. This failure of consistency can be read as more fully "American" than a complete acceptance of disorder would be, since America, the product of the historical encounter between Europe and the New World, cannot be dissociated entirely from the European. And that Williams's work involved a strong European connection at its inception, one that was bound to color his later work as well, is testified to in his early work, which responds particularly to Keats.[18] In his *Autobiography*, Williams acknowledges Keats's importance to his early career but claims to have passed beyond his influence fairly quickly. His first substantial works—an unpublished early long poem (Williams destroyed one version of this poem but he apparently neglected to do the same with his second copy, which survives) and *The Wanderer* (1914)—chart the progress of this standard "abandonment."

Williams described his first long poem as a rewriting of *Endymion*, imitating Keats's line and form as well as *Endymion*'s concern with the progress toward maturity of a young poet. As Williams recounts it, the poem tells the tale of a prince abducted from his wedding feast, a feast with no survivors other than himself, who awakens in a land he does not know, where no one understands him.

> [What follows was] no more and no less than the aimless wandering, for the most part, of the young prince in his effort to get home again as well as to discover what had happened to him—he had not been able to recall the details, merely "sensed" them: That there had been a beautiful bride, a father, a mother; that a disastrous event of some sort had occurred of which he was the victim. So he went on, home-

> ward or seeking a home that was his own, all this through a "foreign" country whose language was barbarous.[19]

Williams's poem parallels Keats's in being unsatisfactory to its author (Keats apologized for his poem's immaturity in his preface, Williams burned his); and in its antique setting (both poems reach backward for strengths that will carry them across the threshold of the moment and into the future). But where Keats's tale of the wanderings of his hero ends finally in a transcendence that suggests the successful movement of the poet out of the realm of the immature into full poetic power (even if not accomplished in that particular poem), Williams's poem tells only the tale of loss without recovery, arriving at no conclusion.

Williams's poem bears witness to his sense of exile from the world of its model. And his breaking the poem off functions as his version of transcendence, signaling his recognition that the Keatsian model is insufficient to his need. For as one who would be a truly American poet, even though inducted into the ranks of poetry by an Englishman, Williams cannot afford to think his own land barbarous.[20] Like Keats, who in *Endymion* celebrates the special virtues of the English muse, Williams works to be the poet of his own place, and to do so he must silence his early contempt for the New World.

He accomplishes this in his next poem, *The Wanderer*, a second rewriting of *Endymion*,[21] though in a much less directly imitative style. Set in Paterson, by the banks of the Passaic, *The Wanderer* is the tale of an emphatically American poetic novitiate. This novitiate specifically involves affirming value in what is still seen as the degradation of the American present: the poet drinks the river's filthy water and it transforms him. The degradation is revalued and the recognition and acceptance of value in what earlier seemed worthless, even though the acceptance is drenched with despair, are reimagined as the way to glory. Instead of submitting to despair over his surroundings and himself in them, Williams determines to make the most of them.[22]

The poem's Americanness is suggested also, though problematically, in its clear links to Whitman—Williams borrows especially heavily from "Crossing Brooklyn Ferry" (for example, in the second stanza: "But one day crossing the ferry / With the great towers of Manhattan before me, / Out at the prow with the sea wind blowing, / I had been wearying many questions / Which she had put on to try me: / How shall I be a mirror to this modernity?").[23] Whitman serves Williams as a defense against Keats, but it is a defense that presents difficulties of its own. Williams defends against both threats with a neat feint, borrowed again from *Endymion*. He makes the poem at its conclusion into the tale of the abandonment of its own mode, of its poet's departure from the style of his teachers. The poet, transformed by his draught of river water, prepares at the close to go on to "the new wandering" and, presumably, a new poetry, free of all reminders of poetries past.

The renunciation demonstrates just the opposite of its claim, of course. Williams continues invested in the myth of originality that his teachers model for him, and as we will see his revision of that myth in *Paterson* repeats with a different emphasis Eliot's response to the weight of romantic and Whitmanic pressures to be original. Where Eliot demystifies the myth of originality in terms of the works of earlier poets (demonstrating that an earlier poet has always already said it before) and then claims that demystification as the sign of his own originality, Williams extends the demystification to the world at large. His poem too has sources outside itself, but they are not only poetic; they include a much wider range of texts. These he quotes not to suggest his own insufficiency to an ideal model of poetic transformation—the model that Eliot depends on to create through contrast the effect of loss in the first three books of *The Waste Land*—but as signs of his lack of concern with such a model. This poem claims at once to depend on an enormous range of earlier texts and to be completely at home with such a dependence. Williams reverses Emerson's emphasis in "Quotation and Originality" on the power of even the most belated individual to make a real contribution to the cultural store in spite of an enormously rich and various cultural inheritance.

The situation parallels that of Eliot's original unoriginality, again with an opposite emphasis. Where Eliot aims at originality and almost accidentally discovers that it is necessary to subvert the very originality he desires in order to attain (some version of) it, Williams insists on subversion while being less at ease with the extent to which he can neither accomplish it nor even unqualifiedly desire it. While their attempts differ, they are clearly men of the same moment, both caught up in the project of revising the system of valuation in which they feel they count less than their European predecessors. Conflicting impulses operate in both cases, complicating judgment and inscribing the work within the real complexity of history and the process of cultural change. And in Williams's case, as in Eliot's, the demystification of originality creates an essential conflict that is reflected throughout his poem.

Williams's demystification of romantic originality takes a second, more semantic, tack as well. In his chapter on Edgar Allan Poe in *In the American Grain*,

Williams distinguishes between true and false originalities: "Poe's work strikes by its scrupulous originality, *not* "originality" in the bastard sense, but in its legitimate sense of solidity which goes back to the ground, a conviction that he *can* judge within himself."[24] Three senses of the word originality are in play here. The first, true originality by Williams's lights, consists in faithfulness to one's place of origin, one's own ground, so that Poe, who is American by origin, can only be good insofar as his work shows its Americanness. The second, romantic notion of originality as the fruit of its poet's individual genius — the sense that brought the word into wide usage — is rejected here, punningly, as a bastardization (even as its principal tenet, "judging within oneself," is upheld). This opens the way for *Paterson*'s insistently unagonized quotation. Originality in its third sense — temporal originality — is elided here, though an awareness of it pervades the essay, along with an awareness of the issues of belatedness that follow from it.[25] In this respect, Williams's redefinition again follows the pattern of his romantic precursors, whose use of the term "originality" emerges out of a similar attempt to confound the difficulties of belatedness through redefinition. Thus, where both Eliot and Williams assert their originality by demonstrating in differently weighted ways the impossibility of originality, Williams asserts his originality in addition by redefining the word. He will be original in a new way (and in a way he claims is based in a temporally more "original" etymological sense, though this is arguable), by being true to his locality. It only remains for Williams to discover in what such truth consists.

This project is easier set than accomplished, for localism as Williams defines it consists less in a catalogue of particular local details than in the recognition of the basic principles of the relative values of cultures. The Americanness Williams attributes to Poe involves not the introduction of local details within a narrative structure essentially like those used by Europeans — the fault for which Williams and Poe damn Hawthorne — but recognition of the need to discover or fashion a narrative structure appropriate to each new culture. So Williams could claim that the bizarre surfaces of Poe's stories were not the point at all — these were (we can infer) mere reflections of Poe's sense of the bizarreness of his own literary position. Instead, the importance of Poe's work lies in his recognition of the need to turn away from European models.

This abstract doctrine of localism that transcends any particular locale — a translocalism — does not in itself provide a very clear basis to build on. Indeed, Williams acknowledges that Poe had difficulties in determining how to structure his locally representative stories once he had seen the need to do so, and these difficulties—like everything else in Williams's discussion of Poe—suggest a parallel with Williams's own experience. But the doctrine does provide a basis for a beginning. The description that Williams finally formulates of Poe's American realization of the new localist method would serve as well as a description of his own:

> authentic particles, a thousand of which spring to the mind for quotation, taken apart and reknit with a view to emphasize, enforce and make evident, the *method*. Their quality of skill in observation, their heat, local verity, being *overshadowed* only by the detached, the abstract, the cold philosophy of their joining together; a method springing so freshly from the local conditions which determine it, by their emphasis of firm crudity and lack of coordinated structure, as to be worthy of most painstaking study.[26]

Clearly this description can be read as a look forward to *Paterson*'s explicitly local subject matter, its style of quoting local documents (authentic particles), its "firm crudity" (part of a refusal to connect itself with any established tradition of literary language, which Williams discusses elsewhere in the essay), and its "lack of coordinated structure" (the need of a new structure is fulfilled, in the absence of any clear sense of what that new structure should be, as antistructure). But it also describes the principles at work in the construction of the book in which this description appears: *In the American Grain* both depends on an undoing of the traditional memory of American history and employs quotation extensively.

Williams's use of quotation in *In the American Grain* and, later, in *Paterson* is partially explained, rather roundaboutly, in his reading of Poe's use of quotation in his prose. Williams views Poe's borrowings of "the tags of other cultures" as a sign not of a need to pay obeisance to those cultures, but of his strong sense of his own culture: "Poe could look at France, Spain, Greece, and NOT be impelled to copy. He could do this BECAUSE he had the sense within him of a locality of his own, capable of cultivation. . . . If there had ever been another American to use his Greek, Sanskrit, Hebrew, Latin, French, German, Italian and Spanish—in the text—with anything like the unspoiled mastery of Poe, we should have known, long since, what it meant to have a literature of our own."[27] Writing about "The Purloined Letter," Barbara Johnson notes that the story "is riddled with a constant, peculiar kind of intertextuality,"[28] and the same might be said for the tales as a group. Poe's peculiar uses of quotation—purloined words, phrases, and even whole sentences, made to serve covert purposes while sitting, apparently innocently, in plain view—include extensive misquotation and misattribution and go hand in hand with what Williams calls "the witty tricks with bogus Latin which he plays on his illiterate public."[29] These devices work as a kind of rewriting of the past, enabling Poe to take over the present by taking over the past that seemed to preempt the present. In this respect Poe's uses of quotation double the more explicit concern present in all his work, both poetry and prose, with the unceasing repetition of the news of its own haunting by the past's absence, an absence for which Poe claims some (troubled but unrepentant) responsibility at the same time that he mourns it. ("To One in Paradise," the poem Williams judges Poe's best, gives one instance of this pattern.)

Williams's choice of Poe as model American is in some measure guided by his sense that Poe combines Williams's own choice to remain in the United States with the erudition he admires in Pound and especially in Eliot and misses in himself.[30] Poe's unnostalgic use of quotation as the scene in which issues of authority and cultural filiation are worked out models an alternative to Eliot's use of the device (and it is Eliot who is the object of Williams's remark quoted above on the lag in the development of a "literature of our own"). But Williams himself did not adopt Poe's alternative. Rather than correcting Eliot's nostalgic use of erudite quotation, Williams forgoes that kind of quotation (almost) altogether. Eliot's mode of quotation becomes the subject of Williams's revision, initially, as we have seen, in *In the American Grain*, where Williams uses quotation in pointed opposition to Eliot's use of the device in *The Waste Land*. Later, as we shall go on now to consider, he employs the device again in *Paterson*, to multiple effect.

Paterson is filled with quotations (roughly 50 percent of the text), and these quotations are principally of two kinds: summaries of events from Paterson's history, recent as well as not; and contemporary ephemera, such as advertisements, an artesian well report, park signs, and (most frequently) excerpts from letters to Williams. These quotations are generally set off as blocks, and in smaller type, though occasionally borrowings are included in the standard format as well. The summaries come from published histories and from texts provided him by Kitty Hoagland, a neighbor who was writing a history of the area. Williams sometimes quotes these sources directly and sometimes alters them, usually to give the impression that they were written contemporarily with what they describe. Very occasionally he presents material entirely of his own construction as if it were a quotation.[31]

Williams's use of ephemeral and historical quotations revises along two axes the nostalgic stances demonstrated both in Pound's *Cantos* and in Eliot's *The Waste Land* by their borrowings from poetries of the past. Where Pound's and Eliot's quotations from such as Homer and Spenser suggest a winding down of worth in the present from an earlier time of great value, Williams's use of contemporary ephemera urges the value of the present (*qua* present) over that of the past, while the relative lack of literary value of such ephemera, according to the usual scheme of measurement, argues against hierarchical systems of valuation per se. This view is reiterated in the text, around the metaphor of the Passaic Falls:

> Clearly, it is the new, uninterpreted, that
> remoulds the old, pouring down . (*P*, 82)
>
> The past above, the future below
> and the present pouring down: the roar,
> the roar of the present, a speech—
> is, of necessity, my sole concern . (*P*, 144)

And while his use of the historical summaries may at first appear to be part of an attempt to document an American past that can serve as a source of authority to rival that of Europe, the incidents recorded are too consistently proofs of failure and confusion to support such a reading. In section 1 of book 1, for instance, Williams shows us a perverted Eden full of prodigies of nature somehow gone wrong. We see pearls of great size, but the biggest is ruined by boiling; an enormous fish stoned to death; a devout hydrocephalic; and violent Indians and renegade black and white slaves. To underscore the point, the section closes with two literal (and historical) falls—that of Sarah Cumming, the minister's new bride, to her death, and that of Sam Patch, the "famous jumper" whose career began with a plunge into the Paterson falls to prevent the collapse of a bridge and ended with his death after a jump from the Genesee falls.[32] In steadily providing evidence of the absence of an Edenic American past, Williams's historical quotations refuse interpretation as an attempt to substitute one (American) nostalgia for another (European) one.

In scattering these descriptions of episodes from Paterson's past across the poem, Williams suggests also that the faithfulness to place of origin he vaunted in his localist theorizing is achieved in some measure by allowing the city's history to speak for itself. This effect is increased by the fact that the episodes are offered in the form of quotations taken from what seem to be contemporary historical documents. However, the quotations come not from the town archives but from historical summaries, written quite a while after the moments they describe, and even these Williams does not always reproduce verbatim. This undermines any suggestion of greater value in the past that the presence of quotations from earlier moments in itself might make, redoubling the refusal to represent the past nostalgically begun in the un-Edenic choice of historical events.[33]

The quotations are meant to imitate the onrush of experience. In the *Paterson* manuscript at Yale, Williams includes notes to himself on how to present the quotations he plans to include:

> BLOCKS of the Lyle material[34] (impersonating the falls: its meaning) (its particulars) put in across the pages at intervals, long and short (when dramatic emphasis can be obtained by a piece that comes to some sort of conclusion). No indentation, no paragraphing, no stop for ends of sentences even. Ending where it ends and picking up the material when convenient or inconvenient. The poem to go on and on. The Nardi letters. The Gladys and friend letters. No over selection but plenty of cutting for effect. Rearrangement where it will add anything. IN SOMEWHAT SMALLER TYPE FACE THAN THE REST to save room. (not too small) The job now is to cut and s[e]nd the material to typist with instructions to run it all in together in one tumbling stream but using caps or italics for special picking out of especially noteworthy bits. For instance this, here, would be an example of what is intended. The material copied to be run to the end[35]

Williams's methods draw on the understanding at work in early modernist collage,[36] both pictorial and poetic. The technique of juxtaposing markedly various kinds of texts (such as letters, handbills, and historical documents, mixed with varying styles of poetry), set in a variety of typefaces, repeats the collagist habit, borrowed in its turn from the newspaper format, in which articles on quite unrelated subjects are juxtaposed on a page that may also feature advertisements, comics, or serialized fiction.

This technique points to the complexity of experience. Early cubist collage paintings, for instance, blurred the line between reality and art by including within them found objects from the "real" world. In so doing, they directed attention to the constructedness of what we call the real (that is, its artificiality). This point is reiterated in the lines from a poem by the surrealist Louis Aragon quoted in book 5: "'la réalité! la réalité! / la réa la réa la réalité!' " (*P*, 209).[37] Williams's work makes a similar point in juxtaposing found texts with passages of his own composition. But as the note cited above indicates, even the found bits are subject to Williams's editing "for effect" and so cannot fully represent the "real." This failure may in itself suggest the impossibility of ever fully replicating the quality of experience—in art or in any representation—since any encounter with experience involves some shaping on the part of the perceiver (a repetition of the cubist lesson on the blurring of real and artificial with which this paragraph began).[38]

A small percentage of *Paterson* does repeat the words of earlier, well-known poets, a factor that complicates Williams's rejection of the methods of Eliot and Pound and which we will consider further on. For the most part, however, Williams works specifically to obscure the influence of earlier poetry on his work. For instance, and in direct contrast to the quotations at the start of the *Cantos* and *The Waste Land*, the poem begins with an epigraphal "quote" composed by Williams himself. Within the body of the poem, the first quotation comes from a younger poet called Marcia Nardi who in the course of the quotation declares herself "to be more the woman than the poet" (*P*, 7). These lines are most emphatically *not* borrowed from a threateningly successful precursor.

Along with a consistent recurrence of historical summaries, the first two books of *Paterson* include quotations from other letters from Nardi and from several other correspondents that carry the troubled, critical mood of the historical bits into the portrait of Paterson present. Together these support an aesthetic of heterogeneity[39] through their refusals of unity in both their interminglings of kinds of texts, of poetry and prose, and in their representations of divorce, discord, and difficulty as the governing quality of life:

                    Divorce is
the sign of knowledge in our time,
divorce! divorce!   (*P*, 18)

This heterogeneity operates in tension with a concern for order, resolution, and marriage expressed at intervals across the poem. The link between the marriage/divorce and the hierarchic/unhierarchic dichotomies is direct. Even without assuming that there need be a hierarchy in marriage, though in Williams's version there certainly is, the resolution into a settled order of things suggested in his use of the term is consonant with the sense of a clear order necessary to hierarchy.

Plotwise, *Paterson* rewrites "The Wanderer": a character called Paterson (sometimes called Dr. Paterson, sometimes Noah Faitoute Paterson) sets out on a quest to find beauty, and initially finds disappointment instead. Because he seeks beauties of a sort not available in the world he lives in, beauties built of resolution of discord, he overlooks those beauties that are available in the messy world he inhabits:

> beside the water he looks down, listens!
> But discovers, still, no syllable in the confused
> uproar: missing the sense (though he tries)
> untaught but listening, shakes with the intensity
> of his listening (*P*, 100)

As the poem progresses, however, he learns to recognize beauty in what had seemed to be chaos and, concomitantly, he rejects the nostalgia for old beauties that had misled him.[40] At the close of book 4 he has learned:

> the nostalgic sea
> sopped with our cries
> Thalassa! Thalassa!
> calling us home
> I say to you, Put wax rather in your
> ears against the hungry sea
> it is not our home!
> (*P*, 201)

Paterson, like *The Waste Land*, works through a tension between its plot and (some aspects of) its own structure, since the poem the character Paterson appears within embodies (or claims to) the very randomness he does not understand. But the reader's position in relation to this tension differs here. Where in *The Waste Land* the narrative teaches us to see the difference between its laments and the poem's through the reading experience per se, *Paterson* involves direct narrative guides (as in the passage beginning "beside the water," quoted above) that tell us from early on that Paterson does not speak for the poem when he fails to see beauty in the world around him.

The poem's method seems meant to include the world in its complexity. Its refusals of resolution seem to support the overthrow of hierarchies, which require clear orders to operate. At points, Williams tells us precisely this:

> [He] Poet, poet! sing your song, quickly! or
> not insects but pulpy weeds will blot out
> your kind.
> He all but falls . .
> And She —

Marry us! Marry us!
Or! be dragged down, dragged
under and lost

She was married with empty words:
better to
stumble at
the edge
to fall
fall
and be

—divorced
from the insistence of place—
from knowledge,
from learning—the terms
foreign, conveying no immediacy, pouring down.
—divorced
from time (no invention more), bald as an
egg .

and leaped (or fell) without a
language, tongue-tied
the language worn out .

The dwarf lived there, close to the waterfall—
saved by his protective coloring.

Go home. Write. Compose .

Ha!

Be reconciled, poet, with your world, it is
the only truth! (*P*, 83–84)

The province of the poem is the world.
When the sun rises, it rises in the poem
and when it sets darkness comes down
and the poem is dark . (*P*, 99)

The poem's fiction holds that it encounters its nostalgic, orderly impulses and throws them off—but, complicating this, those impulses still exert great force even in the moment of their "final" renunciation, at the end of book 4. It is this force that leads to the eventual composition of a fifth book, in which the nostalgic rage for order reasserts itself. And even before book 5, the orderly impulses sometimes escape the net of the plot.

Paterson's critics differ on whether and to what extent Williams succeeds in embodying the world's complexity and disorganization in his poem. Where some critics find the multitude of materials evidence on the side of his success, others find it unconvincing. Marjorie Perloff in particular finds the poem too organized. "The poet strolling through the park [in book 2, section 1] ostensibly records what he sees, observes, thinks, remembers, but in fact no detail is admitted into the space of the poem that does not relate to the central marriage-divorce tension that is the theme of the book."[41] The marriage-divorce tension serves as metaphor precisely for the tension within the poem about its own form—whether to resolve (marry) and in so doing fit itself into a tradition of poetic unity; or to refuse this kind of coherence (divorce) and so strike out into its own, new territory. Given the importance of this tension to the poem as a whole, it seems hard to blame the poem for not being entirely on the side of divorce (or indeterminacy). But Perloff's one-sided reading responds to the equally but oppositely one-sided readings by the many critics who have found in *Paterson* the model of indeterminacy and freeplay. In fact, there are quite a few such determinedly ordered moments as the one Perloff points to, at all levels in the poem. Even the fiction that the poem resolves on the side of indeterminacy can be read as evidence for its determinacy, its orderliness. While certain aspects of the poem's structure contradict Paterson's views on art, the argument against Paterson's standard views is itself subverted by other aspects of the poem's structure. Finally, what may seem from certain angles to be the poem's rejection of the nostalgic search for unity, and from other angles to be an embrace of such unity, reveals itself as ambivalence. The poem's heterogeneity turns out to inhere not in an embrace of the world's dehierarchized and discordant variety, but in its multiple and divergent attitudes about such an embrace.

An example of such ambivalence comes near the end of the final Nardi letter, when Williams qualifies the movement away from the Eliotic pattern of hierarchic quotation that the inclusion of Nardi's letters suggests in itself. Chaucer, whom Eliot invokes in the first lines of *The Waste Land*, appears for a moment in the signature to this letter—"La votre C" (*P*, 91).[42] This is the signature with which Criseyde closes her farewell letter to Troylus. (Williams continues the identification in the postscript, where he has Nardi refer to herself as "Cress.") Gale C. Schricker accounts for the anomaly of Williams's use of the very technique he objects to in Eliot as an exception made to stress Williams's sense of his connection to Chaucer, a fellow "inclusive, locally oriented poet."[43] While Williams's attraction to Chaucer is apparently quite strong, his decision to quote him is also a response to Eliot. By affirming a strong connection between his work and Chaucer's, Williams sets himself in contrast to Eliot, whose play against Chaucer in *The Waste Land* initially suggests a diminution of poetic power (though this suggestion is subverted later in the poem).

Yet in spite of his efforts to achieve the opposite effect, with this line Williams blurs the distinction between his own efforts and Eliot's. He renames Nardi, whose letters' presence in *Paterson* had been the sign of his reaction against Eliot's methods, by means of a quotation that quietly endorses those very methods. The turn against Nardi is suggested not only in the kind of renaming but in the fact of the renaming; of all the other of Williams's correspondents quoted in *Paterson*, only Nardi's own name does not appear in some form (most of the others are referred to by their initials). At the same time, by linking Nardi with Criseyde, Williams begins the pattern that continues across the poem of characterizing women as whores—a term that operates here as antithesis to the term "poet" and affirms an all-too-familiar gender hierarchy. The invocation of this pattern contributes to the atmosphere within the poem of ambivalence toward its own premises.

The nostalgic hierarchy of past over present takes on specifically literary reference and comes into question in book 3, the Library section. Here the role of the canonic quotations that Williams objects to in Eliot and Pound is suggested in the books that first attract ("Books will give rest sometimes" [*P*, 97]) and then stifle ("a roar of books / from the wadded library oppresses him" [*P*, 100]) Dr. Paterson's imagination. The divergent judgments on books represent a battle between nostalgic and antinostalgic impulses. Using as background a series of disasters that occurred, in slightly different order, in Paterson in 1902, Williams has the library destroyed by tornado, fire, and flood ("—a dark flame, / a wind, a flood—counter to all staleness" [*P*, 100]), and then finds it reasserting itself—still in a stifling manner—in the same flood that seemed to silence it ("And there rises / a counterpart, of reading, slowly, overwhelming / the mind" [*P*, 130]).

In this section, as part of the debate, Williams also introduces into his own poem the same sort of hierarchic quotation that he objects to in Eliot and Pound.

Beautiful Thing!

. . . .

And as his mind fades, joining the others, he
seeks to bring it back—but it
eludes him, flutters again and flies off and
again away .

O Thalassa, Thalassa!
the lash and hiss of water

The sea!

How near it was to them!

Soon!

Too soon .

—and still he brings it back, battering
with the rest against the vents and high windows
(*P*, 101)

This passage may seem to go back on all the antinostalgic claims of the poem to this point. But while it does represent a nostalgia, it is a mitigated nostalgia. Williams uses "O Thalassa" [The sea!]—in Xenophon's *Anabasis*, the cry of the Greeks who have been fighting for Cyrus as they approach the sea and the ships that will carry them home—not to suggest that beauty exists only in the past and thus that this quotation brings the reader closer to the "beautiful thing" than can Williams's poem, written in the present. Instead Williams uses this quotation to give us the lesson that all poetry is nostalgic and, on the basis of the equality that understanding can be read to imply, to argue against the need for nostalgia for any particular moment in the actual history of poetry. Where earlier in the poem Williams suggested that he meant to contradict nostalgic claims by denying nostalgia value per se, here he rejects particular nostalgia while defending it in the abstract as a necessary condition of poetry.

The line "How near it was to them" works both as comment on Xenophon's story, suggesting the nearness of the sea to the soldiers who shout at the sight of it, and as comment on the phrase's resonance across centuries, suggesting a greater nearness of earlier writers ("them") to the inspiring "beautiful thing" (the "it" that eludes the poet figure six lines above). But at the same time, the word "near" in that same line repeats the old tale of eternal belatedness, the story that all poetry—all speech even—is constituted at and through a (nostalgic) distance (even if the distance is small) from its object. The soldiers are read as Xenophon's figures for his own situation as a writer, speaking of the sea not when they have arrived at it, but when it is within sight.

Once the discovery is made that nostalgic lament can be understood as a figure for the poetic calling itself, Williams can represent himself on an equal footing with his predecessors, equally near to the still-elusive muse. He does this three lines later in the claim "and still he brings it back" and in the sequences that follow, in which the "beautiful thing" appears in the persons of a young woman in contemporary Paterson. The elusiveness of direct meaning is represented in the failures of the beatings and rapes performed upon this woman, who continues beautiful though bruised, to make her yield her secrets. The figure is a particularly unpleasant version of the old image of the whored muse, here assaulted and jeered at by her frustrated poets.

As a correction to the complaint at the start of *The Waste Land*, this passage does not succeed, since it actually repeats Eliot's gesture at the close of his poem. As we have seen, Eliot too discovers nostalgia and unoriginality to be the condition of all poetry, suggesting that the (necessarily slight) element of difference introduced in his own work (the version of originality left to him after his demystification of its myth) lies in the explicitness of his demonstration of the same unoriginality acknowledged by all the poets he quotes. On the other hand, in its argument for the nostalgic principle per se, the passage does serve Williams well as one pole in the debate over his own relation to the poetic tradition that he carries on throughout the poem and which he represents explicitly in book 3.

The other half of this debate reappears soon enough, as Williams moves on in the next pages to reassert the antinostalgic stance taken earlier in the poem through an explicit rejection of Eliot:

> Who is it spoke of April? Some
> insane engineer. There is no recurrence.
> The past is dead.
> (*P*, 142)

"Unlike the recuperative dream of *The Waste Land*," writes Joseph Kronick explicating this passage, "*Paterson* abjures the desire to recapture a lost plenitude and, instead, commits poetry to a perpetual beginning."[44] It is this logic of perpetual beginning that fuels the destruction of the library by fire and flood earlier in this section. But this logic is only half the story.

Two sets of quotations appear in manuscript drafts of book 3 but do not continue into the published version. These excisions confirm that the contest of nostalgic and antinostalgic impulses functions not merely as part of the poem's fiction, but was waged at the level of composition as well. The first of these excisions involves the texts of two business letters (one quoted in full, the other in excerpt in the draft) written by Williams's father (the notes in parentheses are Williams's).

THE STYLOGRAPH
or
RAPID LETTER COPYING
BOOK
No 4
Pto. Plata 10th Oct. '77

To the

Butcher of the Trans-
Atlantic Ship sailing for
St. Thomas on the 12 Oct (-Columbus landed in
the West Indies Oct 12
1492.)

Sir,

This letter will be
handed to you by the Butcher
of the _____by which Str
I ship today _____fine
fresh turtles, which I re-
commend to your care.
Enclosed is an order
for Dr. H. Brillen to whom
the fish go, and he will pay
you as a remuneration for
your attention Two shilling
and sixpence (2/6) a head
for all landed alive.
Your ob't servant
W. G. Williams

How to recover that clarity and directness, I do not know.
an era in a few words, ended.

(In blue crayon, rapid scrawl)

20 Nov '80

Knoeppel & Co
Remt. Ca $300 . by
Miss Hoheb.
W.G.W.

(Excerpt)

Your esteemed favor of 17th ult'o. is . etc

I must confess that Meaar[sic] Schuyler Hartley and
Graham are a libel on the American character for
business-like promptness.—I have had to make
so many excuses to the parties interested in the receipt of
these goods, that I regret having undertaken to
order them.—
I should have got far better articles for the money
from England.—
(Yale, 188-L1)

After the first letter, a lading notice for a shipment of turtles to travel on a boat set to sail on October 12—the same date, as Williams notes in his manuscript, that Columbus reached the New World—Williams comments: "How to recover that clarity and directness, I do not know, an era in a few words, ended." His father's letter seems intended to work here as an example of a paradisal clarity, now lost. The second letter complains about American lack of promptness and shoddy goods, comparing them unfavorably to English goods. The fall occurs in the movement into the New World between the two letters. But the two together are made as well to serve as an exhibit for the lost Eden. The use of these letters here would seem, then, to be the most nostalgic variety of quotation, a direct repetition of his own father's words, within a discussion of paradise lost—a use dependent on the same backward-looking stance Williams objects to in Pound and Eliot.

But even within the context of a weighing of nostalgic and antinostalgic alternatives, Williams decides against giving this much play to the nostalgic position. In excluding these letters, Williams severely restricts the suggestion of the existence of an Eden that the letters implied, but he does not erase the suggestion altogether. He covers the gap left by omission of these letters with a near-quotation of a line from a poem by Marianne Moore and a brief reference to, instead of a quotation from, his father—the Englishman William

George Williams, who came from the West Indies to the area near the Passaic River called in the time of the Revolution New Barbadoes Neck:[45]

> There was an earlier day, of prismatic colors   :   whence
> to New Barbadoes came the Englishman   .
>   Thus it began   .
>
> (*P*, 109)

The words "an earlier day, of prismatic colors" refer us to Marianne Moore's "In the Days of Prismatic Color." Moore's poem opposes modern complexity to a simple early world, but the poem's own complexity belies attempts to read it as a (simple) defense of either. In choosing to use this phrase from Moore, Williams problematizes the suggestion of an Edenic world that even this shortened reference to his father makes.

Moore's poem, like Williams's, involves specific rejection of simplistic nostalgia, ironically dismissing those who condemn complexity and desire a return to early simplicity—as, for instance, when the (female) author of "Marriage" looks back longingly to a time "when Adam / was alone." But Moore, again like Williams, does not simply reject simplicity for complexity. Her poem, like Williams's, addresses the complexity of response to complexity, acknowledging the attractions of simplicity. While simplicity is emphatically not the milieu from which Moore's obscure discussion with its difficult line breaks comes, neither is the complaint against the murkiness of meaning in the complex fallen world ironized entirely out of existence.

In substituting Moore's words for his father's, Williams acknowledges a relation of influence.[46] While his use of quotations from historical summaries gestures toward Pound's inclusion of historical texts in the *Cantos* (and likewise toward Eliot's borrowings from valued sources in the past), the mode of citation of noncanonic texts is learned from Moore. Her work, as we shall see, makes a point of relying on unauthoritative sources and in so doing of questioning the definition of authority. Relying on two such different models, Williams (again) occupies a position of ambivalence. This particular borrowing blurs the modes of quotation and allusion, for it both indicates a direct influence (and so operates allusively) and models the results of that influence (the quotation technique in itself).

Williams's decision to borrow from Moore here counteracts the effect of an earlier decision to not acknowledge the relation between them. The first of the passages from Nardi (*P*, 7) included in a manuscript version a reference to "M. M." (Moore) and Emily Dickinson, whom Nardi speaks of as exceptions to the pattern of difficulty for women poets that she describes. In deleting that line in later versions, Williams avoids calling attention right at his poem's start to the model for his counterpoetics of quotation. But in citing Moore further into the poem, Williams gestures toward acknowledgment of his debt.

The second set of borrowings present in an early version of the manuscript but not in the published poem consists of a pair of quotations from Eliot—one set in quotation marks, one not—and a clear allusion. "Violence! / 'in a dry month' " (Yale, 188-L3, p. 60) follows the announcement of the tornado that appears in the final version on page 111. The deleted lines "sooner or later a wind will come—/ bringing rain" (Yale, 188-L3, p. 17) were included in a section developed as part of the same discussion. The third reference to Eliot expands the censure implied in the others:

> river has been broken, broken
>   to a purpose
> that is not its own, lost
>   its identity
>
> a triviality. The purpose
> has been made to feed—not
>   the MEASURE but
>   another's need
> unrelated to the measure : beside
>   the point
> as much as a flood is
>   (Yale, 187, p. 66)

While Eliot's lines are a catalyst to Williams's, he omits them, at least in this form, from the final poem. But if quotation of Eliot's lines, even on purpose to refute them, seemed too direct a tack, Williams did bring them into the poem in a new guise a bit further on in book 3.

The flood begun in response to Eliot's drought in the drafts of section 1 builds threateningly through section 3 ("The sullen, leaden flood, the silken flood /—to the teeth / to the very eyes" [*P*, 130]; "the water two feet now on the turnpike / and still rising" [*P*, 135]; "—it's undermining the railroad embankment" [*P*, 136]). Against this flood of old books in the poem's plot, the structure of the poem offers a flood of uncanonic, unnostalgic quotations, which culminates in the series of three, insistently collagist, page-long quotations. One page (*P*, 137) features phrases from various sources set overlapping and askew like bills posted on a public wall. The second (*P*, 138) reprints a letter from Pound at St. Elizabeths. The third (*P*, 139) reports on the substances found at various depths in an artesian well at Paterson.

At the same time that the enervating flood of books is reaching its peak, we are presented in these three pages with an argument for this poet's continuing independent strength. These texts demonstrate his energetic refusal to surrender to the kinds of traditional authorities the flood of books represents. Both the kinds of texts he chooses to cite (all ephemeral and contemporary) and what they say support this refusal. The first page includes slang expressions, a salute to Antonin Artaud, and a pun on funeral plants "(it should be explained that / in this case 'plants' does NOT refer to interment)" (*P*, 137). The Pound letter offers a reading list:

> . . . re read *all* the Gk tragedies in
> Loeb. — plus Frobenius, plus
> Gesell plus Brooks Adams
> ef you ain't read him all. —
> Then Golding 'Ovid' is in Everyman lib. . . .
> (*P*, 138)

But this list is rejected rather than endorsed. The great works of the past included here are the kind of texts that Pound (like Eliot) does quote in his work, and that Williams pointedly refuses to depend upon in his. The borrowing from Pound's letter in itself works as a rebuff to the tradition Pound offers (though Williams did not oppose reading these books, they did not constitute a tradition in which he chose to situate his poem). This rebuff continues on the next page, where Williams reprints the local artesian well drilling account, which reports that

> At [2,100 feet] the attempt to bore through the red sandstone was abandoned, the water being altogether unfit for ordinary use. . . . The fact that the rock salt of England, and of some of the other salt mines of Europe, is found in rocks of the same age as this, raises the question whether it may not also be found here.
> (*P*, 139)

This jibe manages to suggest both that there's no use in looking to the past for sustenance in Paterson, New Jersey (a counter to Pound's line in the *Cantos* about finding water at great depth), and that England and America may be understood to be on a par. (This argument is continued later when Williams cites Pound's retort to his Artesian punning: "just because they ain't no water fit to drink in that spot [or you ain't found none] don't mean there ain't no fresh water to be had NOWHERE" [*P*, 183]. Elsewhere in the poem Williams cites Pound again, less polemically, as support for his [Williams's] questioning of United States economic policy [*P*, 185; 217–18].)

On the page following the artesian well report, the flood of books reaches its full height:

> — to the teeth, to the very eyes
> . uh, uh
>
> FULL STOP
>
> —and leave the world
> to darkness
> and to
> me
>
> (*P*, 140)

The poet's death by drowning—parodying the proceedings in Eliot's "Death by Water" section—is announced by the presence of the final line of the opening quatrain of Gray's *Elegy Written in a Country Churchyard* (1751). On their own, the associations with death implied in the elegiac form make the quotation work here as an epitaph, as does the way it is set, which mimics the style of the lettering on gravestones. Within the framework of the flood of books, Gray's line also seems to play an instrumental part in the death it marks—the (one last) canonic reference that killed the camel.

Though it ostensibly marks a low point in the poem, Gray's line is employed playfully here, by a poet who has just dramatically displayed his anticanonic credentials. The sculptural reshaping of the *Elegy* means to suggest the achievement of a consummate control that allows its poet to wander into the camp of hierarchic quotation, which he pointedly avoided at the poem's start, even as he tells of the dangers of that camp. In setting this quotation here Williams suggests that he is now firmly out of reach of the dangers such backward reference posed earlier, that he is able now to transform it where before it might have acted badly upon him.

The line from Gray serves Williams's point here not only in its graveyard reference. In choosing a line from the *Elegy*, Williams goes to one of the most insistently traditional poems ever written. It is at once an elegy for a passing social order and for the kind of poetry that Gray associates with that social order, one aimed at a select audience versed in a very specific tradition, of which Gray clearly considers himself a part. In this elegy for poetry set in a cemetery, an enormous quantity of allusions to earlier works is buried—Dante, Virgil, Spenser, Milton, Pope, Gay, Horace, Shakespeare, and Dryden are among the many whose words echo through Gray's stanzas. Source hunting has been among the principal occupations of Gray's critics. In fact, Gray suggests that he identifies this kind of poetry with poetry per se, and his reflection on the role of the poet in society concludes with the death of his poet figure and with a sympathetic epitaph for him.[47]

Gray's backward-looking lament in the *Elegy* parallels that of Eliot in *The Waste Land*, and Gray's line does double duty as a reference to Eliot in Williams's poem, serving both as an instance of Eliotic quotation for Williams to correct and as a stand-in for Eliot's poem per se. In quoting Gray here, Williams finds an alternative to the direct quotations of Eliot he introduced and suppressed in the drafts. Where direct quotation of Eliot would have specified the derivation of Williams's technique too directly, in citing Gray thus Williams suggests he has achieved, in a limited but sufficient degree, the skill in quoting without copying (both literally in his use of Gray and figuratively in his "quotation" of Eliot's quotational technique) that he had earlier attributed admiringly to Poe—a skill that he held could in itself be the basis for development of a "literature of our own." But at the same time, in citing Gray he suggests despite himself that his "correction" of Eliot evolves in some degree out of sympathy. Though the quotation seems to be offered in parody, its appearance, like the earlier appearance of the phrase from Chaucer, also suggests an abiding reverence and nostalgia for the great works of the past and for the hierarchy within which such greatness can be established.

And the effects of Gray's line within Williams's poem continue. At the same time that Gray's poem laments the increasingly democratic nature of his society, it was itself an agent of democratic forces and the poem is as importantly proto-romantic as it is post-classical. Its (relatively) unsentimental valorization of the experience and reflections of its speaker—exactly the isolated "me" of the line Williams borrows—presages the similar stance of the romantics, a stance that evolved in part at least as a mode of coping with and correcting for the threat of meaningless anonymity implied in democracy's equal valuation of everyone. The paradox of this poem about the incapacity of poetry to speak effectively any longer was continued in the extremely enthusiastic reception it received, a reception that argued that its report of poetry's death had been exaggerated.

But while poetry did not die, it certainly did change to meet the world's new ways. Gray's liminal situation parallels that which both Eliot and Williams fear and hope will be their own, anticipating as they both do a major modernist break with the poetry of the period before. In addition to the other roles this quotation plays in *Paterson*, Williams's use of Gray's line here can be read as a figuration of the contradictory responses people often have toward change. And like both Gray and Eliot, Williams aids the cause of the mode he favors less, even as he combats it. At the same time that he claims to most effectively reject the tradition through his use of Gray, the comparison his use of the line sets up within the poem demonstrates parallels between his work and that of Gray. His use suggests as well the continuation of his nostalgic impulse even as he disclaims it—for he has, after all, quoted Gray, importing his authority in the usual manner of hierarchic quotation. Only in this instance he seeks authorization for subversion.

Book 3 ends with a rejection of past and future as sources of poetry ("I cannot stay here / to spend my life looking into the past: // the future's no answer" [*P*, 145]). But in spite of the claims to having overcome the pull of the past, the debate over nostalgic and antinostalgic stances is not settled, and it continues throughout book 4. As we saw above, at the close of book 4 (which Williams considered the end of the poem at the time he wrote it), the nostalgic argument is explicitly denied:

> I warn you, the sea is *not* our home.
>   the sea is not our home
>
> The sea *is* our home whither all rivers
> (wither) run   .
> . . . . . .
>   Listen!
>   Thalassa! Thalassa!
>   Drink of it, be drunk!
>   Thalassa
> immaculata: our home, our nostalgic
> mother in whom the dead, enwombed again
> cry out to us to return   .
>   the blood dark sea!
> nicked by the light alone, diamonded
> by the light   .   from which the sun
> alone lifts undamped his wings
>   of fire!
> .   .   not our home!   It is NOT
> our home.[48]
>
>   (*P*, 201–2)

The poem goes on in the page and a half that remain to endorse the refusal of nostalgia further in the portrait of a swimmer emerging from the sea and heading inland (toward the "true" America Williams had spoken of in *In the American Grain*). The poem ends with a "quotation" from another moment in Paterson's history, that of the hanging of the murderer John Johnson in front of a large crowd, which reaffirms the poem's valuation of dissonance, and a five-line (fourteen-word) windup declaring the poem ended.

But of course the poem did not end there. Williams's need to add another book suggests that the issue of nostalgia in particular and of the place of hierarchic structures in the new world generally was not so settled for Williams at the end of book 4 as he insisted it was. Book 5 carries on the ambivalence of the first four books. It suggests on the one hand an acceptance of dissonance, for instance in the quotation from an interview with Mike Wallace in which Williams explains that poetry need not make sense and in the inclusion of a Sappho poem that questions standard structures of authority. On the other hand, it speaks against dissonance in its uses of a clear symbolism from a standard mythology, in its macho insistences on the need to "whore the virgin" (a familiar transformation from one to another term in a mutually defining pair that involves no real change in the traditional image of the feminine), and especially in its pointed resolution of dissonance in the rather upbeat close. Williams's quotations from his poem *The Wanderer* near the end of *Paterson* explicitly endorse the very kind of return to origin rejected at the poem's start ("'the river has returned to its beginnings" / and backward / [and forward] / it tortures itself within me / until time has been washed finally under: / and 'I knew all [or enough] / it became me'" [*P*, 233]).

Where at the poem's start Williams emphasized more explicitly the subversive tendency in his work, at its close the emphasis shifts toward the more conservative side. But it does not settle there definitely. Williams's late effort to write a sixth book countervails the understanding that he was satisfied with his addition of the fifth, with its apparently cheerful resolution in a dance of the difficult resolution-in-irresolution of book 4. Williams's ambivalence at least is consistent to the end. His inability to definitely conclude the poem gives further evidence that the poem's essence is ambivalence, and that *any* conclusion would be inadequate to that essence.

The ambivalence Williams expresses about changes in traditional hierarchies is nowhere more insistently represented than in his treatment of gender, both within *Paterson* and outside it. Outside the poem, his tributes to his mother—

an artist in her youth—and to his strong-willed grandmother lift the hatch on generally repressed preoedipal identifications. Likewise his acknowledgments of feminine aspects of himself depart from the macho norm. For instance, writing to his friend Viola Baxter in 1911, Williams declares, "You are quite right, Viola, quite right, men are not strong enough to 'bat air' with women. That forever proves to me I am not a man; they, men, disgust me and if I must say it fill me with awe and admiration. I am too much a woman."[49] I suggest that this reworking of traditional gender roles is at least in part a carrying through of the principle of dehierarchization, demanded as part of his American modernist attempt to disclaim secondary ranking. The attempt to acknowledge the feminine serves as a metaphor for the acknowledgment of value in what had formerly been considered secondary and dismissed. The ambivalent denigration of the traditionally masculine and equally ambivalent lauding of the traditionally feminine in the letter to Baxter figure the ambivalence Williams experiences over the project of dehierarchizing. He is troubled by loss of the pleasures of hierarchy—particularly of aspirations to originality, of identification with the British (an American quandary especially pertinent to Williams, whose British-born father never became a United States citizen), and of the privileges of maleness within the traditional gender structure. While changes in gender roles were themselves an immediate concern, they also operated within a larger context of change in social hierarchies generally. The representations of gender in *Paterson* (and in some other modernist work) speak at once literally and metaphorically. They figure secondariness in general as feminine and suggest that specific gender concerns interact with concerns about the dismantling of other social hierarchies.

A similar departure from the macho pattern is suggested in the early poem "Transitional":

> First he said:
> It is the woman in us
> That makes us write—
> Let us acknowledge it—
> Men would be silent.
> We are not men
> Therefore we can speak
> And be conscious
> (of the two sides)
> Unbent by the sensual
> As befits accuracy.

I then said:
Dare you make this
Your propaganda?

And he answered:
Am I not I—here?[50]

These lines may be understood to signal the poet's recognition of a stage of identification with the mother through which all children pass, and which continues a part of all men as well as all women. This stage is often denied in our culture, with its strong gender polarities and gender hierarchies. These lines need not be understood, however, to overturn the standard hierarchization of masculine/feminine relations, if the poet is read here not as the representative of all men but as the special case, unusually in touch with his feminine self. Again, both of these readings can be understood to apply at once: Williams's claims about feminine aspects of himself (a use of the term feminine that itself continues standard definitions) walk a thin line between affirmation of the feminine per se as valuable and denial of such value.

Relatedly, in the closing chapter of *In the American Grain* Williams speaks approvingly of what he represents as Lincoln's womanishness:

> The Great Railsplitter's "All I am or ever hope to be I owe to my angel mother"; the walking up and down in Springfield on the narrow walk between the two houses, day after day, with a neighbor's baby, borrowed for the occasion, sleeping inside his cape upon his shoulder to give him stability while thinking and composing his coming speeches. . . .
>
> It is Lincoln pardoning the fellow who slept on sentry duty. . . . The least private would find a woman to caress him, a woman in an old shawl—with a great bearded face and a towering black hat above it, to give unearthly reality. . . .
>
> The age-old torture reached a disastrous climax in Lincoln. Failing of relief or expression, the place tormented itself into a convulsion of bewilderment and pain—with a woman, born somehow, aching over it, holding all fearfully together. It was the end of THAT period.[51]

Here Williams corrects Whitman's portrait of Lincoln as heroic father in "When Lilacs Last in the Dooryard Bloom'd" and especially in "O Captain! My Captain!" The old woman, antithesis of the hero, emerges as a response to the excesses of masculinity associated here with the Civil War, but which can as well be read as that broadly defined earlier period from which modernism insists it is itself a departure.[52] Again, the image of the woman presented here raises problems. Born to piece together the wreck of the earlier period, this womanly man receives no joyous welcome; she is accepted rather as the necessary next step.[53]

Figuring the secondary as female is not, of course, new with Williams. We can locate a direct ancestor of his use of the metaphor close to home in the practice common among Victorian poets of using women as poet figures to communicate their sense of belatedness and cultural impotence (Tennyson's Lady of Shalott provides a good example). But Williams's use of the figure is particularly highly wrought. At the same time that femininity represents his belatedness, as it did that of his Victorian predecessors, it serves also as an important site for his reinterpretive attempt. Affirmation of value in the feminine is one of the principal routes by which Williams works to challenge traditional hierarchic assumptions. The shared concern of feminists and of American moderns with dehierarchization and with valuing the traditionally secondary suggests a parallel between their efforts. But the strong ambivalence that (both male and female) modernists feel about their attempt unpleasantly colors many male modernists' representations of women, making the parallel problematic.

Sandra M. Gilbert, while acknowledging that *Paterson* seems "almost uniquely 'liberal' in its granting of a voice to Woman," notes also that the poem enacts an ambivalence toward women writers and its own gestures at overturning standard gender hierarchies.[54] She offers a brilliant reading of Williams's anxieties about female literary competition and of his appropriations of the work of Marcia Nardi. Gilbert stresses, however, only the macho side of the ambivalence (for her, *Paterson* only "appears, at least on the surface, to be . . . 'liberal' "), an approach that finally subverts its own reading of the text as ambivalent.

As we have seen, in a period of cultural revaluation such as the one within which Williams works, the judgments of both old and new systems obtain at once and compete with each other directly, creating an ambivalence toward everything that comes under scrutiny. For Williams, this means that where he will often stress the value of the "feminine" (using the term normatively as a fair synonym for passive) within the male (as in the examples cited), he has difficulty with acknowledging the "masculine" (or active) within the female. Thus Gilbert's critique of Williams's attitude toward women writers. His valuing of the feminine within the male makes one step toward overturning gender hierarchies, but it has little effect without the follow-up step. This second step

Williams takes only hesitatingly. To the extent that he still judges within the framework of the system that has taught him that the modern and the American, along with the feminine, are secondary, he condemns the female figures in his work. In the long run this constitutes a self-condemnation, since these hierarchies seem interdependent, though in the short run it is crudely misogynistic. At the same time, insofar as he attempts to revalue what is traditionally judged of small worth, including himself as an American, he values those same female figures.[55]

The mixed attitudes of the modernist poet toward his position are manifest in *Paterson* in Williams's representations of women, which insist frequently on very standard gender relations. The poem opens with a mating of one man and many women—"Innumerable women, each like a flower. But / only one man—like a city" (*P*, 7). And as the poem proceeds, women are again and again marked as either whore or virgin, terms that signal lowness or highness (though still within a secondary frame) but never an equal relation. These images suggest the same will to preserve familiar structures as do his other reaffirmations of the very hierarchies he seems to want to overturn. But the vehemence of the macho stance he takes at some points is born of anxiety over the questioning of standard gender roles that he conducts at other points, and particularly, as we shall see, in his representations of the process of poetic filiation across *Paterson*.

In his analysis of the tensions within modernism, Andreas Huyssen takes the evident antipathy present in male modernists' portraits of female characters as demonstration of an essential modernist antifeminism.[56] Huyssen's argument raises questions about whether the condemnation of female figures in the work of male modernists, even when those female figures are understood to represent the poet's attempt at restructuring the entire system of valuation, can be taken as anything but misogynist vitriol. But while his point is important, Huyssen's argument elides the complexity of experience. In arguing that Williams's work may also serve feminist ends, I do not disregard Huyssen's point. The poem, like history, works at once to antithetic ends.

That issues of filiation must be of central importance to a poem called *Paterson* has been remarked by several critics, but the poem's working out of what it renders as an extremely problematic issue has never been considered carefully. Those studies that have addressed it follow the poem's lead and assume that the matter is one of understandable concern for the perpetuation of hard-won knowledge of world and craft.[57]

Williams's rejection of poetic parents in *The Wanderer* is followed in *Paterson* by an almost total absence of parental figures—both in terms of the dearth of borrowings from past literary greats and in terms of the absence of letters from older poets. Pound might be construed as an exception; though he was Williams's peer, he constituted himself as a mentor to everyone. But even granting him such status, as we have seen, the letters from Pound included in *Paterson* provide little sense of the handing on of a poetic tradition.

In speaking of poetic parents in *Paterson*, I depart from the understanding operative in discussion of *The Waste Land* that the acknowleged precursor figures will be consistently male. Williams's introduction of poetic daughters opens up the possibility of poetic mothers as well. Likewise, his citations from nonpoetic sources represent a rejection of the hierarchy of inspiration implicit in Eliot's anatomy of influence. Where Eliot admits only poetic texts as influences, and marks these masculine, Williams admits texts of all kinds and so acknowledges the possibility of influence from sources marked "feminine" in the terms of the hierarchy Eliot employs. More directly, Williams does include mention of Emily Dickinson in his poem, via Edward Dahlberg's letter at the close of part 2 of book 1 (*P*, 28).

Though we do not see much evidence of Williams's poetic parents, we do see affirmation of Williams's own status as potent poetic parent. Instead of citing works by established, older writers from whom he can borrow authority, Williams cites unauthoritative, younger writers, who are presented as his (querulous) poetic children. The quotations from six younger poets and writers that punctuate the poem offer evidence of a literary progeny. Though their relation to him is embattled, like that of many children to their parents, their presence does imbue Williams with an authority on which they seem to depend. Both Nardi and Ginsberg, the two poets of the group and the successors most prominently featured, are cited mentioning that Williams wrote introductions to their work.[58] In denying the parental model with regard to himself, only to go on to assert its operation when it works to his advantage, Williams would seem to be making no real change in the system of authority of past over present. But in opening his poem with a quotation from Marcia Nardi, a female heir, Williams claims to be a potent parent with a difference.

To recap what has lately become a well-known story, on March 29, 1942, Marcia Nardi came by appointment to Williams's office to discuss arranging her son's release from Bellevue's psychiatric ward. She had gotten in touch with Williams at the suggestion of a mutual friend, Harvey Breit, and she brought with her a sheaf of poems.[59] Williams read and liked these well enough to recommend them to James Laughlin for publication,[60] and he discussed plans for including excerpts from her letters in *Paterson*. Nardi and Williams corresponded for some time after that, during which period Nardi, who never seemed able to hold a job for long, occasionally asked Williams for small loans as well as assistance in getting grants and in being published. Though he continued to admire her work, Williams stopped corresponding with Nardi in 1943 and she disappeared from his life until 1949, though he tried to find her twice, in 1945 and 1947, for permission to use the letters in *Paterson* books 1 and 2. The correspondence resumed upon Nardi's resurfacing in 1949 with a request for a few hundred dollars, by implication in payment for her contribution to his poem. Williams sent $20, calling it a token of his "good will and appreciation for your assistance to me in the past."[61]

Early on in the development of *Paterson*, soon after meeting her, Williams began incorporating versions of Nardi's letters into his poem. The first of these, following up on the initial visit, identifies her immediately as a poet with problems of self-confidence tied to gender:

> In regard to the poems I left with you; will you be so kind as to return them to me at my new address? And without bothering to comment upon them if you should find that embarrassing—for it was the human situation and not the literary one that motivated my phone call and visit.
>
> Besides, I know myself to be more the woman than the poet; and to concern myself less with the publishers of poetry than with . . . living . . .
>
> But they set up an investigation . . . and my doors are bolted forever (I hope forever) against all public welfare workers, professional do-gooders and the like. (*P*, 7; ellipses are Williams's)

In later letters she discourses insightfully upon the position of the woman writer in society. In the final letter, about 3000 words of which Williams uses to close book 2, Nardi castigates him for his failure to assist her in the real-world ways necessary to establishing a position from which to write:

> My attitude toward woman's wretched position in society and my ideas about all the changes necessary there, were interesting to you, weren't they, in so far as they made for *literature*? That my particular emotional orientation, in wrenching myself free from patterned standardized feminine feelings, enabled me to do some passably good work with *poetry*—all that was fine, wasn't it—something for you to sit up and take notice of! And you saw in one of my first letters to you

> (the one you had wanted to make use of, then, in the Introduction to your Paterson) an indication that my thoughts were to be taken seriously, because that too could be turned by you into literature, as something disconnected from life.
>
> But when my actual personal life crept in, stamped all over with the very same attitudes and sensibilities and preoccupations that you found quite admirable as *literature*—that was an entirely different matter, wasn't it? . . . (*P*, 86)
>
> Your whole relationship with me amounted to pretty much the same thing as your trying to come to the aid of a patient suffering from pneumonia by handing her a box of aspirin or Grove's cold pills and a glass of hot lemonade. I couldn't tell you that outright. And how were you, a man of letters, to have realized it when the imagination, so quick to assert itself most powerfully in the creation of a piece of literature, seems to have no power at all in enabling writers in your circumstances to fully understand the maladjustment and impotencies of a woman in my position?
>
> . . .
>
> A completely down and out person with months of stripped, bare hardship behind him needs all kinds of things to even get himself in shape for looking for a respectable, important white-collar job. And then he needs ample funds for eating and sleeping and keeping up appearances (especially the latter) while going around for various interviews involved. And even if and when a job of that kind is obtained, he still needs the eating and the sleeping and the carfares and the keeping up of appearances and what not, waiting for his first pay check and even perhaps for the second pay check since the first one might have to go almost entirely for back rent or something else of that sort. (*P*, 88–89)

These analyses apply both to the situation of the financially impoverished writer and, in metaphor, to the situation of the woman writer deprived of cultural support for her endeavor. The words Williams employs are Nardi's own, but the order of the sentences is slightly altered at points, and large sections, some included in earlier drafts, are omitted.[62]

Williams's biographer Paul Mariani describes Williams's interest in Nardi as the product of the realization that in her he had found "the exact monstrous female voice to complement his own monstrous hydrocephalic self."[63] Clearly the letters appealed to him not only because they offered a complement to his voice, but also because the femaleness per se of the complement spoke particularly pertinently to Williams's inquiries into the issues of gender and poetry that he and Nardi both explore. In other words, Williams's confused response to his own sense of himself as feminine—he affirms it insofar as it is part of the rewriting of the structures he inherited and fears it insofar as he is not prepared for such a rewriting—is echoed in Nardi's consideration of her own participation in what she perceives to be a masculine domain. And he is intrigued with the extent to which her perceptions can repeat his own. Her very different position within the literary hierarchy makes the parallel less exact than Williams suggests, however, and makes possible the kind of extensive borrowing of her language that he indulges in. But while Nardi's words are taken over by Williams in a manner related to that in which Eliot takes over those of Kellond, the takeover is acknowledged here; Nardi's complaint is aired, and her words are partnered with those of other young poets, male as well as female.

Her treatment does differ, however, in the extent of the borrowing and in the fact that she is renamed (as we have seen, where the others are referred to by their initials, Nardi's letters are signed "Cress," after Chaucer's Criseyde). This renaming suggests Williams's ambivalence toward acknowledging living females in active roles, though he feels no compunction about endorsing the abstract value of "the feminine." In a letter to Robert D. Pepper, Williams characterizes the Nardi letters as "a reply from the female side to many of my male pretensions. It was a strong reply, a reply which sought to destroy me. If it could destroy me I should be destroyed. It was just that it should have its opportunity to destroy."[64] Though Nardi's letter certainly complains of Williams's treatment of her, to read it as an attempt to destroy him seems exaggerated. Williams's response suggests that the reply in itself—qua reply, or qua sign of agency—is what threatens here, hardly a model for complete revision of gender hierarchies.

Nonetheless, Williams's decision to quote Nardi here varies the familiar pattern of poetic filiation. Within this filial model, the son questions his father's authority not in itself but in order to maneuver himself into a position to take it over for himself. Where the father/son relation excludes females from succession, thus repeating and perpetuating the gender hierarchy Williams questions, his introduction of a poetic daughter here attempts to circumvent that repetition. Williams's poetic attempt mirrors Nardi's real-life struggle against standard patterns of filiation, an attempt she delineated in the letter Williams quotes from at the poem's start. The mysterious trouble mentioned in the last paragraph of that quotation was explained in an earlier draft, which included an additional paragraph on the nature of that problem. Williams altered only the initials:

> But I was, believe me, in a most desperate situation that Sunday. I didn't know a soul except P. T. (at least no respectable person) outside the world where only standardized conceptions of parenthood prevail; and there I was faced with an investigation of my decidedly irregular private life which would have amounted, for me, to the most ghastly kind of inquisition—especially since my son, by the way, was illegitimate.
>
> (Yale, 186-L3, p. 10)

Williams too attempts an irregular kind of parenthood in including Nardi among his chosen heirs.

In figuring the combative familial relation between himself and his "heirs," Williams also represents metaphorically his understanding of his own quarrelsome relation to the poetic parents he refuses to acknowledge directly. The first two books include letters from Nardi (seven) and Edward Dahlberg (one) that call Williams into question, just as he questions the methods of his predecessors. Nardi complains about his friendship and Dahlberg urges Williams to abandon his medical practice in order to devote himself to his writing. Dahlberg also foreswears interest in the literary past:

> . . . whatever snares I make for myself, I won't weep over Poe, or Rilke, or Dickinson, or Gogol, while I turn away the few waifs and Ishmaels of the spirit in this country. . . . You see, I am always concerned with the present when I read the plaintive epitaphs in the American graveyard of literature and poetry. (*P*, 28–29)

In this respect too, Dahlberg is made to speak for Williams (whose jottings in the pages of the Yale *Paterson* manuscript include such self-motivating maxims as "I shall never be satisfied until I have destroyed the whole of poetry as it has been in the past" and "I will entirely destroy poetry as it has existed in the past, if necessary, to put over what I want" [Yale, 187, p. 100]). A letter from "T," Williams's friend Alva N. Turner, a young male writer of ambiguously gendered first name (*P*, 26–27), deals with challenges to standard gender roles. Turner writes of his sister Billy, another ambiguously gendered first name. Billy hits her husband, disparages Alva's housework (while doing none herself), and generally "want[s] to boss" (*P*, 27). Though, as the poem advances, the letters from his literary young become less confrontational, in books 1 and 2 they represent challenges to standard gender and generational hierarchies.[65]

If the younger writers may be understood to represent Williams in some measure, the introduction of daughters invokes by implication an awareness of mothers and of the feminine, in all its threateningness, in general. Femininity is represented in quite a variety of ways in *Paterson*—from the very standardly patterned to the apparently unhierarchized, with many positions in between. As we've seen, the poem opens with an image of one man and many women, which suggests a certain lack of subjectivity among the women. And throughout we get images of women as bodies, or more particularly as genitalia—the "beautiful thing" (the phrase recurs throughout), punning via the poem's Chaucer references on the Wife of Bath's phrase, "bele chose."[66] This phrase also repeats Columbus's description of the New World, cited in book 4, section 2 (*P*, 178). Both references characterize the women they are then linked with as inspiring objects rather than as subjects in themselves. The "beautiful thing" passages and the discussions of women as whores (and later as virgins) are interlinked, sometimes literally and sometimes simply in sharing the view of woman as passive source of the poet's inspiration, or muse. In the most prominent of these episodes, Dr. Paterson visits a rape victim in the basement of her employer's house:

> Persephone
> gone to hell, that hell could not keep with
> the advancing season of pity.
>
> —for I was overcome
> by amazement and could do nothing but admire
> and lean to care for you in your quietness—
> . . .
> You showed me your legs, scarred (as a child)
> by the whip .
>
> Read. Bring the mind back (attendant upon
> the page) to the day's heat. The page also is
> the same beauty : a dry beauty of the page—
> beaten by whips
> . . .
>
> Beautiful Thing!
> And the guys from Paterson
> beat up
> the guys from Newark and told
> them to stay the hell out

of their territory and then
socked you one
          across the nose
          Beautiful Thing
for good luck and emphasis
          cracking it
till I must believe that all
desired women have had each
          in the end
          a busted nose
and live afterward marked up
          Beautiful Thing
          for memory's sake
to be credible in their deeds

Then back to the party!
          and they maled
and femaled you jealously
          Beautiful Thing
as if to discover whence and
          by what miracle
there should escape, what?
still to be possessed, out of
          what part
          Beautiful Thing
should it look?
          or be extinguished—
Three days in the same dress
          up and down   .
          I can't be half gentle enough
half tender enough
          toward you, toward you,
inarticulate, not half loving enough . . .   (*P*, 125,126,127–8)

The "quietness" and "inarticulate[ness]" of this patient (compared here to the blank page upon which the poet writes) constitute the large part of her appeal. The poet and the thug are joined here in marking their "pages" with blows.

This passage and its partners directly deny any possibility of authority (in its root sense) to women—the silent whore/muse is the (active) poet's (passive) opposite. These images operate in tension with the Nardi letters, in which a female speaker argues for her right to be taken seriously as both a poet and a person, and with Dahlberg's mention of Dickinson and its reminder that a history of women poets is already in place, invalidating any attempt to reduce the world to the "orderliness" of traditional gender role assignments. In book 4 we are offered the example of Mme Curie—the pregnant scientist—as a cross between the poem's contradictory tendencies, representing her as at once both active and passive. This character is sometimes seen as the embodiment of Williams's refusal of images of women as passive, but such readings overlook the rather passive nature of her "activity": she sits stirring, waiting for the radium to emerge.

Further complicating things, we have references to Williams's actual mother and grandmother, both of whom are quoted at points.[67] Though reference to these women would not necessarily mean a departure from standard role assignments, in Williams's case those standard roles are affected by two facts. He was himself, as a general practitioner with extensive obstetrical experience, very much involved with the female world of physical creativity. And his mother, a painter and singer rather than a poet like Charlotte Champe Stearns Eliot, was likewise involved in the "male" world of artistic creativity and played a major role in the evolution of her son's artistic aspirations.

Williams's unusually close identification with his mother suggests an undoing of the oedipal pattern of repressing such identification, with its inherent structure of domination. In its place we get not a clear alternative, but signs of an attempt to revise the pattern. Brian Bremen reads *Paterson*'s polyphony as evidence of Williams's movement away from the traditional hierarchies of interpersonal relationships (of gender, race, and class) and from the oedipal model on which such patterns of domination are based. Bremen understands Williams to move instead toward adoption of a "mother-based" psychological model, along lines suggested by Jessica Benjamin. In such a model, the possibility of sympathetic recognition of the other that flourishes in the preoedipal period continues into adulthood. That such a model might be understood to function within *Paterson* is suggested by the poem's equal valuing of many voices—those of others as well as that of self, both valued within an expanded narcissism. Bremen reads the progress across books 1 through 4 as a movement from pointed exposure of oedipal gender polarity toward overcoming that polarity in the merger of "male" and "female" aspects in Mme Curie.[68] I find this carefully nuanced argument a very useful account of Williams's complexity, though Bremen places Williams more definitely in the relativist camp than do I. In my view, while Williams does move toward a freeing of the anchor of gender roles, his complex relation to real women and to women's words throughout the poem demonstrates his inability to come quite as near to the accomplishment of that end as Bremen suggests he does. It might be argued that the variety of images of women signals the insufficiency of any of them to represent the poem's view of the feminine, and that Williams's effort in representing women so variously is precisely to suggest the inadequacy both of these images and of the attempt to come up with a stable image of the feminine—just as the poem as a whole critiques Dr. Paterson's limited views of art and life. This argument has its attractions, but such a reading must be balanced by recognition of the poem's reflection of Williams's profound investment in the freedoms that standard gender hierarchies offer men and thus, again, of his ambivalence about change.

Williams's early plans for *Paterson* involved including Nardi's letters throughout. In the poem as published, the quotations from Nardi's letters end with book 2, in the extended excursus on the inadequacy of Williams's response to her as a person and as a poet. This borrowing works as further evidence for the poem's case for the world's disunity. The case is made also in the letter from Dahlberg that concludes section 2 of book 1, the critical tone of which meshes well with Nardi's. The role of poetic successor goes unfilled in book 3, but is filled again in books 4 and 5, this time by Allen Ginsberg, from whom three letters appear in all. In the first of them, Ginsberg introduces himself to Williams in terms perfectly suited to Williams's purposes:

> Dear Doctor:
>
> In spite of the grey secrecy of time and my own self-shuttering doubts in these youthful rainy days, I would like to make my presence in Paterson known to you, and I hope you will welcome this from me, an unknown young poet, to you, an unknown old poet, who live in the same rusty county of the world. . . .
>
> As to my history: I went to Columbia on and off since 1943, working and travelling around the country and aboard ships when I was not in school, studying English. I won a few poetry prizes there and edited the Columbia Review. I liked Van Doren most there. I worked later on the Associated Press as a copyboy, and spent most of the last year in a mental hospital; and now I am back in Paterson which is home for the first time in seven years. . . .
>
> I do not know if you will like my poetry or not . . . I envision for myself some kind of new speech—different at least from what I have been writing down—in that it has to be clear statement of fact about misery (and not misery itself), and splendor if there is any out of the subjective wanderings through Paterson. This place is as I say my

> natural habitat by memory, and I am not following in your traces to be poetic: though I know you will be pleased to realize that at least one actual citizen of your community has inherited your experience in his struggle to love and know his own world-city, through your work, which is an accomplishment you almost cannot have hoped to achieve. . . .
>
> (*P*, 173–74; my ellipses)

If Williams could not have hoped for this, he certainly welcomed it.

In transferring Ginsberg's letter to his poem, he reinforces the sense of the familial relation between them by excluding one, and only one, paragraph. Ginsberg's discussion of his history had originally begun thus:

> As to my history—my father is Louis G., of whom you know. He would send his regards, if he knew I was writing, and also an invitation to come to supper, as we have bought a house in Eastside and are able to entertain for the first time in years. He was remarried last week.
>
> (Yale, 189-L7)

Ginsberg suppresses mention in his letter of his problematic mother, whose creation of difficulty for her family is hinted at in the linked references to a history of not being able to entertain and the remarriage. In a parallel move in *Paterson*, Williams suppresses mention of Ginsberg's father, also a poet, in order that he can appear as the only father figure on the scene.

Williams's move away from Nardi signals his inability to continue supporting the degree of transformation of the system of filiation he had initially proposed in introducing her. In presenting Ginsberg as heir apparent in books 4 and 5, Williams modifies his transformation of the pattern of succession. In replacing Nardi with Ginsberg, Williams moves from a female to a male heir, but a male heir whose homosexuality complicates the standard gender and familial model, even if only by revealing the depth of the male/male bond that the homosocial system represses. In choosing a feminized male (a man who offers himself as a love object to another man) as his poetic son, Williams continues the questioning of the "standard" family model, with its assumptions of domination (of male over female, masculine over feminine) that the nomination of Nardi as heir began. But where Nardi's presence acknowledged the poet's bonds with living females as well as with abstractly feminine parts of himself, Ginsberg's presence acknowledges the feminine while perpetuating a pattern still standard in its maleness.

Just as Dahlberg's and Nardi's criticisms of Williams in books 1 and 2 figure Williams's own critical relation to his predecessors, so does his choice of Nardi and Ginsberg as successors represent his own sense of his relation to his predecessors as a variation on the traditional father/son pattern of poetic filiation. Insofar as the relation between poetic fathers and sons is understood to follow and endorse a standardly hierarchic model, his general attempt to break with such models leads him to represent his relation to his predecessors as a subversion of the traditional pattern of filiation. The figures of the woman writer and the feminized male writer interest Williams in important measure as figures for his own challenge to traditional structures. In them he represents an aspect of himself.[69]

In selecting Ginsberg as successor, Williams also brings into question the standardness of the father/son tradition that precedes him. In his final letter, Ginsberg, about to set off for the North Pole, describes himself as having "a whitmanic mania & nostalgia for cities and detail & panorama and isolation in jungle and pole, like the images you pick up." He then goes on to plan his return to Paterson: "When I've seen enough I'll be back to splash in the Passaic again only with a body so naked and happy City Hall will have to call out the Riot Squad" (*P*, 213). The references to Whitman and to pleasure in nakedness suggest both a freeing from repression ("a body so naked" speaks of a more profound revelation than simply the removal of clothes can effect) and, more specifically, an awareness that the repression of the feminine within the male has never been a fully successful enterprise.

The letters from Nardi and Ginsberg—with their qualified transformations of familiar patterns of filiation—are further qualified in book 5 by three letters from other younger writers that reaffirm standard hierarchic patterns in various ways, though with less emphasis on the filial relation per se. The first letter in book 5 comes from Josephine Herbst, condescendingly and inaccurately described in Williams's *Autobiography* as an "unsuccessful novelist," whose work he never much liked, though "to Jo herself," he writes, "I constantly have my hat off."[70] Herbst writes an extremely gracious letter in response to Williams's rather bleak description in the *Autobiography* of her life in a country house, where he and his wife used to visit Herbst when she was married to the rather less successful novelist (though of *his* first novel Williams firmly approves), John Herrmann. Herbst's letter, or at least the portion of it Williams employs, gives no sign of rancor at Williams's representation of her harsh life or of the unhappy end of her marriage. Instead, it gently corrects that representation with mention of all the flowers growing there and of the happy progress of children and friends. Within the context of *Paterson*, the letter from "Josie" serves as a model of benign relations between the past and the present. Thanking Williams for his memories, Herbst speaks from Williams's past, approvingly, insisting that he is missed ("I wish you and F. could have come. It was a grand day and we missed you two, one and all missed you" [*P*, 209]). And her descriptions of happy children and birds nesting ("the wren . . . is sitting warm and pretty on five eggs" [*P*, 210]), accompanied by no mention of her own work, oppose the disturbance of familiar gender roles and of patterns of filiation suggested in the letters from Nardi and Ginsberg.

Ginsberg's final letter follows Herbst's, and is itself followed by what actually was part of a short story submitted to Williams by Gilbert Sorrentino, but which is here presented as a letter, with initials (G.S.) given as signature. This passage set in a Mexican border town describes a man bargaining with a whore ("she is smooth-faced and wants four dollars but you make it three but four she says and you argue . . . " [*P*, 214–15]) before going with her. It concludes with the judgment that the wisdom of the experience is "deep as birth, deeper than death" (*P*, 215), a statement that suggests little possibility of change in the hierarchical status quo.

The final letter, from Dahlberg again, tells of yet another woman writer.

> In socialist Denmark I knew a highly intelligent author, a woman, who had come to America and there had a child by a wretched scribbler. Poor and forsaken she returned to Copenhagen, where she earned her niggard indigence doing reviews for the Politiken, and giving occasional lectures on Middle English and early Danish. She lived in the slummy part of that beautiful city, trying to support a wonderful boy, sturdy, loving, and very masculine. . . .
>
> (*P*, 229)

As was the case with the borrowing from Herbst, though more evidently here, this quotation speaks ambivalently. On the one hand it presents us with a woman writer—another sign of movement in the familiar pattern of poetic filiation. But we see her represented as a teacher not a writer, and we get no evidence of her artistry firsthand, since, unlike Nardi and all the other poetic children Williams presents, she does not speak for herself. In addition, it is her capacities as a mother—instilling the principles of his traditional gender role in her son—that move Dahlberg most. This excerpt offers parallels with the introductory quotation from Nardi (woman writer and mother of an illegitimate child) at the start of book 1. The likeness of the situations given in the two quotations provides a sense of roundedness and of closure. While the image of the Danish woman is still presented with ambivalence, it stresses much more the traditional feminine role, where the Nardi quote stressed a change in that role, as well as considerable trouble as accompaniment to that change. Though Nardi referred to herself as "more the woman than the poet," she is represented as one actively engaged in her writing, and that writing makes her of interest to Williams. The lessening prominence given the woman writer figure as his work proceeds suggests a diminishing sense of his difference from the system with which he earlier sought to break. The contrast might be taken as evidence of Williams's growing conservatism, or it might be understood to represent sequentially across the poem an ambivalence about dehierarchization that was present all along. Williams's refusal to conclude the poem also suggests such a reading. Where book 4 ends on a fairly relativistic note, book 5 counters with an opposite emphasis. Perhaps book 6 would have moved back in the other direction, had it been developed further.

This same ambivalence toward the transformations he proposes, manifest in his choices of whom to quote, is represented also in a figure offered explicitly as reflection on that ambivalence. Lesbians appear at three points in the poem, all in the last two books. These appearances reflect the complications of sexual relations and of patterns of inheritance that fill *Paterson* in spite of and in tension with the claim inherent in the poem's title that it will concern itself with a standard model of inheritance (from father to son) and with the sexual hierarchy of male over female that this model implies. In *Paterson* 4, section 1,[71] Williams represents a love triangle composed of an older woman and an older man who compete for the affection of a young woman. The section seems to operate as an allegory of the competition between Williams (represented in the man Paterson) and those American poets he condemns for their European manners (represented in the old woman Corydon) for the body and affections of America (represented as Phyllis, and as innocent of any poetic tradition).[72] Here change in gender roles is specifically tied to a wider set of issues. We get no examples of Paterson's poetry, but Corydon's is represented extensively, echoing a combination of Eliot ("At the / sanitary lunch hour packed woman to / woman [or man to woman, what's the difference?]" [*P*, 166]) and Crane-as-imitation-Eliot ("Condemned . / but who has been condemned . where the tunnel / under the river starts? *Voi ch'entrate* / revisited!" [*P*, 164]). The poetry is rather precious, and, in another dig at Crane, Phyllis has trouble with some words ("what's a guerdon?" [*P*, 167]).

But clear as these role assignments seem, the section is rather confusing. In the first place, the condemnation of Corydon, who wins Phyllis's affections in the end, is effected with suggestions of a good amount of sympathy. Williams noted in a letter to Robert Lowell that though he had begun the portrait of Corydon as satire, "she won me quite over. I ended by feeling admiration for her and real regret at her defeat."[73] Since Corydon does win Phyllis (though the young woman chooses her without passion as the best of the available lot), the defeat Williams speaks of occurs outside the allegory, where both Corydon and Dr. Paterson want to write a poetry that can move the girl, not merely get her grudging endorsement. Williams's affection for Corydon may spring in part from the fact that her poetry is not entirely distinct from Williams's own, having at least one interest in common with his:

> If this were rhyme, Sweetheart
> such rhyme as might be made
> jaws would hang open .
>
> But the measure of it is the thing . None
> can wish for an embellishment
> and keep his mind lean,
> fit for action .
> such action as I plan
> (*P*, 161–62)

Like Williams, Corydon sees the key to poetic success in the measure.

The idyllic style is in itself rather precious, and this preciousness informs the heavy symbolism of this section. The presence of these formal elements has an inconsistent effect. While they seem on the one hand to support the point of mocking Corydon's style, they remind us on the other hand of how much this structure is of a piece with the highly, if not consistently, symbolic structure of the rest of Williams's poem, beginning in the preface with the dog/poet symbolism and continuing through the representations of discord as divorce that fill the pages that follow. But we need not follow the back and forthing exactly to recognize the basically ambivalent position that Williams understands as his own, and which he works to affirm as a position of value from which to continue the challenge to hierarchy that begins the poem. In associating himself with both the nostalgic and the unnostalgic forces in this allegory, Williams continues the debate of the library section. And, as in the library section, the ambivalence remains unresolved.

The competition for Phyllis turns out thus to occur between two possible figures for Williams himself. But the ambivalence continues even in the characterization of these two figures, for while Dr. Paterson seems meant to figure a break with poetry past, his standard masculinity (defined through its controlling relation to a passive female, or at least the attempt at that) suggests no such break. That his relation with Phyllis fails, when she doesn't prove inclined to give herself to him as demanded ("He took her nipples / gently in his lips. No / I don't like it" [*P*, 164]), argues once again for Williams's sense of the insufficiency of old structures. Corydon also represents Williams's ambivalence, in modeling both a nostalgic bent and an alternative gender relation, which would seem to represent not just corruption—as has generally been understood—but also the kind of challenge to standard structures that Williams himself attempts. In addition, the lesbian as figure for the poet—counterpart to Williams's figuring himself in Ginsberg—represents in herself Williams's bicultural situation and his ambivalence as well, allowing him to retain the traditional controlling role of the lover of women and yet be a (new) "woman" himself. His reuse of the lesbian figure at two points in *Paterson* 5 suggests that she holds particular interest for him.

Those of Williams's critics who celebrate his embrace of complexity in books 1 through 4 generally dislike book 5. Written seven years after book 4 was published, and after a stroke had limited his physical capacities, book 5 reflects a new frame of mind for Williams, one that emphasizes the conservative side of his ambivalence. The book has as central metaphor the medieval unicorn myth, as represented in the Unicorn tapestries at the Cloisters in New York City. Via this metaphor, Williams presents images of intensely normative gender roles: "every married man carries in his head / the beloved and sacred image / of a virgin / whom he has whored . . . keep your pecker up / whatever the detail!" (*P*, 234–35), "the virgin and the whore, / an identity, / both for sale / to the highest bidder! / and who bids higher / than a lover? Come / out of it [the woods] if you call yourself a woman" (*P*, 237–38). On the one hand, these lines point to the commodification of female sexuality in patriarchal culture that makes virgin and whore identical; both being available for sale, though in different markets (wedding chapel or brothel). In so doing, the lines may be read as an attempt to begin to transform gender stereotypes by holding them up to scrutiny. On the other hand, these lines perpetuate the stereotypes by offering no alternative image of femininity. The normative, sexist effect of such freshly minted lines is seconded in the quotations, by such material as the Sorrentino tale of bargaining with whores in Mexico (*P*, 214–15), Dahlberg's letter on the Danish woman, and even—in the most dramatic assertion of standard quotational authority—a biblical citation (Matthew 1:18) on the appearance to Joseph of an angel explaining the pregnancy of Mary. And in harking backward to the middle ages for the adequate metaphor, Williams argues for a union of past and present, giving over the effort to break with the past urged throughout the first four books. The book ends on a note opposite to the embrace of complexity and dissonance of book 4: "We know nothing and can know nothing . / but / the dance, to dance to a measure / contrapuntally, / Satyrically, the tragic foot" (*P*, 239). While the passage acknowledges the importance of counterpoint, its effect is of a giving over of the earlier gesture toward wider knowledge and toward change. Here again the total effect is complex and ambivalent, but the emphasis has shifted.

But for all its reiterations of standard hierarchies and of the status quo, in this book Williams also quotes what survives of a Sappho poem,[74] with attribution, suggesting again his own identification of himself as a "woman" who loves women through his acknowledgment of a (the original) lesbian precursor (*P*, 217). In mentioning Sappho's name, Williams erases the possibility that her poem's sphere of reference might be understood to shift to the heterosexual when he writes it into *Paterson*, as happens with Catullus's translation of the same poem.[75] This is one of the few quotations of poetry in *Paterson* and the most extensive (all the others borrow a few words at most), but it is not a swerve toward the kind of effects Eliot achieves through such borrowings.[76] Rather than serving simply as sign of nostalgic, "masculine" desire, the quotation signals Williams's admission of his own ambivalence about such desire and about its alternative, an antinostalgic, present-minded, "feminine" desire. But in establishing a link between Sappho and himself, Williams continues the revision of patterns of filiation begun in the choice of Nardi as his first heir. Here and only here he acknowledges a predecessor openly, and this predecessor is female. The nature of her authority becomes an issue immediately, via a quotation from Arnold Post (A.P.), a classics professor at Haverford College, who introduces the poem thus:

> " . I am no authority on Sappho and do not read her poetry particularly well. She wrote for a clear gentle tinkling voice. She avoided all roughness. 'The silence that is in the starry sky,' gives something of her tone, . " (*P*, 217)

This paragraph manages at once to dismissively characterize Sappho as a standardly feminine poet (with "a clear gentle tinkling voice") on whom one would not want to waste much time and to establish her as one over whom authority is not had.

As it happens this is not the first mention of Sappho in the poem; Williams invoked her earlier as well, also with regard to issues of authority.[77] In the library section (book 2, section 2), she is made to represent those authorities whose work Williams has burn:

> Beautiful thing! aflame .
> a defiance of authority
> —burnt Sappho's poems, burned
> by intention (or are they still hid
> in the Vatican crypts?) :
> beauty is
> a defiance of authority :
> (*P*, 119)[78]

In citing her in book 5, Williams might seem to be bending to the kind of authority he had refused to honor earlier on. Such a reading would fit with the view of the fifth book as a surrendering of the positions held in the earlier four books. But the particular poem complicates this reading, for in choosing this poem Williams aligns himself with Sappho rather than bowing before her precedent, since this is a poem in which she too disclaims authority. Sappho's poem is about a woman watching a man in conversation with a woman whom the first woman desires. I quote it in Williams's version:

> Peer of the gods is that man, who
> face to face, sits listening
> to your sweet speech and lovely
> laughter.
>
> It is this that rouses a tumult
> in my breast. At mere sight of you
> my voice falters, my tongue
> is broken.
>
> Straightway, a delicate fire runs in
> my limbs; my eyes
> are blinded and my ears
> thunder.
>
> Sweat pours out: a trembling hunts
> me down. I grow paler
> than dry grass and lack little
> of dying.
>
> (*P*, 217)

In Sappho's poem, we do not know whether the object of this affection has feelings for either of her admirers, or even whether the man has any interest in her; we know that the speaker envies anyone, male or female, who has the girl's attention and may also be understood to envy the capacity to sit before her with any self-control. Sappho's poem specifically refuses gender hierarchy, rank here being determined instead by individual capacity to gaze at the beloved (the one who succeeds is a "peer of the gods").

Similarly to Eliot, with his precedents whose complaints of unoriginality provide the sources of their claims to originality, Williams finds in Sappho an example of a predecessor's claim to lack of authority that turns out to be the basis of her authority. The beloved's presence makes Sappho mute ("my voice falters, my tongue is broken"), and this muteness becomes her subject in part. But in addition to repeating Eliot's gesture, a move which alone would simply affirm the status quo, Williams opens up his representation of authority to include not just the feminine, as with the recognitions of the importance of the muse to the poem, but the female as well.

When Sappho's poem is embedded in Williams's, it does not matter which of her suitors the girl prefers. At issue is, rather, the position from which she is regarded. Sappho's poem repeats the configuration present in the idyl of book 4, of male and female competitors for the love of a woman. In book 4 the lesbian role is not definitely assigned to Williams. In quoting Sappho's poem, Williams does align himself with the role of the poem's lesbian speaker. This alignment does not, however, work simply as an endorsement of the undoing of gender hierarchies, contrasting the very standard gender pattern featured elsewhere in book 5. Instead, it operates as itself an emblem of ambivalence. Williams's ambivalence about the feminine, American position he feels thrust into surfaces in this quotation as envy for the male figure—the "peer of the gods." The envy here springs not, as in Sappho's version, from the attention lost to the speaker (here linked to Williams), but from the position the male figure takes vis à vis the feminine (another beautiful thing): a position of self-control that leads in itself to a control of the situation; a position quite different from that of the speaker's uncontrol before the beloved. In Williams's poem, Sappho's poem becomes a statement of his envy of the situation of his precursors, who did not (or so he imagines) feel pulled as he does between competing systems. This reading puts the quotation back in the camp of the prohierarchists, very much in line with the rest of book 5. But the fact that Sappho is acknowledged as one of the envied precursors pulls it out of that camp again. Within Williams's poem, Sappho's poem, like the poem's speaker, trembles on the threshold of contradictory significations, which together portray Williams's complex position.

Williams's lesbian identification continues a page later, with the passage beginning "There is a woman in our town." This woman, who dresses not to please a man ("her / face would attract no / adolescent") but *as* a man (apart from a somber flower on her right breast "to / say she was a woman," she "was dressed in male attire, / as much as to say to hell / with you"), might well be a lesbian (though the poet still wants to ask her if she's married, if she has children). At any rate, she undoes standard gender distinctions. This woman represents Williams's readers; it is for her, we are told, that he has written all his work (*P*, 219–20). Here again, as with the Sappho, the lesbian is presented with no hint of disapproval, in a manner distinctly at odds with the insistent macho stance adopted at other points in the poem. In representing his readers at once as lovers of women and as women, Williams suggests that even at this late point in his career he understands these readers to be, like himself, the products of two systems. These systems reflect on the one hand an Old World, to which hierarchy is appropriate because the old tends to be rated highly within such hierarchies, and on the other hand, the New World, which must renounce hierarchy in order to find grounds for arguing its own value. In *Paterson*, Williams represents the ambivalence that the tension between these two systems creates through his inconsistent portraits of male/female roles, particularly as regards poetic filiation, and in his lesbians.

Williams's use of quotation in *Paterson* reflects his ambivalence about his position as an American modernist. His rejection of canonic literary quotations of the kind Eliot employs seconds his general effort to overturn traditional hierarchies and so to revalue the categories "American" and "modern," which rank secondary within such hierarchies. Similarly, his choice of quotations concerning the history of Paterson suggests value in the American, while the messiness of the historical examples he selects refuses to simply substitute one nostalgia for another. The gesture implicit in Williams's use of quotation situates the poet's concerns in the world of authority, and his flouting of canonic quotation suggests a will to undo standard patterns of authorization. His inclusion of letters from younger writers, however, works to establish him in the same position of authority over them that he refuses to others over himself (even as the quarrelsome nature of many of these letters acknowledges the struggle involved in any intergenerational handoff—an acknowledgment that does not, however, challenge the basic hierarchic pattern of authority).

This same ambivalence is demonstrated in Williams's treatment of gender, a pivotal issue in the poem, dealt with emblematically in the quotations. The transformation of the standard model of poetic filiation to include a woman and a gay man does challenge hierarchic patterns by releasing the feminine from the position of silence and domination. Williams does not feel altogether comfortable, however, with this attempt to undo the gender hierarchy in which the feminine is marked secondary (both in general, as qualities that both men and women might share, and in particular, in women as a group). The move involved—acknowledging a male identification with the traditionally "feminine" and a female identification with the traditionally "masculine"—radically questions the standard model of male self-definition, a process Williams finds not easy to undergo. This process may be understood to suggest a revision of the oedipal model, through which the pattern of masculine domination of the feminine is enforced. Rather than silencing the women around him and the feminine aspects of himself, Williams works to unrepress them. Because such an attempt at unrepression involves a great threat to his sense of self and to his concept of masculinity, he does not work to this end consistently, and at moments vehemently expresses views on the feminine that follow the pattern of repression. But ambivalence about change is not the same as simple conservatism. In endorsing and emphasizing his own ambivalence in *Paterson*, Williams gives evidence of the real complexity of change, which rarely happens all at once or exactly as expected.

Chapter Four

Marianne Moore's Poetry of Quotation

Marianne Moore's use of quotation differs markedly from that of both the poets we have considered so far. While Eliot and Williams employ the device occasionally, to specific effect, Moore's poetry involves quotation from the start. Of the twenty-four pieces in her first book, *Poems* (1921), ten include at least one phrase set in quotation marks, and in later volumes the proportion increases.[1] The kind of texts from which she chooses to borrow differs also from the kinds the other poets select. Moore borrows most often from pointedly unvaluable work, including what Marie Borroff calls "promotional prose"—language used in newspaper and magazine feature articles and advertisements, a kind of literary half-world[2]—and such little-regarded sources as conversations overheard, park monuments, and books of the sort we generally consider "secondary material," such as biographies, religious commentaries, and natural-history texts. The sources themselves generally are unrecognizable, except when identified in the notes (for example, "Lines 14–15: 'Water in motion is far from level.' *Literary Digest*").[3] Where Eliot quotes from the works of literary greats (or those he would have us come to regard as greats) in order to establish the authority of his text, and Williams quotes from local historical summaries and from the letters of younger poets in order to suggest his own complex American authority, Moore emphasizes the secondary qua secondary, the pointedly unauthoritative. And in quoting so frequently she brings the integrity of her own texts into question. In the long run, this emphasis too reveals itself to be fueled by an ambivalence toward the notion of authority not unrelated to that at work in the poems of Eliot and Williams. It too functions as a sign of originality and so serves as a source of authority. Moore's work reflects at all levels her paradoxical position as a poet who both aspires to authority and questions the hierarchical terms on which authority circulates.

Of the two poets considered so far, Marianne Moore's use of quotation shares most, at least on initial inspection, with that of Williams. Both Moore and Williams take the overwhelming proportion of their quotations from texts not valued in the established literary tradition. In each case the decision to cite little-valued work develops as part of an attempt at revaluing secondariness; but while they share a common direction, the attempts are not entirely coincident. Where Williams is drawn to the project of revaluing secondariness because he belongs to two groups judged secondary, the modern and the American, Moore comes to it as a member of three such groups. As an American modernist woman poet, her investment in the revaluation of secondariness is more firm than that of Williams. Where femininity serves Williams as a metaphor for his secondariness, in Moore's case it is a literal concern, both an obstacle to poetry of the familiar sort and a source of pressure toward innovation.

Many of her poems deal with Moore's sense of the American tradition and her place within it, as several critics have pointed out.[4] In "England," for instance, she defends the American against imputations of secondariness, arguing for the equal value of its culture to those of Europe and the East:

> England
>
> with its baby rivers and little towns, each with its abbey or its
> cathedral,
> with voices — one voice perhaps, echoing through the transept — the
> criterion of suitability and convenience: and Italy
> with its equal shores — contriving an epicureanism
> from which the grossness has been extracted:
> . . . and America . . .
> the wild man's land; grassless, linksless, languageless country in
> which letters are written
> not in Spanish, not in Greek, not in Latin, not in shorthand,
> but in plain American which cats and dogs can read!
> . . .
> To have misapprehended the matter is to have confessed that one has
> not looked far enough.
> The sublimated wisdom of China, Egyptian discernment,
> the cataclysmic torrent of emotion

compressed in the verbs of the Hebrew language,
the books of the man who is able to say,
"I envy nobody but him, and him only,
who catches more fish than I do"—
the flower and fruit of all that noted superiority—
if not stumbled upon in America,
must one imagine that it is not there?
It has never been confined to one locality.
(*CP*, 46–47)

Notes (*CP*, 268)
Lines 34–36: "I envy nobody," etc. *Compleat Angler*.

The poem begins with negative comparisons of Europe and America and then turns them around. Not only is America found equal to its fellows, we are told as well that within America there are no hierarchies: in this land cats and dogs read as well as men and women. The overstatement works at once ironically and fondly to suggest that America is perhaps no better than other places, but is at least as good. Moore's use of quotation here invokes the "authority" of an English source text (the *Compleat Angler*, not a usual source of literary authority) to argue against the view that English texts are more authoritative (fishing ability, not nationality, becomes the criterion for judgment). The American poet claims her place on the stage here. But while, as it is in "England," nationality is a concern throughout her oeuvre, Moore's use of quotation interrogates hierarchy most markedly in terms of gender, and it is that aspect of her work, understood to refer through analogy to hierarchies of all sorts, that will receive the great part of this chapter's focus.

A number of critics have recently explored the difficulties encountered by women poets in entering the poetic realm. Most basic is a difficulty in establishing voices for themselves within a tradition that has been composed almost entirely of men. This tradition operates on an understanding that the feminine is properly the object of poetic description, and is therefore of secondary importance, while the describer—the poet—is defined as masculine and primary through the opposition.[5] A second difficulty emerges when, the first hurdle jumped, these newly articulate women poets are refused entry into the set of "high-cultural" writers. The distinction between high and low, or mass, culture that evolved in the nineteenth century seems to have developed at least in part as an attempt to exclude the increasing numbers of women writers (principally novelists in the nineteenth century, and poets as well in the twentieth century) from the world of "good" literature.[6]

Moore engages both difficulties, working at once to establish a (feminine) position from which she as a woman could engage the poetic tradition, in spite of its equation of femininity and silence, and to disguise or mitigate the same femininity in order that she might enter the world of "high" art. Quotation serves Moore as an instrument for meeting both difficulties. It provides her with a means of entry onto the poetic field by masking the fact that she attempts such an entry, by seeming to affirm the understanding that her work—composed as it is of borrowings—involves no speech at all. The suppression of the feminine gestured at in this mimicking of silence also aids her in crossing the boundary of "high" modernism; she was one of a very few women to do so.

At the same time, the presence of quotations from "secondary" sources in the middle of a poem (a site associated with high value) suggests the possibility that things considered secondary (her own feminine voice among them) might be reassessed. This circuitous approach involves the risk that the poetry will be understood actually to be secondary, the same risk that Eliot runs in filling the first pages of *The Waste Land* with borrowings. But, as with Eliot, the risk is balanced by the evidence of originality given in the acknowledgment of unoriginality (and, also as with Eliot, originality is at once welcome and problematic in Moore's work).

Moore's effort at revaluation of the secondary and particularly of the feminine has ties also to a revision of the oedipal model. Like that of Williams, her work unrepresses the feminine; moving beyond his, it redefines what may be understood to be the feminine role in the plural, as *roles*. Jessica Benjamin's rearticulation of the process of development charted in Freud's story of the Oedipus complex can assist reading of Moore's poetry, as it did Williams's. The oedipal model codes the maternal (and by extrapolation, in our culture, the female in general) as site of early attachment and merging, which must be repudiated by the developing male child. This process is accomplished through identification with the paternal (and thus the male), which is associated with separation and agency. Female children in this model remain principally identified with the passive maternal model, though somehow achieving enough autonomy to speak and act in basic ways. In Benjamin's rereading, Freud's oedipal model and its assumptions become not a description of an inevitable process, but "no more than descriptions of our culture."[7] Again, she argues that mothers and fathers may each model both nurturance and agency, and that girl and boy children can identify usefully with both parents equally, without being confused about their gender identity. Expanding the discussion to include the Lacanian gendering of discourse, a Benjaminian argument might suggest that the maternal can also be understood to possess some of the prohibitionary authority associated in Lacan's model with the paternal and with the phallus. Such an argument, insofar as it attempts to move beyond description of the norm in our culture, would seem to require a new, less gender-specific term to represent the source of authority.

Moore's familial relations reflect the much more mobile role identifications that Benjamin's model points to, and these familial relations are likewise reflected in her poetry. Moore's father, John Milton Moore, had a mental breakdown and left the family before she was born. She and her brother were raised by their mother, Mary Warner Moore. Mrs. Moore was educated, an assiduous musician, a watercolorist, an English teacher at the Metzger Institute (a girls' high school in Carlisle, Pennsylvania, at which Moore studied), the editor of a collection of her own father's sermons, and at once extremely pious and generally ambitious. Her ambitions as well as her strong taste and strong will were echoed in her daughter.

Mrs. Moore actively involved herself in her children's education, teaching them French and music and reading to them. Moore particularly remembered her mother reading aloud *Paradise Lost*.[8] This piece of information calls up the image of a complex scene of instruction—the lesson both enforcing the authority of the text being read in the very fact of its selection, and at the same time questioning that authority via the association in name with an absent and incompetent father figure. This double lesson seconds, while resituating, the complexity of Milton's exploration in that poem of the means of establishing poetic authority (within a family structure writ large). These issues interest Moore deeply, and in several of her poems she returns to Milton's story to reflect on them. A brief look at the gendering of authority in *Paradise Lost* will serve as a helpful backdrop to the discussion of Moore's poetic development.

The Miltonic pattern of rebellion of son against father is designed pointedly to exclude both daughters and mothers from authority. There are after all two families in *Paradise Lost:* one, about to begin, on earth, which includes both a man and a woman; and another, in heaven, made up of males only. The apposition of these two families marks and insists upon a distinction between two kinds of creativity—one, earthbound, is regenerative, literally creative, and linked to the feminine. The other, composed itself through metaphor (it is only by stretching the imagination that a family made entirely of males can be conceived of), and associated with more lofty regions, transcends literal, human creativity. The creativity associated with this family has two aspects, both linked to the masculine: God the Father's creation of all the heavenly beings as well as of Adam and (through Adam) of Eve; and poetry. While the two aspects are distinguishable, they are not discrete.

The transfer of female generative powers to the male God is a clear enough maneuver: womb envy is compensated for by an assertion of bigger and better powers of generation, if not in the individual male per se then in the original male, and through him by analogy in all men. This superogation by God and even by Adam of female powers of childbearing (the process by which Adam is made to give life to Eve comes very close to a male parturition scene) operates to deny women *any* special realm of creativity. Since we see it demonstrated that God the Father and Adam can create life if they choose, we are left with the impression that literal, physical creativity is less the special ability of women than a task alotted them—perhaps because men are too busy for the tedium and trouble of actually bearing everybody. This portrait of the division of labor manages at once to acknowledge that male powers of childbearing are metaphoric—most men do not bear—and to claim that the metaphor is more powerful—in a manner, more "real"—than the literal activity of giving birth.

That the creativeness of God the Father is of a sort linked to metaphor is suggested by, among other things, the pun at work in the word *inspiration* (from the Latin *spirare,* to breathe). In both Genesis and *Paradise Lost*, God gives Adam life by breathing into his nostrils (Gen. 2:7; *PL*, book 7, lines 525–26). In the invocation to book 1, Milton reminds us that great poets are inspired (breathed into) when he calls upon the "Heav'nly Muse, that on the secret top / Of *Oreb*, or of *Sinai*, didst inspire / That Shepherd, who first taught the chosen Seed, / In the Beginning how the Heav'ns and Earth / Rose out of *Chaos* . . ." (*PL*, book 1, lines 6–10). The pun works subtly (many lines separate book 7 from book 1), but effectively.[9] It works as support to the poem's larger pun on creativity, which Milton establishes in the poem's first lines by setting the sacred story of human generation in the frame of a reflection on the methods of poetry. It is in turn supported in the lines from book 1 cited above, where Milton blurs the line between poetic and prophetic inspiration in his reference to Moses' "Muse." Where poetic inspiration involves being breathed into by a minor goddess from a large pantheon, prophetic inspiration involves being breathed into by the same, single God who breathes life into Adam. Because the same breath accomplishes both literary and literal creation, we are asked to understand the two as versions of the same process, as tropes of one another.

Indeed, *Paradise Lost* is as much interested in the story of its own origins as in that of the origins of the human race in general, and it tells a story of poetic generation, as Harold Bloom has effectively demonstrated.[10] While the creation of humanity and of the universe provides the background, the poem's principal actions both concern tests of skill in creating meaning (this power to make meaning I will call "literary creativity" here, building upon the Derridean understanding of the priority of the written to the spoken, which allows us to view any use of language as literary). In heaven Satan battles with Gods the Father and the Son for the last word on interpreting their right to office. Later on earth, again in a contest with the Father and Son—this time with Eve as the battleground—he interprets the prohibition of the Tree of Good and Evil in such a manner as to lead Eve to interpret for herself (where the Father and the Son insist that their interpretation is not an interpretation but the only possible right reading, Satan introduces the possibility of alternate readings of all sorts—not only his own). In *Areopagitica* Milton suggests that the Tree of Good and Evil is dangerous specifically because it introduces a choice of knowledges, undermining implicitly the claim of any truth to status as absolute.

Of the two abilities—to create physical things and to create meaning—the latter may well be the greater. As any number of critics and philosophers have pointed out of late, the interpretation we are convinced to give events does at least as much to shape the universe we perceive as does the presence of physical entities and properties. And in *Paradise Lost* the ability to interpret is pointedly (though not uncomplicatedly) gendered. All the principal characters are skilled speakers. Most of them belong to the forces of God, whose speech claims not to be interpretation but to be instead stable truth (a claim the poem both endorses and undermines). Opposed to these "truthful" speakers are Satan and Eve, imaginative interpreters both. As interpreters they must be explicitly condemned by the poem that purports to endorse the truth of God's argument, and both are. But Eve's treatment in the poem involves a great deal less respect for her literary capacities than does Satan's treatment. Where Satan wins for his deviance a kingdom of his own appropriate to the literariness of the sin—a kingdom of alternate interpretation—Eve's prize is completely unliterary and unrelated to her interpretative enterprise. Rather, she wins literal creativity per se: she is to become the "Mother of all Mankind" (*PL*, book 11, line 388). While in its implicit argument the poem sympathizes with Satan's choices,

Eve's exercise of her imagination and then her persuasion of Adam to follow her example get little sympathy. Instead, the poem offers warning against future such exercises by women.

Having said all this, I must now add that Milton does qualify his gendered dichotomizing of literal and literary creativity. Indeed, the poem's premises require such qualification, in terms of both its status with respect to religion (that is, its relation to the sacredness of its source story) and, relatedly, its story line. At the same time that it draws on a sacred story, *Paradise Lost* reflects on the nature of sacred and secular texts and on their claims to authority. Sacred texts, as noted here in chapter 1, operate as such through a fiction of their textual stability—their authority stems in part from the understanding that they represent the voice of the deity and that they do not change. The reputation for stability goes hand in hand with authority. In bringing the Genesis story into the world of secular poetry, where revision rules, Milton challenges the stability and so the sacredness of the story. It is the possibility of interpretation—of offering his own version of things—that opens the poetic field to Milton (and to the poets who follow him). Thus for him the fall is fortunate, though for different reasons than for Adam and Eve, for whom the fall is an unpleasant but necessary step toward the opportunity for redemption in Christ. But at the same time that Milton challenges the stability of the Genesis story, he draws on the fiction of its stability to support the authority of his own secular text.[11] And he reflects on the methods of authority through the opposition of the pre- and post-fall worlds.

The prelapsarian world as Milton represents it has stable meaning and thus would seem to be synonymous with the world from which the sacred text claims to stem and with which it claims to be able to reconnect us. In this world Adam can name the animals on sight (*PL,* book 8, lines 342–54) and Eve can do the same for the flowers (*PL*, book 11, lines 273–77); it is a world in which a direct relation obtains between words and their referents. The postlapsarian world—our world—on the other hand, is linguistically unstable; its words have no direct relation to their referents, all its texts are open to interpretation, and no single interpretation has in and of itself authority over others. Our postlapsarian language is closest to pre-fall language when it is most "literal." Because post-fall language can never actually be "literal," since it always involves some measure of interpretation, "literal" use of language in the postlapsarian world is our metaphor for the kind of emphatically unmetaphorical language which we may posit as an ideal, though its realization (as with many ideals) would be stultifying. The postlapsarian world is the one in which Milton writes, one in which a sacred text may be reinterpreted into a secular poem.[12]

Hierarchies of meaning, as of social order, are attractive at least in part for the simplicity associated with them. The freedom from the need to make choices operative when there are no alternatives has its pleasures. Conversely, along with the different pleasures that go with making one's own decisions, acceptance of the relativity of meaning involves enormous difficulty. This is the difficulty of having endlessly to recognize both the possibility of other readings and the viability of other people's points of view, without the ease of resting on received opinion. In offering his own reading of the Genesis story, but at the same time suggesting gender limits to the group that may partake of a similar freedom in reading, Milton takes a self-contradictory position, which combines the vigorous pleasures of interpretation with the relaxing pleasures of hierarchy. This position is ripe for challenge on its own terms. The postlapsarian world as Milton represents it can only be a world of unstable meanings, an unending series of undulating metaphors. In such a world, in spite of the poem's suggestions of firm gender divisions, gender and gender roles too operate as metaphors and as such are themselves in flux. In taking up the challenge left by Milton's self-contradiction, Moore must embrace the difficult position of relativism, and she must work out her own relation to the attractions of hierarchy and of authority.

The lessons of Milton's poem are revised within the context in which Moore first heard them. As we will see, Mrs. Moore's reading sessions bore fruit later in Moore's poetry. The coincidence of Milton's and Moore's father's names does not account for Moore's fascination with either the processes through which one may claim poetic authority or the gendering of that authority, subjects Milton's poem treats pivotally. But the image of the mother reading in the place of the father this story of poetic rebellion against the powers that be (or have been), written by a poet whose name happens to repeat that of the replaced father, represents aptly the opening up before Moore of possibilities for reconfiguring both literal and literary parenting roles and the life roles a young female with an aptitude for poetry may imagine for herself.

Following from this, the complexity of Moore's relation to her mother, with whom she was extremely close, seems predictable. With the exception of her four years away at college, Moore, who never married and seems never to have been involved in a romance, lived with her mother until Mrs. Moore's death in 1947, when Moore was 59. Though Moore's brother, John Warner

Moore, remained an intimate part of her daily life and participated also in an ongoing familial discourse, the two women shared a particularly tight bond. According to Moore's biographer Charles Molesworth, Mrs. Moore, angry at one point with her son (for greeting a female acquaintance with a kiss in a public place), "confronted him with the charge that he was a separate person, but that she and her daughter [were] not."[13] This kind of talk has more than overtones of excessively close mother/daughter ties, unbroken by the "civilizing" intervention of the prohibiting father, following the oedipal model. But the Moores' relationship included a prohibitionary aspect as well—a sort of "nom/n de la mère"—embodied in Mrs. Moore's deep concerns with issues of principle—at all levels of private and public life—and her often judgmental attitude toward everything around her, including her daughter's poetry.[14] Elizabeth Bishop described Mary Warner Moore's manner toward her daughter as "that of a kindly, self-controlled parent who felt that she had to take a firm line, that her daughter might be given to flightiness or—an equal sin, in her eyes—mistakes in grammar."[15] The relation would seem to involve then at least two kinds of threat: that of a too little differentiated parent and, as consequence of that intimacy, that of a too influentially condemning parent.

But while the relationship seems to have created barriers to individuation for Moore, her handling of it turned the relationship to poetic profit as well. At the same time that she severely critiqued her daughter's poetry, Mrs. Moore collaborated in its making.[16] Critic Margaret Holley ventures that "the relationship between Marianne Moore and her mother may well be the most remarkable and influential mother-daughter relationship in the history of literature. It is a kinship that sustained one of the seminal voices of modern poetry."[17] Bishop described the relation of Mrs. Moore's prose to that of her daughter thus: "I found her extreme precision enviable and thought I could detect echoes of Marianne's own style in it: the use of double or triple negatives, the lighter and wittier ironies—Mrs. Moore had provided a sort of ground bass for them."[18] Moore acknowledged her mother's contribution to her work, in terms that argue an even more substantial debt than Bishop's remarks suggest, in a postscript to *Selected Poems* (1935):

> Dedications imply giving, and we do not care to make a gift of what is insufficient; but in my immediate family there is one "who thinks in a particular way;" and I should like to add that where there is an effect of thought or pith in these pages, the thinking and often the actual phrases are hers.[19]

This debt is documented in Moore's conversation notebooks, which record striking examples of her mother's speech. A good number of these phrases reappear in some form in Moore's poetry. Laurence Stapleton has described in detail Mrs. Moore's contributions to "In Distrust of Merits," which include several pivotal lines reproduced verbatim along with several transformed but recognizable phrases.[20] Other poems to which Mary Warner Moore is known to have contributed lines include "A Grave," "An Octopus," "Silence," "The Mind Is an Enchanting Thing," "He 'Digesteth Harde Yron,' " and "What Are Years."[21] Moore's early conversation notebook has been lost, so there is no tracing the transition of Mrs. Moore's phrases into her daughter's early poetry, but the pattern seems to have been consistent across Moore's career during her mother's lifetime. Apart from specific phrases borrowed, the mother's influence on the daughter's work included as well topics that she raised for discussion and quotations that she pointed out. After Mrs. Moore's death, Moore wrote in a conversation notebook: "I don't care for the books that were not worked on by her."[22] Stapleton emphasizes that Moore recontextualized and "translated" her mother's phrases in the process of incorporating them into her poems, an important point to note. But it is equally important to notice both the extraordinary extent of the bond and Moore's comfort with it. In addition to Mary Warner Moore's direct effect on the poems, many of them seem to speak to or portray concerns shared within the family. "The Paper Nautilus," for instance, reflects on the closeness and tensions involved in maternal love. The poems themselves, however, do not comment directly on the relation between mother and daughter.

This relationship of profound influence is not one of the passive, asocial mergings associated with the maternal bond in the Oedipus complex. To begin with, it is a linguistic relation, though given the poetic milieu the realm of language—usually identified with the paternal—might be seen here as a maternal, semiotic realm, defined along Kristevan lines in terms of linguistic play rather than of rational exchange. But the material that the two women worked through together was itself so much concerned with moral issues, prohibition, and self-restraint, and Mrs. Moore's relation to the poetry was so often negative, that it is hard to read this relation as one of uninterruptedly blissful dyadic interchange.[23] Instead, Mrs. Moore seems to have lived beside Moore as a personified superego, the role linked to the male parent in the oedipal model, while at the same time offering her daughter consistent support—of the sort preoedipally associated with mothers—for her literary ambitions.[24] Another side to this complex gendering within the family is evident in the fact that in letters to her mother and brother from college, Moore refers to herself with masculine pronouns and speaks of her youth as her "boyhood." Her family responds in the same terms. Since Moore begins to speak of her poetic vocation in the same period, the "change in gender" may have served as a means of enabling her transition into the "masculine" world of poetry. The role mobility both women demonstrate suggests the inadequacy of the oedipal model to their experience, and Moore's failure to repress the presence not just of female influences but specifically of her mother's influence in her poetry also suggests that such a move is not necessary to her writing, nor by extrapolation to writing in general, even as Benjamin's model suggests. Though Benjamin restricts her discussion to a Freudian developmental model, the Lacanian gendering of realms of language also comes into question along the lines Benjamin explores.

In including her mother's words and thoughts in her poems and in acknowledging them, Moore posits a maternal authority. Such authority revises the oedipal pattern of domination of the feminine by the masculine, represented for instance in Eliot's pointed repression and denigration of feminine voices in *The Waste Land*. For Moore's work, this revision involves revaluation not just of mothers but of the feminine in general, and has the effect therefore of affirming Moore's own authoritative status. While Mary Warner Moore's speech itself relied on patriarchal apothegms (the Bible was her frequent source), Moore reconstitutes her mother's words in including them within her poems, in the process granting them an authority of a different order, which she then calls upon. The revaluation of the speech of the mother and her transformation into a figure of authority parallel the revision of the secondary status of ephemera and of "middle-brow" literature that Moore effects when she quotes such sources; indeed, the two support one another. The quotation of formerly, or rehabilitated, secondary sources may be understood as a quotation of maternal authority. This is not the same as a quotation of no authority, or a rejection of authority altogether. Instead, it revises the model of quotation of paternal authority, which biblical quotation had explicitly built on and which later borrowings from established literary texts had also borrowed on more or less explicitly. Where the paternal model involves a clear authoritative hierarchy fashioned around the oedipal ranking of father over child and male over female, the maternal model, based on this revised pattern of engenderment, is less fixed and involves a more flexible hierarchy. The revised model, which refuses a stable pattern of domination by one role or gender over another while continuing strongly invested in some authority and its exercise, provides the framework upon which Moore's many poetic questionings of authoritative structures build. Quotation, put to a variety of uses in Moore's work, provides the principal instrument of this questioning.

I suggested earlier that the frequency and consistency with which she employed both notes and quotations argue that they were more than merely helpful in Moore's work: that they were instead essential to it.[25] Quotation as device in itself, along with the connotations of secondariness associated with the critical apparatus of quotation and note, provides Moore with a modest and respectfully rigorous screen persona that affords her a comfort in speech that she would not otherwise feel. I would like here to look at Moore's poem "Silence" as a remark on its own methods and on Moore's use of quotation as a device of versification in general.

> Silence
>
> My father used to say,
> "Superior people never make long visits,
> have to be shown Longfellow's grave
> or the glass flowers at Harvard.
> Self-reliant like the cat—
> that takes its prey to privacy,
> the mouse's limp tail hanging like a shoelace from its mouth—
> they sometimes enjoy solitude,
> and can be robbed of speech
> by speech which has delighted them.
> The deepest feeling always shows itself in silence;
> not in silence, but restraint."
> Nor was he insincere in saying, "Make my house your inn."
> Inns are not residences.
>
> (*CP*, 91)
>
> Notes (*CP*, 276)
>
> Lines 2–4: "My father used to say, 'Superior people never make long visits. When I am visiting, I like to go about by myself. I never had to be shown Longfellow's grave or the glass flowers at Harvard.'" Miss A. M. Homans.
>
> Line 13: Edmund Burke, in *Burke's Life*, by Sir James Prior (1872). "'Throw yourself into a coach,' he said, 'Come down and make my house your inn.'"

The poem presents itself as an exercise in the very restraint bordering on silence that the father recommends. This restraint is demonstrated on two levels, and the relation of the two informs the poem's meaning as importantly as any reading of the words. At the first of these levels the *speaker* restrains her speech, repeating two sayings of "her father" and herself offering only the three lines "My father used to say," "Nor was he insincere in saying," and the concluding "Inns are not residences."

At the second level, arrived at through reference to the notes, we learn that the *poet* also has restrained herself, giving place to the words of others in two instances.[26] Thus, the quotation marks function not merely as signs of the difference between reported speeches and prefatory remarks; they note also the actual quieting of a poet, though the notes demonstrate that she has exercised some vocal power as well, altering the material she borrows and adding to it freely.

Though it is full of assertions, the poem does not tell us anything definite. We do not know, for instance, how to take the central lecture on restraint, since the expansiveness of the father's talk works in opposition to its point. This opposition seems to mean to mock the father, but not in an entirely condemning or dismissive manner, since the poem bases itself on his advice. The uncertainty that arises here arises in all Moore's poems that involve quotation marks, since these marks also operate as signs of ironic intention. In none of those poems can we assume that the speaker or the poet endorses the words set in quotes. Indeed, we must assume not only that there is no way to resolve the question, but that failure of resolution is part of the point. Moore's use of irony thus differs from the most simple use of the device to mean the opposite of what is said, a use which specifies a definite meaning, though indirectly. And the irony spreads beyond the quotation marks: the status of the words not set in quotes becomes equally uncertain, since no relation of contrast to those that are in quotes is established. By pointedly opening the poem to all possible readings, Moore ironizes the possibility of being certain about meaning per se. In this way she points up the uncertainty inherent in every text. At the same time that it denies the authority of any single reading, this stance emphasizes the extent to which each reader has authority to determine for himself or herself the meaning of all texts. In modeling the possibility of alternative readings, Moore's work suggests the possibility of rereadings of the larger sociological texts in which her readers construct their existence.

The quotation marks themselves participate in the ambiguity they help establish by signaling things in addition to the fact that a word or phrase is borrowed. As well as suggesting irony and indebtedness, they can indicate dialogue, show that the phrase they set off is not part of the speaker's normal diction, and mark off titles and mottos. And all of these uses come into play at some point or another in Moore's work. The fundamental ambiguity introduced by the quotation marks (not only do we wonder whose speech they indicate, but we also can't be sure whether they are to be understood as speech markers at all, or whether we are to take them as sincere or ironic) figures, among other things, the ambiguity of Moore's position as a woman poet, the two terms having long been effectively defined as mutually exclusive. The ambiguity of the quotation marks, in concert with a number of other effects, serves her also as a means of coping with the ambiguity of her position. To clarify how Moore's use of quotation contributes to her construction of her situation as a woman poet in "Silence," I will look briefly at other means by which she deals with the position of the "other" in her poetry generally. The discussion of quotation's role in "Silence" will develop then upon this background.

Many of Moore's poems make the point that one arrives at real achievement only through overcoming obstacles—especially internal obstacles; that one must be "hindered to succeed" ("The Paper Nautilus"). The other side of this overcoming or self-conquering in Moore's poetry, and its necessary complement, is *not* conquering or being conquered by somebody else. And this means at any level—even down to the level of not possessing them through too accurate description.[27] Moore's poems fight battles against appropriation at all their levels—working to honor the otherness of the animals and objects they describe even as they recognize that they must, to some extent at least, fail. The very act of describing wildness tames it to the writer's terms, and "otherness" is subverted when translated into the language of its observer.

Moore figures this linguistic perplex in the behavior of the animals she picks to populate her pages. These animals are not completely peaceful; for instance, the eponymous animal in "The Pangolin" does eat ants. But he restrains his appetite to the essential and, aside from the ant-eating, "Pangolins are not aggressive animals" (*CP*, 118). The model for poetry that Moore gives us, then, recognizes its inherent tendency to take over the voice and erase the otherness of what it describes, but while recognizing the inevitability of the effect, tries to keep it down to a minimum. Echoing the tension in her relation to authority, the body of Moore's work reflects a tension between a desire to possess in poetry the objects she renders there and an unwillingness to do so.

The project of valuing otherness is not altruistic. What value Moore asserts for the otherness of other things she asserts for herself as well, since her own voice represents an alternative to the mainstream. As a female American modernist poet she has to fight co-optation (the word signifies the elision of difference) by a tradition that is not quite her own, though it isn't quite *not* her own either. Her choice of unfamiliar subject matter is one way of resisting implicit co-optation, for it makes it difficult for both herself and her readers to ignore the extent to which that material does not fit into the network of the known, and it impedes the general tendency to assume that once a thing has been described it is known. Her strange animals mean to estrange us, to resist our knowing: a pangolin on a page fairly shouts at Westerners that we don't know it. This unfamiliarity comes in spite of the fact that Moore's descriptions are extremely detailed; in fact the failure of these detailed descriptions to render these creatures accessible works to remind us of the extent to which no description coincides entirely with its object.

By employing all the odd prosodic devices that make it difficult for us to read them, Moore's poems also resist co-optation by her *readers*. In Moore's poetry quotation is only one of a slew of strange and estranging devices that she employs on purpose to make reading difficult. The others include her syllabic verse; her frequent use of title as first line; her visual rhymes, which do not accommodate speech easily; her juxtapositions of what seem to be unrelated materials; her constant revision of poems over versions (which makes it difficult both to determine what constitutes *the* poem and to possess it in memory); and her notes.

Moore's refusal of co-optation by the tradition of English poetry continues in her valuing and employing the rhythms of prose rather than the traditional poetic rhythms, as well as in her rejection of what we recognize as traditional poetic subjects. That Moore does not write love poems of the conventionally recognizable sort, that she doesn't seem concerned with other *people* much at all (except in grand and unspecific ways that seem to have little to do with individual human relationships), does not of course signal that the work is bereft of normal human concerns. Quite the opposite. Some subjects are so highly standardized and conventional in our culture that it is extremely difficult to think of them in terms that are not culturally predetermined. Moore's resistance to such subjects is both extremely human and quite necessary. It represents a defensive move against traditional definitions of the feminine that make it difficult for her to function as a poet at all. And a need to displace representation of the "animal" elements of her own nature provides at least part of the motivation for her frequent choice of animals as subject matter. Since traditional poetic subjects and prosodic conventions participate in the system that inhibits the writing of poetry by women, those who *would* write have had to develop new kinds of subject matter and new conventions for dealing with them. But whole new ways of meaning are not invented fresh and all at once; changes happen gradually. Moore supplies her own need for new material and techniques by transforming familiar structures.[28]

In one of the most basic of these transformations, her poems about armored animals who conquer themselves revamp the quest myth, used as a paradigm for the poetic enterprise in countless poems, especially of the nineteenth century.[29] For the women poets who encountered it as part of their induction into poetry, the standard version of the myth posed problems in figuring the quester as male and the object of his quest as female.[30] When we take the quester, off in ostensible search of the beloved, as a figure for the poet, his battles along the way to the lady work as figures for poems he writes about his desire to reach her. If ever he found the lady, he would have nothing further to write about. This role division identifies speech with the male/poet and assigns silence to the female/beloved.

The difficulty for the woman poet who accepts this quest model as model for poetry-making is twofold. First, though it may be possible eventually, it is now and has long been difficult for a female poet to put aside the *female* part of that title and not identify at least in part with the passive lady role. And even if she could do it, she has to question the acceptability of simply turning the tables, knowing for herself the stultifying consequences of being made the motivating object of someone else's desire. Pound's call to "make it new" has a particular resonance for the woman modernist poet, who needs not only to come up with a way to write differently (for the sake of writing differently), but also to establish a position from which to write in the first place.

While she recognizes the impossibility of writing about anything without in some measure objectifying it, locking it into the system of her terms and silencing it in order that she may speak of it, Moore does make the effort not to appropriate or co-opt whatever she describes. Moore's attempt here is radical—she works toward altering the relation between author and subject matter, though again not without ambivalence. She deals with the dilemma the quest structure poses for her as a woman poet by taking on both of the roles—playing both knight and lady in her poems and figuring the combinations of the two roles in her many treatments of self-conquering and in her armored-but-unaggressive animals.

To return now to "Silence," we can recognize in the father, whose words his daughter the "speaker" recites in the great part of the poem, a representative of the culture that has long taught its daughters to not speak. And we can recognize that the quotations in this poem stand in metonymically for the quotations that fill so much of Moore's other poetry. Through the interplay of method and discussion in "Silence," Moore's uses of the words of others in this poem and throughout her oeuvre are revealed at once as signs of her speech anxiety and as enablers, the means by which she overcomes the worst effects of that anxiety and, in the guise of not speaking, begins to speak.

The evidence of the notes also suggests this double attitude of simultaneous self-effacement and self-assertion. On the one hand it is the notes that first make clear that the quotation marks in the poem indicate the borrowedness of the words they set off, as well as that these words are offered as dialogue, something we would have had no reason otherwise to suspect. On the other hand the evident variation between the original in the notes and Moore's version of it establishes her skill as maker and, indisputably, her authorship of the poem's poetry—that Moore, and no earlier employer of her phrases, has charge of the poem. The active role of the notes within the poem's total dynamic makes it clear (if it was not before) that they function not apart from but as part of the poems they annotate.

Moore uses the evidence of arting that her notes provide as a means of introducing herself qua poet as a character into her own poems. In "Silence" this poet/character's restraint, demonstrated through her employment of words written or spoken first by others, comments, as I began to suggest above, on the restraint displayed by the poem's speaker in quoting her father. For the speaker/character, not to be confused with the Miss Homans of the note, gives a portrait of a woman stopped at the door of poetic expression—constrained by old structures and able to do nothing more than repeat them in phrases not her own. The poet/character who emerges through comparison of notes and text has made advances on the speaker/character's position. She can speak and does, with her own phrases, though she disguises them as those of others and though she bases them on an already existent structure (the structure of female silence) and on already existent phrases (the actual quotations that she cites in the notes). The new poem transforms both the old structure and the old phrases. In setting up the levels of text to speak *in their relation*, and not in their specific phrases, Moore makes further creative, transformative use of the silence traditionally assigned to women.

This transformation continues in the borrowing from Miss Homans. In being given one of the poem's two notes, this passage from the *speech* of a *woman* of *no fame* (standardly unauthoritative on three counts) is awarded an authority equal to that of Edmund Burke.[31] Equality in this instance, however, does not involve simply the elevation of an unknown to a position parallel to that of an acknowledged Great Man. Since Moore alters the sense of the quotation from Burke in the process of absorbing it into her poem, his authority also comes into question. So instead of having a clear assertion either of the great value of both speakers or of a shared slight value, or of the ranking of either over the other, we get a questioning of what constitutes authority, without any (authoritative) resolution of the issue. This failure of resolution supports the dynamic at work in the poem overall.

The poem's sustained concern with visiting does a turn on the poet's effort to break silence, requesting the silence of others in order that she may work. Visits and visitors that do not much trouble the host either with excessive need of direction or entertainment or with excessive length of stay appear at the opening and at the close.[32] In expressing need of time alone and a place apart from others, Moore makes the point that even with genius and the most fortunate of situations in relation to the tradition to which she responds, a poet with too many social obligations is no poet at all. The poem does not reject visitors altogether or demand total silence on the part of others. Rather, it requests some say in how one's time and space are apportioned, and the right sometimes not to be available to others.[33]

Having offered the argument that the "father" of the poem stands in for the shapers of Western civilization in general, especially in their literary aspect, I would like to go on to suggest that Moore refers to some particular literary fathers as well. The poem shouts Longfellow insistently at us in line 3, and he lies in fact buried not far beneath its surface. Lines 11 and 12 echo and revise the final stanza of Longfellow's "Resignation": "We will be patient, and assuage the feeling / We may not wholly stay; / By silence sanctifying; not concealing, / The grief that must have way."[34] Longfellow's poem gives advice on how to deal with the death of a young girl: he recommends accepting the loss without moan for the time being, in expectation of meeting her, full grown, in heaven. Though its terms differ slightly from the usual, "Resignation" does follow the basic quest pattern. The poet's beloved is lost and their reunion put off until the last possible moment. In the meantime, her loss gives him occasion for song. Although he claims to advise silence to the girl's mourners, himself most prominent among them, it is not they who fall silent (certainly the poem is evidence that *he* does not), but she—another sacrifice to art.

In responding to Longfellow, Moore begins with an echo of his sentiment: "By silence sanctifying; not concealing, / The grief that must have way" becomes "The deepest feeling always shows itself in silence." But in the line that follows, in language that does a turn on the structure of his,[35] she rejects Longfellow's point—"not in silence, but restraint"—thereby making room for her own poetry to develop, not as silence, but, as this poem demonstrates, as restraint. In a parodic turnabout, in Moore's poem it is Longfellow who is dead, and his grave the object of a quest, though the poet is not the seeker. And the quest for his grave does not go on long, for visitors, albeit superior visitors, can find the grave without aid. Her neat settling of accounts with Longfellow demonstrates that his memory did not trouble Moore terribly. She invokes him for the opportunity his heavy-handed blows give her to display her skill in parrying. The phrases of another father figure, whose memory poses more unsettling problems, echo here also, however. The easily-dealt-with Longfellow is present in the poem as a cover for the poem's struggle with Longfellow's friend and contemporary, the more challenging Emerson.

All Americans since Emerson have been essentially informed in some measure by his work. Emerson's image of the self-reliant man who *can* "enjoy an original relation to the universe"[36] strikes a resonant chord in American breasts because it responds to the deep anxiety over secondary status that permeates American culture, isolated offspring of the culture of the Old World. Compelled to deny dependence on what went before, Emersonian men (and in a more complicated maneuver, Emersonian women as well) construct fictions of their independence and originality, which allow them to go forward with a new sense of their importance in the universal scheme. Their self-confidence frees them to act purposively and without hesitation.

This model has immense attractions for Moore. As a woman poet in search of new modes, as a modern poet, and as an American, Moore shares Emerson's obsession with originality. His doctrine of self-reliance makes possible her doctrine of self-conquering, which responds to and revises his. The influence anxiety implicit in such a revision is complicated—based as such anxiety is in the very longing for independence that it feels called upon to revise. In the process of establishing the idea of a self that is independent of earlier sources, Emerson's model tends to obsure all notion of dependency, and this complicates things further for Moore. Rather than honoring others, Emerson's model goes far toward denying that others exist at all—even in a world made of human relations—though this denial lessens the actual dependency of the "self-reliant" man on others not one whit and probably increases it. Like the quest, the transcendent Emersonian self depends on the silence of those who make it possible. The self as Emerson defines it is a general model for suppression of otherness, of which the quest relation of "male poet"/"female object of description" is a particular case.

Emerson is not entirely ignorant of the dependence implicit in his model. In spite of his best efforts, a covert awareness of this "self"-deception haunts his work, expressing itself through troubled tropes and through the very frequency with which Emerson denies it. In "Silence," Moore begins her critique of Emerson and the Emersonian elements of her own work by putting pressure on some of these tropes. We can recognize a response to Emerson in the first few lines of the poem, in the concerns with both superior people and self-reliance. The definition and value of these ideas come into question here and contribute to the poem's general mood of uncertainty. The atmosphere of doubt introduced by the quotation marks (whose ideas *are* these, and how should we view them?) builds progressively, with the poem. Even as the reader recognizes the possibility that the quotation marks may mean to mock the father's speech, other elements of the poem also prove unstable. The validity of the claim to superiority comes fast into question. Do truly superior people go about expounding rules for superiority, after all? And to whom, exactly, are they superior?

What seems at first to be an ordinary simile for self-reliance in lines 5–7 self-destructs when we notice that the cat's self-reliance depends on the sustenance he will take from the mouse. Moore's image redoes Emerson's famous "puss with her tail" parable near the end of his essay "Experience." Emerson, arguing that we all make our own worlds and that what we perceive is not independent of us but shaped by our seeing, offers a kitten as example:

> As I am, so I see; use what language we will, we can never say anything but what we are. . . . Do you see that kitten chasing so prettily her own tail? If you could look with her eyes you might see her surrounded with hundreds of figures performing complex dramas, with tragic and comic issues, long conversations, many characters, many ups and downs of fate,—and meantime it is only puss and her tail. How long before our masquerade will end its noise of tambourines, laughter and shouting, and we shall find it was a solitary performance? A subject and an object,—it takes so much to make the galvanic circuit complete, but magnitude adds nothing. What imports it whether it is Kepler and the sphere, Columbus and America, a reader and his book, or puss with her tail? [37]

In pointing out that "use what language we will, we can never say anything but what we are," Emerson, as Moore will after him, tells us that language silences what it describes. But he presents the notion in a way that realizes his point, managing here to speak of silencing what he describes while barely acknowledging the existence of what gets silenced. "As I am, so I see" does not note the existence of, let alone inquire into the effect on, the "object" onto which this "subject" projects its image.

Of course Emerson does use the word *object*, but the principal metaphor he takes to express the object's status avoids the issue by confusing things. His choice of part of the cat's own body as the object of her pursuit/interpretation blurs the distinction between subject and object. We do not immediately perceive that puss and her tail are not one, and so do not immediately and never quite definitely recognize the tail as object. The phrase "solitary performance" heightens the confusion. It seems most sensibly to distinguish between the cat's fantasy of a drama involving hundreds of others besides herself and the fact that she plays her game with herself alone. In fact, in a rather alienated image, it distinguishes between the cat and her tail, telling us that the tail has no part in the game as far as the cat is concerned. But the oddness of the image makes it hard to register thus. Emerson obscures the aggressive nature of interpretation as well in representing the cat's fantasy so sweetly. Harmless though it may be in itself, the kitten's pursuit provides not merely a good time; it prepares her for hunts to come.

Even without reference to "Experience," the apposition of "self-reliant" and the cat-and-mouse image in Moore's poem strikes the ear dissonantly. The example undermines the statement. With "Experience" in mind, we can recognize in Moore's image a corrective response to the wisdom of the father of American letters; we might call it a subversive clarification of *his* cat-and-mouse game. By revising the cat's tail into a mouse's tail and changing the game into a murderous hunt, Moore makes explicit what Emerson's simile would conceal: the predatory nature of interpretation and the unpleasant fact that the terms of existence forbid anyone's relying on herself or himself solely; that life as we know it requires victims.

Just as her notion of self depends on Emerson's while it takes exception to it, so Moore's use of quotation imitates Emerson even as it provides her with means of overcoming his demands that she be mute. Like Moore, Emerson quotes extensively. In "Quotation and Originality," he notes that all our habits of living quote the habits of our ancestors:

> Our knowledge is the amassed thought and experience of innumerable minds: our language, our science, our religion, our opinions, our fancies we inherited. Our country, customs, laws, our ambitions, and our notions of fit and fair, — all these we never made, we found them ready-made; we but quote them.[38]

His own quotations are not of this democratic sort, however. Emerson quotes for power. In quoting he means to borrow the authority of famous men along with their words. The first of the many quotations with which Emerson studs this essay comments on this very intention: "'He that borrows the aid of an equal understanding,' said Burke, 'doubles his own; he that uses that of a superior elevates his own to the stature of that he contemplates.'"[39] Emerson's witty setting of this quotation so that it compliments his enterprise even as it feeds his argument prefigures the sly multiple uses Moore makes of the quotations she weaves into poetry.

Having acknowledged the importance of the past, Emerson then goes on to recuperate the argument for independence and to assert the reconstitutive powers of individual genius.[40] Moore's habits of quotation build on Emerson's, but where Emerson emphasizes borrowings for power and the assertion of individuality through transformation of the material quoted, Moore stresses the interconnectedness of all elements of our culture. The fragmentary text her quotations create, along with the fact of Moore's insistence on acknowledging debts, stresses the attenuated nature of inspiration. In many cases the acknowledgment of debt is made quite unnecessarily, according to usual definitions of quotation. Comparison with the original, either given in a note or sought out by the reader, often demonstrates that Moore has substantially altered the phrase in the process of incorporating it. In such instances there remains small similarity between her line and the line she cites as source, so there is no formal need to direct attention to her indebtedness.[41] But time and again she makes a point of highlighting that debt. Like Eliot's, Moore's notes shake the myth of the self-reliance of the poem, and moving beyond Eliot's, Moore's open the realm of reference to include nonliterary, middlebrow sources. Moore's borrowings from ephemeral sources — the stuff of daily life in all its impermanence — emphasize her dependence as a poet on the world around her. At the same time, in a tension that repeats her paradoxical relation to authority, Moore's re-use of the texts insofar as it gives evidence of her skill in transforming them can be read as a joke at their expense. It is a joke that furthers the distance between the high and the low through the understanding that it is only when these borrowings enter her poem and are, as William Carlos Williams put it, "washed of all association with their origin," that they become valuable. Likewise, in the manner of many such rebellions, her quotations contradictorily declare her independence from Emerson and in so doing give evidence of her debt to him.

Not in spite of, but as a result of, these efforts, Moore's method does not cease to be "original" in that attenuated but nonetheless sufficient sense of the word that Emerson argues for. If Emerson precedes her in quoting widely, she quotes a very different sort of text, and to very different purpose, and in poetry, where previously the device had not been much used. Moore does not resolve the vexed question of originality but handles it effectively, insofar as she calls its terms into question even as she meets those terms.

Moore continues an Emersonian then, though with important differences. The unresolved nature of her relation to Emerson gives rise to her inability to deal with him directly or to name him in her poem. But he is present in the two direct references to famous men she does make. Where Longfellow enters the poem as Emerson's follower, Burke enters as his model—the one to whose height Emerson claims, obliquely, to aspire in "Quotation and Originality."[42] In quoting Burke at the close of "Silence" (or, more precisely, quoting Prior quoting Burke), Moore plays on Emerson's playful use of his quote from Burke at the start of his essay. Her quotation alludes to Emerson's quotation, and again we are treated to a sophisticated display of skill at making silence speak. In making punning use of a quotation from Burke, Moore "quotes" Emerson, and thus, like Emerson, she too makes claims to the stature of her model. Her concluding line, which interprets and revises the precise meaning of the line from Burke in the process of explaining it (his line is much more hospitable than hers), can thus be read as a revisionary response to Emerson, whose method she adopts, with altered emphasis.

In a wider sense, the revisionary reading in the final lines suggests the situation of the woman poet, working to redefine the tradition that inspired her to poetry. The evidence of reworking given in the final lines supports the understanding that the poet transforms the father's legacy even as she embodies it. And she saves the final word for herself.

A further complication enters with the evidence from Moore's notebooks that the poem involved an additional, unnoted, borrowing—from Mary Warner Moore. The passage "The deepest feeling always shows itself in silence; / not in silence, but restraint," with which Moore responds to Longfellow's recommendation of silence, had a second original in Mrs. Moore's remark that

"The deepest feeling ought to show itself in restraint."[43] Insofar as it goes unacknowledged, this borrowing holds a place like that of the allusions to Emerson and even Longfellow in the poem. All three operate in tension with the noted borrowings as evidence of an influence struggle, as opposed to an intentional charting of an anatomy of influence. The dynamic repeats that of Eliot's various genesis narratives in *The Waste Land*, with the difference that Moore's notes extol the influence of exactly the sort of secondary sources, linked by analogy with the feminine, that Eliot's notes repress.

Unlike her treatment of the sources of the noted borrowings, Moore does not include the fact of this phrase's maternal source in the dynamic she establishes between the principal poem and the notes. In fact, she directly denies such a source by tagging this line onto the passage attributed to the "father" of the poem and, via the first note, to Miss Homans's actual father. But the anatomy of influence, or deconstruction of the myth of poetic self-reliance, effected by Moore's notes to this poem and to all her poems works oppositely to suggest that all sources, including this one, have roles in the poems they contribute to.

The failure to acknowledge her mother suggests a number of things within this poem, as well as raising a general question about the status of personal reference throughout Moore's work. First, it should be noted that Moore never cited her mother's contributions in the notes to individual poems, so this example is not anomalous. These omissions of maternal reference might be understood as signs of Moore's need to hold her mother's powerful influence in check, and to assert her independence from her at the level of literal authorship of the poem (even as the possibility of fully independent authority is denied). Second, the overlap of mother and father figures points both to the complexity of Moore's own history (since her mother was, practically, both "mother," and "father" to her, in the sense that those words have of fulfilling both supportive and challenging roles) and to the complex blurring of standard gender roles in relation to questions of authority that the poem as a whole argues for.

Joanne Feit Diehl suggests, in relation to a similar moment in "An Octopus," that the failure to acknowledge the maternal source might be understood as a failure on Moore's part to dare to acknowledge the maternal lineage on which her work depends, a sign of her sense that she must invoke "fathers" to lend her poem credibility. In "An Octopus" a comment by Mrs. Moore on Henry James goes unacknowledged, but Henry James's authority is called upon. "This move participates," writes Diehl, "in a more widespread tendency in Moore's work not merely to obscure the biographical . . . but also to supplant the original mother-daughter dynamics of poetic origin with a more 'neutralized' veneer of impersonality in order to speak with the universalized authority of the masculine poetic tradition."[44] But while Moore's search for authority meant direct engagement with the male literary precursors from whom she intended to wrest some, "Silence" is so much an interrogation of the "father's" authority that the decision to not cite the mother seems less a retreat from acknowledgment than a negotiation of the grounds on which mothers may eventually claim authority directly. An emergent feminine, or maternal, authority does appear here, through the citation of Miss Homans (similarly complexly cited citing her father); through the general interrogation of the father's position; and through the poem's privileging of "secondary" sources, including speech. All of these devices suggest the complexity of the enterprise of claiming authority while holding it in question.

At the same time that quotation offers Moore the means for speaking without seeming to, it serves her as a technique for redefining as authoritative what had been considered secondary. The poem "Poetry" provides a fairly explicit argument on this point. This poem exists in several versions: here I cite the "longer version" given in the notes to the *Complete Poems*.

Poetry

I, too, dislike it: there are things that are important beyond all
this fiddle.
Reading it, however, with a perfect contempt for it, one
discovers in
it, after all, a place for the genuine.
Hands that can grasp, eyes
that can dilate, hair that can rise
if it must, these things are important not because a

high-sounding interpretation can be put upon them but because
they are
useful. When they become so derivative as to become
unintelligible,
the same thing may be said for all of us, that we
do not admire what
we cannot understand: the bat
holding on upside down or in quest of something to

eat, elephants pushing, a wild horse taking a roll, a tireless wolf
under
a tree, the immovable critic twitching his skin like a horse that
feels a flea, the base-
ball fan, the statistician—
nor is it valid
to discriminate against "business documents and

school-books"; all these phenomena are important. One must make
a distinction
however: when dragged into prominence by half poets, the result
is not poetry,
nor till the poets among us can be
"literalists of
the imagination"—above
insolence and triviality and can present

for inspection, "imaginary gardens with real toads in them," shall
we have
it. In the meantime, if you demand on the one hand,
the raw material of poetry in
all its rawness and
that which is on the other hand
genuine, you are interested in poetry.

Diary of Tolstoy, p. 84: "Where the boundary between prose and poetry lies, I shall never be able to understand. The question is raised in manuals of style, yet the answer to it lies beyond me. Poetry is verse: prose is not verse. Or else poetry is everything with the exception of business documents and school books."

"Literalists of the imagination." Yeats, *Ideas of Good and Evil* (A. H. Bullen, 1903), p. 182. "The limitation of his view was from the very intensity of his vision; he was a too literal realist of imagination, as others are of nature; and because he believed that the figures seen by the mind's eye, when exalted by inspiration, were 'eternal existences,' symbols of divine essences, he hated every grace of style that might obscure their lineaments."

(*CP*, 266–68)

This poem distinguishes poetry from that which is not poetry on the basis not of form (no distinction between poetry and prose is admitted), not of content (bats, critics, and baseball fans must be admitted, in spite of their lack of pedigree), and not of the source of image ("nor," we are told, "is it valid / to discriminate against 'business documents and / school-books'; all these phenomena are important"). Instead, the criterion is genuineness. What the genuine consists of is never stated explicitly, but it becomes apparent, as John Slatin has argued, that the genuine represents for Moore exactly what hasn't become hackneyed, what hasn't joined the realm of "poetry in general"[45]—the very realm in which authority is usually understood to inhere. In Moore's rendition, true poetic authority (or the authority of being true poetry) springs from a very different realm—the realm of what had not formerly been recognized as valuable, the realm of the "secondary," here redefined as essential. In the *process* of recognizing authority in the unauthorized lies real poetry, in Moore's definition. The struggle to see value where it has not been seen before constitutes the poetic effort in this view. Once an image has been recognized and presented it becomes familiar and crosses into the ranks of the conventional, and so it quickly becomes in Moore's terms no longer eligible to be poetry. As a result, the category of the genuine is always in flux.

"Poetry" makes the case for attribution of authority to traditionally "secondary" texts in its insistence that "business documents and school-books" may be poetry. Throughout Moore's work her many quotations from secondary sources—precisely the realm of "business documents and school-books"—argue for the value of such sources by claiming her work's dependence on them for its (redefined) authority. Of the 278 attributions of phrase[46] given in the notes to the *Complete Poems*, only 34 refer readers to works that might be said to belong to the broad category "literature" (including poetry and novels, many of them noncanonic), while another 7 are references to works of renowned essayists, and 2 refer to the private papers of literati. In addition the attributions include name-only mentions of 25 famous persons, some of whom are literary, and three references to the Bible. The rest of the attributions (210) refer to the world of secondary material of all varieties, including popular magazine and newspaper articles, advertisements, lectures, conversation, critical texts, TV shows, mottos, natural history books, and so forth. The mixture of "authorities" on which the poems build suggests that ephemera and standardly unauthoritative texts may claim a new importance as acknowledged sources of poetic inspiration and authority. And they support by analogy the argument that, like that of the sources cited, the secondary position in which the fact of Moore's Americanness, her modernity, and her gender initially locate her may be revalued. In addition, they raise questions about the poem's own claims to authority and about what authority is.

Along with the citation from Tolstoy, the two other phrases set in quotation marks in "Poetry" can be understood to remark on Moore's quotation technique. "[I]maginary gardens with real toads in them" (the original of this line has yet to be found)[47] may be read as a metaphor for Moore's quotation-studded poetry, if the quotations, imported from the "real world" outside the poem, are understood as the toads and the poems in which they appear as the gardens. Likewise, the term "literalist of the imagination" seems a fair description of a poet such as Moore who includes literal borrowings in her poems rather than borrowings of a more figurative, allusive sort.

The argument of "Poetry" continues in the interplay between the poem and the notes. Moore provides notes to two borrowed phrases (each transformed slightly). Both of these phrases come not from "secondary" sources but from attempts by established literary authorities (Tolstoy and Yeats) to define the field of poetry, and both Moore borrows in order to disagree. Moore employs this turnabout technique frequently. Her attempt in arguing with these authorities is to claim authority for the unauthoritative, a complex move with the principal intent of maneuvering Moore into a position of authority. In the same gesture, it subverts the possibility of authority of the old sort by removing its basis in stable, familiar orders and by redefining authority as flux. This is not merely a cynical move, nor is it unfamiliar; in fact the move has an authority of its own, which Moore points to obliquely via her footnote to Yeats on Blake. In aligning herself with Blake against Yeats, Moore lines up on the devil's team; that is, the team of literary insurgency represented in Blake's cosmology by Milton's Satan.[48] (Laurence Stapleton's suggestion to Holley that "imaginary gardens with real toads" may refer us to Milton's paradise, "the prototypical poetic garden . . . in which Satan, embodying evil, sits 'Squat like a Toad, close at the ear of Eve' " [*PL*, book 4, line 800], strengthens the link to Milton and, absent the view of Satan as evil, to Blake.[49]) For Moore, as for Blake, established authority is by definition a fraud. As with money, the value of which is dependent on its circulation, in the model Moore presents here poetic authority maintains its cultural currency only when it too is in motion, from generation to generation, from poet to poet. But where money may move in limited circuits and maintain its strength, Moore's model specifically insists that the circuits of poetic authority be opened wide. Again, her refusal to rank kinds of poetic material applies by analogy to kinds of poets as well. And again, like Blake and Milton before him, Moore treads a fine line in struggling to open the gates to authority for herself through calling authority into question.

Another manifestation of the interrogation of authority in "Poetry" developed across Moore's revisions of it over the years. The poem was well known and well liked, in all its subversive playfulness. But its argument created problems for its poet. For if it was "genuine" on first publication, once it became well known, by its own lights it lost some of its genuineness. For later publications, Moore revised the poem substantially and managed in so doing to disperse some of the familiarity. Finally Moore cut the poem to three lines, and printed one of the longer versions in the endnotes. The short version reads:

Poetry
I, too, dislike it.
Reading it, however, with a perfect contempt for it, one dis-
covers in
it, after all, a place for the genuine.
(*CP*, 36)

By relegating the well-known longer version to the endnotes, Moore again brings into question this and any poem's claims to stability and authority. Even as she demotes the longer version, she re-creates it as a kind of guarantor, with an authority based in priority, that can lend some of its weight to the newer, shorter version to which she appends it. At the same time, she creates a sense of alienation for the reader, who does not know how to take a poem exiled to the notes, and this unfamiliarity allows for (though it does not ensure) the prerequisite genuineness.

Moore's paradoxical position in relation to authority is continued in her religious and moral concerns. These concerns are demonstrated both through explicit consideration of what constitutes respect for others and right action and through specific reference to religious source texts. Though most of her religious references are to commentaries and other secondary texts, very occasionally Moore borrows directly from the Bible, doing a turn on the traditional paternal authority structures such borrowing usually involves. One early poem, we are told in the note, takes its title from Isaiah:

"The Bricks Are Fallen Down, We Will
Build with Hewn Stones. The Syca-
mores Are Cut Down, We Will
Change to Cedars."

In what sense shall we be able to
secure to ourselves peace and do as they did—
who, when they were not able to rid
themselves of war, cast out fear?
They did not say: "We shall not be brought
into subjection by the naughtiness of the sea;
though we have 'defeated ourselves with
false balances' and laid weapons in the scale,
glory shall spring from in-glory; hail,
flood, earthquake, and famine shall
not intimidate us nor shake the
foundations of our inalienable energy."[50]
Note [*Obs.*, 95]
Isaiah, 9:10

The virtue of the biblical quotation here comes not, it would seem, from its prophetic source but from its economy of phrasing. This suggestion is continued in "The Past Is the Present" and "Novices," where the beauty of biblical Hebrew is specifically discussed. For instance, in "Novices" we get:

"split like a glass against a wall"
in this "precipitate of dazzling impressions,
the spontaneous unforced passion of the Hebrew language—
an abyss of verbs full of reverberations and tempestuous energy"
in which action perpetuates action and angle is at variance with angle
till submerged by the general action;
obscured by "fathomless suggestions of color,"
by incessantly panting lines of green, white with concussion,
in this drama of water against rocks—this "ocean of hurrying consonants"
with its "great livid stains like long slabs of green marble,"
its "flashing lances of perpendicular lightning" and "molten fires swallowed up,"
"with foam on its barriers,"
"crashing itself out in one long hiss of spray."
(*CP*, 61)

The sources of these phrases are various: some secular (Flaubert, Leigh Hunt), others religious commentaries (A. R. Gordon, *The Poets of the Old Testament;* P. T. Forsyth, *Christ on Parnassus;* George Adam Smith, *Expositor's Bible*). The mixture of sources complicates any attempt to read this borrowing as of the same order as that featured in its religious source texts. Instead, Moore's invocation of religious texts works in large measure to set a framework for understanding her quotations and her aspirations to authority.

The religious contextualization points readers both to the precedent for her borrowing in invocation of biblical authority and to her variation on the precedent. In fact, Moore's biblical borrowings and allusions seem to grow less from a model of paternal authority than from her literal maternal model. Mary Warner Moore's style of speech apparently had an aphoristic weightiness informed by her history as a minister's daughter. (Bishop described her as speaking "more slowly than I have ever heard anyone speak in my life," and called her sentences Johnsonian.[51]) Had she been given the opportunity, Mrs. Moore seems to have been a likely candidate for the ministry herself. Certainly she (as did Moore) regularly offered suggestions for sermons to her son; and, like that of her daughter, Mrs. Moore's conversation was punctuated with quotations—of both biblical and literary sources.[52] All of these elements operated to suggest an authority linked to biblical authority. But, though both Moore and her mother were very pious, we can recall here Compagnon's remark that "the dream of the commentary or of the discourse of scriptural quotation is always to be the first, to take the place of the first."[53] Moore's quotations borrow on the authority of her mother, and both of their quotations at once call on the authority of the father and take issue with the way in which that authority excludes them from the ranks of the official invokers of the word of God. Moore's religious references, like those of Milton (her father's namesake), occur within a frame of aspiration to poetic power that draws on the tradition of the prophets, and within a dynamic of rebellion against her own exclusion from authority. Moore has a model for this as well in Blake's assertion in "The Marriage of Heaven and Hell" that *prophet* was the operative word for *poet* in the days of the Old Testament. Just as Milton's claiming some of the authority of the prophets meant mitigating the extent of the authority he claimed, so for Moore claiming some of Milton's authority means problematizing that authority.

But for all its questioning of the absoluteness of regnant authorities, Moore's poetry does not advocate a complete relativization of value. Indeed, her poems often concern themselves with discrimination and judgment. For instance, in "Picking and Choosing," remarking on a Latin student's mistranslation of "summa diligentia" ("to the humbug whose name is so amusing—/

very young and very rushed, Caesar crossed the Alps / on the top of a '*diligence*'!"), the poem's speaker protests: "We are not daft about the meaning, / but this familiarity with wrong meanings puzzles one" (*CP*, 46). Likewise, in "Novices" puerile critics are themselves judged harshly, here through ironic mockery of their underdeveloped judgments: "Yes, 'the authors are wonderful people, particularly those that write the most,' the masters of all languages, the supertadpoles of expression" (*CP*, 60–61).

"When I Buy Pictures" walks the line between clear hierarchy and relative valuation in its discussion of how to judge art. The poem gives what seems to be a strict criterion of aesthetic judgment, but it specifically excludes ranking on the basis of belittling what is not judged successful:

> It must not wish to disarm anything; nor may the approved triumph
> easily be honored—
> that which is great because something else is small.
> It comes to this: of whatever sort it is,
> it must be "lit with piercing glances into the life of things";
> it must acknowledge the spiritual forces which have made it.
> (*CP*, 48)

The system envisioned here admits the possibility that all things might be judged successful if they meet the criterion laid out at the close. But the opposite possibility, that hierarchy might be necessary to judgment after all, enters the poem as well in the phrase "nor may the approved triumph *easily* be honored" (my emphasis). The poem is not at ease with its own hierarchic yearnings, but it acknowledges them nonetheless. The poem's ardent desire for success and its competitiveness are "playfully" demonstrated in the interplay between the poem and the note on the phrase quoted in the penultimate line: "Line 18: '*Lit by piercing glances . . .*' A. R. Gordon, *The Poets of the Old Testament* (Hodder and Stoughton, 1919)" (*CP*, 268). The note documents Moore in the act of acknowledging the literally spiritual force (a religious commentary) that contributed to this poem's making, and informs us thereby of this poem's success on its own terms in "acknowledg[ing] the spiritual forces which have made it."

Similarly, in "To a Steam Roller" the grounds on which authority is established are found to be arbitrary and its means of expression duplicitous, but authority is not condemned out of hand. Instead, the poem explores the means by which Moore might claim some authority for herself while avoiding the methods she deplores:

The illustration
is nothing to you without the application.
  You lack half wit. You crush all the particles down
    into close conformity, and then walk back and forth on them.

Sparkling chips of rock
are crushed down to the level of the parent block.
  Were not "impersonal judgment in aesthetic
    matters, a metaphysical impossibility," you

might fairly achieve
it. As for butterflies, I can hardly conceive
  of one's attending upon you, but to question
    the congruence of the complement is vain, if it exists.
      (*CP*, 84)

The poem gives a clear instance of a direct challenge to authority at the level of the argument. But in the first two stanzas the poem itself exercises the same kind of crushing authoritative judgment for which it castigates its addressee. Even as it condemns such judgment, it emulates it. The final sentence, in the third stanza, mitigates the bossy tone of the poem's start with its statement of the need to acknowledge the existence of what one cannot conceive of for oneself. This suggests an ability opposite to that displayed in the first two stanzas—an ability to acknowledge one's lack of authority. The combination of the two stances makes the poem as a whole an oddly congruent complement. Again, we have an example of an ambivalent relation to authority—at once desired and condemned for its association with "the parent block" (a nice image of a blocking father or mother figure—perhaps Milton in particular, or fathers or mothers, poetic or otherwise, more generally). The relation of the butterfly and the steamroller represents the paradoxic union of the two responses to authority that exist simultaneously in Moore.

Though in central effect Moore's poems share more with Williams's than with Eliot's, they do share with Eliot's and not Williams's their interaction with appended notes. These notes make knowledge of the sources of the borrowings part of the poetry, and the degree of precision of the annotations becomes an issue therefore. In the main, Eliot's notes give fairly precise information about where to find the originals of the lines they annotate (for example, "192. Cf. *The Tempest*, I, ii"). A note to "Cf. Baudelaire" would in itself be fairly imprecise were it not followed up with two lines of a poem ("Les Sept Vieillards") that readers can track down easily if they care to. We have seen, however, that these notes do not give a thorough account of all the poem's dependencies. Instead they operate to create a frame of reference within which Eliot asks us to consider his work.

Moore achieves a similar frame of reference in her use of notes. As we have seen, the notes overwhelmingly refer us to standardly unauthoritative texts. Notes were not included in versions of the poems published in magazines; they were a bibliographic and not a journalistic feature. They appear in all but the first of her books, and Moore apparently introduced them into *Observations* in response to Scofield Thayer's inquiries about sources.[54] The majority of these notes acknowledge sources from which phrases were borrowed. The forms of these acknowledgments vary from the very precise, "See *Brooklyn Bridge: Fact and Symbol* by Alan Trachtenberg (New York: Oxford University Press, 1965)" (*CP*, 294), to the extremely imprecise, "'A wife is a coffin' Ezra Pound" (*CP*, 272). The form only rarely comes so close to the scholarly model as in the first example. References to journals are by and large fairly precise, usually including date of publication, though not the page number. Of the 317 notes in *Complete Poems*, 25 refer us simply to an author; 16 refer us to an informal comment or lecture; and 170 give us some amount of information that directs us to a book or magazine. But not all of the 317 correspond to quotations set in the poetry: some are keyed to phrases that were borrowed but not set in quotation marks, others explain terms, and still others comment on the method of composition.

While Moore uses quotation marks to multiple effect, she does not use them cavalierly. We may generally assume that where there are quotation marks we are presented with a borrowed line (except in the cases where quotation marks indicate words used as words, as in "'Avec Ardeur,'" and in instances like that of the set-off phrases of "Granite and Steel," where the impression of quotation is pointedly played upon). As with Eliot, however, we cannot assume that all or even most phrases not set in quotation marks and/or noted are not quotations. On occasion Moore knew the sources of lines she quoted and failed to cite them. The editors of the *Marianne Moore Newsletter* discovered that a "copy of *Observations* (1924) recently sold at auction contains an inscription by MM to Helen McGlade and Mary H. Tolman. Added in MM's hand to the notes for 'Marriage,' with reference to the quotation beginning 'I am such a cow . . . ,' is the identity of the speaker, 'M. Tolman,' and this name is also added to the index."[55] In some instances Moore deleted notes that had provided correct source information, though the facts they contained had not ceased to be accurate. For instance, a note to the *Observations* version of "Bowls" tells us that a three-line passage set in quotes comes from an "advertisement in [a] French magazine" (*Obs.*, 101). Though the line continues in quotation marks through all later versions, the note disappears. Moore cites the source in a reading diary, so we know that this was not a case of her correcting an inaccuracy. Similarly, Moore sometimes cites sources in her notes for lines not marked with quotes in the poems proper.[56] And the archives give evidence of instances in which Moore refrained pointedly both from noting borrowed words and from setting them in quotation marks.[57]

Until recently, Moore's critics have tended to ignore the repercussions both of the fact of her quotations within the poems' systems of meaning and of her notes, except insofar as they shed light on sources for the quotations. Moore authorized this overlooking in a "Note on the Notes," which first appeared in *What Are Years* (1941) and continued in all later collections of her work. Responding to the criticism of "some readers," she suggested in this note that her use of quotation marks and notes was prompted purely by a desire to acknowledge debts.

> A willingness to satisfy contradictory objections to one's manner of writing might turn one's work into the donkey that finally found itself being carried by its masters, since some readers suggest that quotation-marks are disruptive of pleasant progress; others, that notes to what should be complete are a pedantry or evidence of an insufficiently realized task. But since in anything I have written, there have been lines in which the chief interest is borrowed, and I have not yet been able to outgrow this hybrid method of composition, acknowledgements seem only honest. Perhaps those who are annoyed by provisos, detainments, and postscripts could be persuaded to take probity on faith and disregard the notes.

Even setting aside the irony implicit in a note that gives permission to disregard notes, the tone and phrasing of this apology are ambiguous.

The "Note on the Notes" at first may seem to suggest that the notes and quotes might be ignored with no loss in understanding of the poems, once we note the poet's desire to give credit as due. But a criticism of those who would forgo the extra effort of attention that quotation and notation involve is implicit in the first sentence of the note. The image of the donkey carried by its masters involves no censure of the donkey; it points instead to the stupidity of the human beings who carry it. The sentence begins by speaking of "a willingness to satisfy," which might at first be understood to represent the sentiments of the writer, suggesting that the poet's tractability on this issue would involve her in assisting her readers' slide into inanity, a slide for which she refuses to take responsibility.

The peculiar phrasings Moore employs here are, of course, disruptive and give rise to a kind of backtracking that, if it is not unpleasant, certainly forbids easy progress. After having read this crafty paragraph, any reader should be warned off ignoring any element Moore has judged appropriate to her meaning. She plays with words when she says her acknowledgments are "only honest." They *are* only honest, but they are not *only* honest. Though in some cases phrases set in quotation marks without matching endnotes may be left noteless only because Moore did not remember the source, in general aesthetic demands rather than (or in tandem with) a will to acknowledge sources determines the presence or absence of both quotes and notes. The proliferation of evidences of omissions of attribution suggests that Moore was discriminating in her use of notes as well as in her use of quotation marks. Where Moore appended notes but did not set off the phrase referred to in quotes, she omitted the marks because she did not consider them appropriate to the poem.

Given this understanding of their artfulness, the roles played by the notes might seem relevant to discussion of each poem, as they have been in the discussion of "Silence" and "Poetry" herein. In general critics have not found them so, however. Discussion has centered around the extent to which we are meant to be or to become familiar with the texts Moore cites in the notes. "[Moore's] notes (unlike those of *The Waste Land*) are not part of your education, we are not meant to look up the sources," writes Hugh Kenner.[58] Stressing the stylistic attractions Moore finds in the lines she borrows, Bonnie Costello, also working through comparison with *The Waste Land*, notes that "Moore's quotations and notes are entirely different from Eliot's. Her borrowings do not extend the meaning of her poems into the worlds they allude to."[59] Perhaps because of the lack of direct link between poems and source texts, Margaret Holley goes on to conclude that the notes operate as a general remark and should not be understood to interact with the individual poems to which they are keyed:

> The fabric woven by the whole list [of notes] taken together . . . makes its collective point, and that is the cumulative impression of the many-sided literate culture of which both the poet and the poems are products. In short, the notes appended are not so much to poems as to a book, to "the poetry." They are occasioned solely by the quotation marks, and there is no real reason to append many of them except

> to recognize this complicity of texts. They are a reflection of the process by which the literary artifact is fabricated out of the materials of its culture—out of the debris, so to speak, the odds and ends of discourse that converge in the literate mind. . . . They are one of the first and most direct and vivid images we have of the self-conscious intertextuality of the literature of our century.[60]

While the notes do function with reference to the poetry in general, there are important instances in which the interplay of text and note can be understood to be particularly meaningful, as we have seen. And it seems likely that upon further consideration more instances of such counterpoint will emerge. Part of the slowness of Moore's critics to conclude thus may stem from the difficulty such an assumption poses—both in terms of finding the texts in question and in contextualizing them. But just such an effort to search out what is good wherever it lies would seem called for by Moore's overall enterprise—an ongoing struggle against the limitations on vision imposed by the easy availability of beauties ranked highly within conventional hierarchies.

Sometimes the interplay between note and poem is made humorously apparent. In the poem "To a Snail," for instance, the first lines read "If 'compression is the first grace of style,' / you have it. Contractility is a virtue / As modesty is a virtue." The original of the quotation is given in a note: "The very first grace of style is that which comes from compression." The original works out to be more extensive and much less graceful on its own terms than Moore's version. So the poem ends up showing off its own grace—not being modest at all. And the note clearly plays an integral part.

As a group, Moore's notes interact with and inform her quotations in many ways: they complicate reading, by making each reader's experience of a poem potentially different from every other reader's experience (according to when or whether he or she turns back to the notes), and they point out the oddness of her sources. The notes also assist Moore's effort to avoid co-optation, principally in giving evidence that her borrowings are emphatically mediated. Many of the notes in the *Complete Poems* refer us to secondary sources rather than to an original. This mediational emphasis is carried further in the fact that the "originals" Moore cites through layers are often themselves full of quotations or about quotations. Moore's preference for employing the material she quotes at a remove springs from the same desire to honor otherness by keeping a respectful distance from it as characterizes her descriptions of animals.[61] The poem "New York" highlights the understanding behind such method by comparing mediated and unmediated modes and, while not directly condemning either, suggesting problems with each:

New York

the savage's romance,
accreted where we need the space for commerce—
the center of the wholesale fur trade,
starred with tepees of ermine and peopled with foxes,
the long guard-hairs waving two inches beyond the body of the pelt;
the ground dotted with deer-skins—white with white spots,
"as satin needlework in a single color may carry a varied pattern,"
and wilting eagle's-down compacted by the wind;
and picardels of beaver-skin; white ones alert with snow.
It is a far cry from the "queen full of jewels"
and the beau with the muff,
from the gilt coach shaped like a perfume-bottle,
to the conjunction of the Monongahela and the Allegheny,
and the scholastic philosophy of the wilderness.
It is not the dime-novel exterior,
Niagara Falls, the calico horses and the war-canoe;
it is not that "if the fur is not finer than such as one sees others wear,
one would rather be without it"—
that estimated in raw meat and berries, we could feed the universe;
it is not the atmosphere of ingenuity,
the otter, the beaver, the puma skins,
without shooting-irons or dogs;
it is not the plunder,
but "accessibility to experience."

(*CP*, 54)

Notes (*CP*, 269)

Line 4: *Fur trade*. In 1921 New York succeeded St. Louis as the center of the wholesale fur trade.

Line 8: "*As satin needlework . . .*" George Shiras, Third, *Forest and Stream*, March 1918; *The Literary Digest*, March 30, 1918. "About the middle of June 1916, a white fawn only a few days old was discovered in a thicket and brought to the hotel. Here, in the company of another fawn, it grew rapidly. During the earlier months this fawn had the usual row of white spots on back and sides, and although there was no difference between these and the body color, they were conspicuous in the same way that satin needlework in a single color may carry a varied pattern . . ."

Lines 18–19: *If the fur is not finer*. Frank Alvah Parsons: *The Psychology of*

Dress (Doubleday, 1920) quotes Isabella, Duchess of Gonzaga: "I wish black cloth even if it cost ten ducats a yard. If it is only as good as that which I see other people wear, I had rather be without it."

Line 25: "*Accessibility to experience.*" Henry James.

In this poem's Old World, firmly entrenched poetic conventions mediate experience heavily so that what is perceived is altered beyond possibility of recognition—a coach here looks like a perfume bottle. These problematic, misrepresentative conventions are opposed to what is presented as a New World approach to poetry, which reaches out and catches on the hoof the beast it would describe and drags that beast home to dissect it in minute detail. This rougher method too presents problems, marked by the presence of all the dead animals, which suggest the lethal nature of too-precise description. The poem has it then that overly conventional, highly metaphorical speech obliterates what it would describe, but so does too precise speech. The poem concludes with an endorsement of a combination of the two approaches: "it is not the plunder, / but 'accessibility to experience'" (lines 24–25). Accessibility to experience (especially in quotation marks) differs from experience plain, suggesting distance and mediation—though not the highly conventional, perfume-bottle kind; a potential for action, but not the action itself. The poem offers another endorsement of restraint; of a way of writing poetry that at once describes and points to the difference between its description and the thing described; a method of description without co-optation.

The interplay of notes and poem in "New York" gives good example of the variety of Moore's styles of documentation in her notes. Both the notes to "New York" and the quotation marks within the poem, which also act as mediators, reinforce the distanced effect suggested by the word "accessibility." The first of these notes gives a bit of contextualizing information. The second cites a source and makes clear that the quotation it annotates is almost exact. But Moore makes sure that we know that she does not take the phrase from Shiras's article; instead she has read an excerpt in *The Literary Digest* and borrows it from that source. The poem's second quotation (line 11) is not identified. (The *Observations* version of the poem notes its absence of information on this borrowing thus: "'queen full of jewels':—" [*Obs.*, 99].) The third note tells us that the line it corresponds to in the poem is a variation on a theme from the Duchess of Gonzaga's original. The quotation marks here do not mark a direct quote, they seem instead to be signs of a desire to acknowledge that the idea is borrowed. They also serve in the poem to give an effect of dialogue; to suggest that a person other than the poem's principal speaker says this line.

The fourth of these notes points us to Henry James without going into particulars, and without providing the original statement for comparison. As it turns out, this "quotation" from James transforms a statement James did make, in the manner of the transformation made earlier of the phrase from the Duchess of Gonzaga. But Moore did not make this transformation herself. In the blurb to the English edition of a collection of his stories entitled *The Finer Grain* (1910), James is cited describing his intent: "By the 'finer grain' the author means, in his own phrase, 'a peculiar accessibility to surprise, to curiosity, to mystification or attraction—in other words, to moving experience.'"[62] Though Moore may have seen this blurb, she takes her phrase from Dixon Scott's *Men of Letters*, in which Scott, interpreting James, argues that James's style is actually simple and run by a reverent desire to render fairly and with good conscience what he describes (a position with which Moore would feel very sympathetic, and which suggests again some relevance of the source text to the poem). In a section about the influence of James's father on his writer son, Scott writes, "All he cared to produce was that condition of character which his son calls 'accessibility to experience.' You were very interested only when you were interested—your very conscience ought to work unconsciously—and so our Henry James was equipped for life without plundering it."[63] Moore's poem borrows not only Scott's contraction of James's statement, but his link of that statement with lack of plunder. In choosing to acknowledge James and not Scott, Moore departs from her emphasis on layering, but it might be argued that she does so in a way consonant with her point. Her reference to James provides a general direction toward the origin—access if you will—but not enough detail to get you to the direct experience.[64] All of the quotes in "New York" are in some manner indirect; none refers us to the immediate source of the line quoted. This habit of mediation provides an "accessibility" that both preserves the integrity of the original and acknowledges the authority of secondary sources as a class.

As I have discussed in the preceding chapters, Eliot and Williams employ quotations as documentation for substantial statement and effect, in each case with a large historical scope. In *The Waste Land* Eliot makes a brief but sweeping survey of Western culture with a nod at the close to Indian religion. Williams's *Paterson* gives the history of a New Jersey town founded with the nation, and so offers in synecdoche a history of the United States. (For all his emphasis on the present, Williams's quotations focus readers often on the past—through the historical summaries—and on the future—through the letters from the next generation of writers who will continue Williams's poetic line.) While they did write lyrics, both poets limited the great part of their uses of quotations to long work. Though their purposes vary widely in other respects, Eliot and Williams share a concern with the relation of their moment to times past and to come, and they employ quotations as means of demonstrating what they feel that relation is or could be.

Moore's concerns also are with history. Strongly aware of the past, she works as poet to situate herself in relation to poets who went before, while at the same time entertaining hopes for the future (and for herself in it). But she focuses frequently also on dealing with and finding value in the here and now. Her uses of quotation support this temporal focus. Unlike Eliot and Williams, Moore employs quotation in work of all length. Though her longer poems involve a slightly higher proportion of quoted lines than do her shorter lyrics, the proportion in the shorter poems remains high nonetheless. In Moore's work, as in that of the other two poets, quotation documents. But a document of present value is by definition a different sort of document than a document of value in the past or to come. The present is essentially unfixed, and to represent it properly its documents—things usually characterized by their fixedness—must body forth this flexibility. Moore manages this effect by quoting ephemeral material not intended to survive its moment, by revising her quotations, and by moving around her quotation marks from version to version so that the quotations—both in text and in status as quotations—do in fact change.

"The Past Is the Present" offers a good example of Moore's ahistorical aspect. The statement of the title posits an identity of past and present and suggests thus a denial of the whole idea of movement across and through time. The basis of comparison that allows for the negative judgment of present that characterizes nostalgia disappears. We can see here also, of course, the remains of an impulse to honor the past and to value it highly (with all the implications of judgment that that implies) in the poem's very premise, which means to value the present by comparing it with a valuable past and finding it just as good.

The poem's first sentence suggests that the poem will be structured to import the value of the past into the present through comparison of Moore's own work with that of a biblical prophet:

The Past Is the Present

If external action is effete
   and rhyme is outmoded,
      I shall revert to you,
   Habakkuk, as when in a Bible class
      the teacher was speaking of unrhymed verse.
He said—and I think I repeat his exact words,
      "Hebrew poetry is prose
   with a sort of heightened consciousness." Ecstasy affords
      the occasion and expediency determines the form.
         (*CP*, 88)

Notes (*CP*, 276)
   Lines 7–8: *"Hebrew poetry is prose with a sort of heightened consciousness."* Dr. E. H. Kellogg in bible class, Presbyterian Church, Carlisle, Pennsylvania.

The poem defeats the expectation it sets up, when instead of the biblical authority it calls upon the words of a modern-day bible-school teacher (the note gives us the name E. H. Kellogg, a man of small renown).

At the same time that it asserts the value of the present and seems therefore to overturn the hierarchical basis for discrimination, the poem makes claims for the importance of Moore's methods, and so lays claims to the benefits of hierarchy. It is Moore's poetry, with its prosy rhythms and its fierce enthusiasms, that the final three lines mean to describe, not just any or all poetries of the present. Again, Moore does not abandon the competitive aspects of poetry in her development of a place for herself within its borders; instead she introduces alternatives to competition, along with evidence of her own competitiveness to balance and to begin transforming the field of possibility.

The questioning of assumptions about history is developed further, again backhandedly, in the poem that faces "The Past Is the Present" in the *Complete Poems*. "'He Wrote the History Book'" speaks in teasing tones to a young boy, the son of a historian. The boy, with the unashamed egocentricity of childhood, assumes that his father's history book must be the only history book.

"He Wrote the History Book"

There! You shed a ray
   of whimsicality on a mask of profundity so
      terrific, that I have been dumbfounded by
it oftener than I care to say.
         The book? Titles are chaff.

Authentically
  brief and full of energy, you contribute to your father's
    legibility and are sufficiently
synthetic..Thank you for showing me
      your father's autograph.
    (*CP*, 89)

Notes, (*CP*, 276)

At the age of five or six, John Andrews, son of Dr. C. M. Andrews, said when asked his name, "My name is John Andrews; my father wrote the history book."

Moore plays upon the boy's phrasing ("*The* book?") to call into question all historians who assume their version of the story is the only version. The importance of the issue she raises here to her own position as poet is stated both outright and obliquely in the four-line sentence that makes up most of the first stanza. It is the historical valuing of one set of voices over others that has been dumbfounding for women poets throughout history (another reason for questioning the value of the past), and that continues to make it difficult for Moore to speak in her own voice.

Moore's remarks to the boy do not seem to be merely ironic, however. The blatancy of his childish self-centeredness can serve as a model for understanding the tendency that animates his father's work (and that of many, perhaps all, storytellers); the boy's enthusiasm "contributes to [the] father's / legibility." And the father of "'He Wrote the History Book'" can of course be understood to represent not only historians but poetic fathers as well—the dumbfounding weight of the great works that have gone before, which comes under scrutiny also in "Silence."

While those two poems represent moments in which Moore employs quotation to contribute to the breaking down of the hierarchies that would exclude her and to accommodate alterity, the ambivalence she feels toward this transformation surfaces as well in poems that do concern history specifically. "In the Days of Prismatic Color," the Moore poem Williams cites briefly in *Paterson*, represents this ambivalence well:

In the Days of Prismatic Color

not in the days of Adam and Eve, but when Adam
  was alone; when there was no smoke and color was
fine, not with the refinement
  of early civilization art, but because
of its originality; with nothing to modify it but the

mist that went up, obliqueness was a variation
   of the perpendicular, plain to see and
to account for: it is no
   longer that; nor did the blue-red-yellow band
of incandescence that was color keep its stripe: it also is one of

those things into which much that is peculiar can be
   read; complexity is not a crime, but carry
it to the point of murkiness
   and nothing is plain. Complexity,
moreover, that has been committed to darkness, instead of

granting itself to be the pestilence that it is, moves all a-
   bout as if to bewilder us with the dismal
fallacy that insistence
   is the measure of achievement and that all
truth must be dark. Principally throat, sophistication is as it al-

ways has been—at the antipodes from the init-
   ial great truths. "Part of it was crawling, part of it
was about to crawl, the rest
   was torpid in its lair." In the short-legged, fit-
ful advance, the gurgling and all the minutiae—we have the classic

multitude of feet. To what purpose! Truth is no Apollo
   Belvedere, no formal thing. The wave may go over it if it likes.
Know that it will be there when it says,
   "I shall be there when the wave has gone by."
      (*CP*, 41–42)

Notes (*CP*, 268)

Lines 23–25: "Part of it was crawling," etc. Nestor. *Greek Anthology* (Loeb Classical Library), Vol. III, p. 129.

Moore's tone here is anything but straightforward: the easy disposing with of Eve (in lines 2 and 3) makes it impossible to read without irony, but the lament over the loss of clarity operates consistently throughout the rest of the poem, challenged only (though integrally) by the pointedness of the poem's own complexity.

The concern with originality stated in line 6, in combination with the reference to Whitman in the title (the phrase "prismatic colors" comes from the end of "As I Ebb'd with the Ocean of Life"), indicates at the start that a principal concern of the poem is the relation of its own method to that of its predecessors. As was the case with Williams's borrowing from Moore discussed earlier (his addition of "day of" to "prismatic color" marks it as a borrowing from Moore rather than Whitman), Moore's borrowing from Whitman blurs the boundary between allusion and quotation. The borrowing invokes, through allusion, the original world lost—the paradise of Whitmanic or Miltonic speech (the latter suggested via the references to Eden and to snakes), represented here as free from the need to acknowledge the world's complexity. And at the same time, it unnostalgically offers example of this poem's own originality, insofar as it is a quotation and thus points to Moore's "original" use of the device throughout her work. In so doing it counters its own lament. In Whitman's poem the prismatic colors are linked with the return to the world of pure presence through death, in an image that argues the necessity of nostalgia to poetry. Moore's ambiguous use of the phrase would seem in this context both to revise and to affirm Whitman's point, since she employs nostalgia here, but in a way that is at once both ironic and sincere (a meta-irony).

Understanding this borrowing from Whitman as a reference to Moore's own technique directs us to the poem's first overt borrowing, set in quotation marks in lines 23–25. These lines come from a fragment from Nestor of Laranda in the *Greek Anthology*, which speaks evocatively of yet another version of a fall (in which the serpent swallows Eden): "Part of it was crawling, part of it was about to crawl, and the rest was still torpid in its lair. But it thirsted and put its jaws in the stream. Then all Cephisus ran into them, and horrid gurgling sounded in its throat. As the water sunk, often did the nymphs lament for Cephisus that was no more."[65] The nymphs' lament echoes Moore's own (and in so doing gives further evidence that, if it is not necessary to an understanding of the poetry, knowledge of the contexts of Moore's quotations can inform reading helpfully). But again the lament is qualified by the investment in modern complexity evidenced by Moore's difficult setting of the fifth stanza (the "init- / it / fit-" rhyme) and by the presence of the line from Nestor in the poem.

The poem's final line gestures toward the possibility of a return to a world of truth and clarity. Here Moore abandons the syllabic pattern operative in the earlier stanzas so that Truth can suggest the truth of its own assertion by analogy with the prosodic straightforwardness of the line "I shall be there when the wave has gone by." Compared to the complex pattern of line breaks that rule the poem to this point, this line sails by triumphantly. John Slatin, who sees no irony in Moore's condemnation of Eve, argues for a reading of the poem as sincere lament.[66] But while the line does give voice to a yearning toward a simpler world, even this last, plainer statement is complicated by its setting within quotation marks, which echo and complicate the uses of the device earlier in the poem at the same time that they, as Moore's quotation marks always do, introduce a radical, ironic uncertainty. Rather than taking a clear stand for or against nostalgia, the poem's tensions are finally unresolvable, suggesting that Moore shared with Eliot and Williams an essential ambivalence toward the changes she, nonetheless, assisted and which were necessary to her work. And the admission of some element of nostalgia into the mix complicates the dynamic further, rather than simplifying it.

References to Milton recur in Moore's pair of long poems, conceived together, "An Octopus" and "Marriage." These poems, which each involve reference to the fall, the garden, and Adam and Eve, both take up where *Paradise Lost* leaves off: "An Octopus" tells the story of life in exile from Eden, while "Marriage" gives an account of the institution of marriage after the first couple. These poems include an especially high concentration of quoted lines. In both poems the high proportion of quotations, mostly from texts of little standard value ("An Octopus," for instance, depends largely on phrases from the Department of the Interior's *Rules and Regulations: Mount Rainier*), bespeak an attempt to resituate authority in the ordinary, in the present, and (via the originality of the attempt) in Moore herself.

"An Octopus" describes a trip up Mount Rainier (or Mount Tacoma, by its Indian name) in Washington State (Moore and her brother had scaled it in 1922). The Octopus itself refers to the glacier that covers the mountain's top. The scenery along the way is described in terms borrowed from a variety of sources, both religious and touristic. Though the climbers' staging point, called Paradise Park, goes unmentioned in the poem, many other allusions let readers know they are in Edenic territory. Mentions of falls proliferate. An anxious animal is described, Eve-like, as "the victim on some slight observatory, / of 'a struggle between curiosity and caution'" (*CP*, 74, lines 108–9). Patricia Willis points to specific Miltonic echoes: "Milton's paradise is a garden on a mountain with blossoms of 'gay enamel'd color,' 'rapid current,' sapphires, gold, rich trees, 'Grots and Caves / of cool recess,' waterfalls, and a lake holding 'Her crystal mirror.'" Moore's poem is set on a mountain covered with flowers, some of which stand in "'an arrangement of colors / as in Persian designs of hard stones with enamel' (ll. 134–35)," and on which there appear "'rapids and high pressured falls' (l. 85); 'sapphires in the pavement of the glistening plateau' (l. 144); 'dumps of gold . . . ore' (l. 30); 'grottoes from which issue penetrating draughts' (l. 61); a 'waterfall which never seems to fall' (l. 57); and the lake 'The Goat's Mirror.'"[67] But Moore's is a postlapsarian Eden; access to the origin is emphatically denied. Here

> . . . "guns, nets, seines, traps and explosives,
> hired vehicles, gambling and intoxicants are prohibited;
> disobedient persons being summarily removed
> and not allowed to return without permission in writing."
> (*CP*, 75, lines 157–60)

The particular crimes substitute for the "first disobedience" of which we all stand convicted.

This poem attempts to write its own permission for an access to authority, but under heavily qualified terms. For while a return to a simpler world with which such authority might be associated has some allure here (happiness, presumably a desideratum, is declared to have departed with Adam [*CP*, 75, lines 146, 152]), the poem holds on to the doctrine of the fortunate fall, feeling "the love of doing hard things" (*CP*, 76, line 171) and refusing to follow the Greeks in their attempt to resolve "'complexities which still will be complexities / as long as the world lasts'" (*CP*, 75, lines 144–45). This acceptance of complexity goes along with an insistence upon a virtue in America, for all its distance from the origin. The complexity that distance introduces becomes a kind of originality in itself (the same maneuver accomplished with the initial romantic use of the concept), and Moore can mention "the original American menagerie of styles" (*CP*, 74, line 125), speaking ostensibly of flowers but pointing at the same time to the mixture of styles included in her own poem via the wide variety of texts quoted.[68] The poem ends with a tableau of fallenness:

> the white volcano with no weather side;
> the lightning flashing at its base,
> rain falling in the valleys, and snow falling on the peak—
> the glassy octopus symmetrically pointed,
> its claw cut by the avalanche
> "with a sound like the crack of a rifle,
> in a curtain of powdered snow launched like a waterfall."
> (*CP*, 76, lines 188–94)

With its shot that suggests the source of the wound the earth feels at the fall in *Paradise Lost*,[69] the closing image offers no nostalgic hope for a way out of the difficulties of the world Moore inherits.

Joanne Feit Diehl offers an excellent reading of this poem's encounter with issues of gender and poetry. Her reading concludes, however, that although ambitious, the poem finally fails to achieve sublimity because it closes without transcendence. We see no evidence, Diehl holds, of Moore's having succeeded in throwing off the grip either of male precursors or of the too-strong maternal influence, represented in the strangling octopus image at the close ("Creeping slowly as with meditated stealth, / its arms seeming to approach from all directions" [*CP*, 76, lines 176–77]).[70] Instead, the argument continues, we see in the poem's thicket of quotations evidence of the deflection of Moore's own voice, which given rein would have spoken more directly of the woman poet's difficulty in exercising her voice, particularly in combination with her sexuality. The problem with such a reading, of course, lies in its failure to recognize the quotations as an apt means both of expressing precisely those difficulties met by women poets and of critiquing the standard methods of authority that assert self-reliance by denying the assistance of other texts.

Instead of deflecting expression of Moore's profound concerns, the quotations allow it. As we have seen, they are themselves enablers, representing in themselves almost allegorically the difficulty in speech Moore encounters and handles. At the same time, the texts she chooses to quote from support her argument by representing in themselves a critique of standard authority structures. In her notes Moore gives credit for phrases borrowed to a series of Christian moralists: Richard Baxter's *Saints' Everlasting Rest;* Ruskin; W. D. Hyde's *The Five Great Philosophies;* and Cardinal Newman's *Historical Sketches*. These "authorities" of various degree allude as a group in the notes to the biblical model of "original" authority, to which the poet might be assumed, like Milton, to aspire. But beside these authorities Moore cites, along with the Parks handbook, M. C. Carey and "W. M." in the *London Graphic*, W. P. Pycraft and Francis Ward in the *Illustrated London News*, John Muir, Clifton Johnson's *What to See in America*, W. D. Wilcox's *The Rockies of Canada*, and a conversation "overheard at the circus." This juxtaposition brings the authority of the first set into question, substituting the complexity of unranked sources for the clear hierarchies of both ecclesiastical and traditional literary authorities.

Thirdly, through the difficulty they introduce for readers, the quotations reiterate the point made in the poems' endorsements of complexity (themselves set in quotations), which echo the principle of the fortunate fall (a principle not unrelated to Moore's notion that one must be "hindered to succeed" ["The Paper Nautilus," *CP*, 121]). In Christian doctrine the fall away from the single truth into the mazes of error is fortunate specifically because it opens the way to Christ's sacrifice and to redemption. Within the logic of Milton's poem, however, the fortunateness of the fall consists in opening the way to interpretation (a capacity modeled by both Satan and Eve). The possibility of interpretation, of recontextualizing what has been said and making it speak anew, is the ground upon which the new poet builds, and so is essential to Moore. Quotations offer her this opportunity both literally, in allowing her to recycle used material, and metaphorically, in giving her an original way to write poetry. Dedication to (re)interpretation as mode also seconds her investment in bringing authority into question. For Moore, and for others who make them, the sticking point in such investments is always how long the principle of questioning authority holds once the old authorities have been tumbled.

The second of the two long poems, "Marriage," addresses related issues, also against a Miltonic backdrop. The poem, which sets itself up from the start as an inquiry into Adam and Eve's view(s) of the institution they inaugurated, neither strongly endorses nor disparages marriage outright. Instead, it offers paired sets of portraits in which both husbands and wives appear equally attractive (both are acknowledged to be beautiful) and flawed:

> he loves himself so much,
> he can permit himself
> no rival in that love.
> She loves herself so much,
> she cannot see herself enough—
> (*CP*, 68)

Occasionally, however, the inequality of influence is noted, as when the passage ". . . experience attests / that men have power / and sometimes one is made to feel it" is followed by "He says, 'What monarch would not blush / to have a wife / with hair like a shaving-brush?'" (*CP*, 68).

While the poem apparently supports the value of efforts at affection per se, its deep concerns lie with the gendering of the role of writer. The poem is remarkable, as Randall Jarrell has noted, for its lack of discussion of sex and children, generally central to discussion of marital relations.[71] The division demonstrated in *Paradise Lost* between literary creativity and literal creativity (usually gendered male and female, respectively) leads to a trade-off in this poem. While portraying the standard gender economy in the foreground of the poem, behind the scenes we get Moore, unmarried, childless, writing the poem. The lack of children in the foreground discussion reminds readers of the trade the poet has made, as does the final image, of a Central Park statue of Civil War rhetorician Daniel Webster with its motto. This image gives us

> ". . . the essence of the matter:
>
> > 'Liberty and union
> > now and forever' ;
>
> the Book on the writing-table;
> the hand in the breast-pocket."
> (*CP*, 70)

Though the motto espouses union, we are presented here with a solitary figure—an authoritative man who is associated specifically with writing in the second-to-last line. This in itself can be read as a critique of the gendering of creativity (opposed to the woman near the poem's start who is "able to write simultaneously / in three languages" [*CP*, 62], but who seems not to put this skill to much direct use, since she is never allowed to be alone). The opposition of these two images makes dubious the possibility that "liberty and union" can be accomplished under patriarchy. A reminder that women may find ways to write nonetheless appears in the poem's final line, with its gesture at a breast (in disguise as a pocket), which, blended with the awareness that it is in fact a woman who writes this poem, gives us Daniel Webster as cross-dresser. This image works not to deny femininity, but as a step toward changing the definitions of both masculinity and femininity.

In "Marriage," the quotations serve as enablers and ironizers, as they do throughout Moore's work. In addition, in this poem that weds 29 noted quotations of varying length (occupying 83 of the poem's 289 lines, and the number would increase if unnoted borrowings were included as well), the borrowings allow the poem to demonstrate both the troubles and virtues of its namesake in its own construction. These borrowed phrases, Moore informs us in a headnote, are "[s]tatements that took my fancy which I tried to arrange plausibly," a statement that itself might be read as a metaphor for the randomness of romance and the efforts couples must make to deal with its consequences. Operating at once at liberty and in union, the quotations make the most positive case in the poem for the possibility that marriage may work under altered conditions.[72]

In these poems and in many others, Moore's work carries further the logic in *Paradise Lost* of Satan's rebellion (and Milton's own) against authority and hierarchy, bringing it into the twentieth century. In Moore's work the rebellion expands into a struggle against the gender roles espoused by the same text that gives the model for rebellion. Moore's treatment of the story involves both a departure from the gender model Milton employs and a thickening of the logic behind the rebellion he describes and enacts. Her work carries further the process of undoing fixed hierarchies that his work implements so pivotally.

In "The Steeple Jack" Moore herself takes on the role of Satan. In this poem set in a quiet New England town, a figure dressed in scarlet works on the steeple, the pitch of which we are told is "not true." Below on the sidewalk are two signs, one "says C. J. Poole, Steeple-Jack, / in black and white; and one in red / and white says // Danger" (*CP*, 6–7). The image is again one of a fallen world, in which nothing is "true," and the eventual repair of the steeple seems unlikely (in fact the steeplejack does not even attempt it, we learn later). The poem closes with a lie:

> It could not be dangerous to be living
> in a town like this, of simple people,
> who have a steeple-jack placing danger-signs by the church
> while he is gilding the solid-
> pointed star, which on a steeple
> stands for hope.
> (*CP*, 7)

Indeed, dangerous is exactly what it always is, and if the devil led us into this world in which all signs are danger signs, specifically because they must be interpreted, at least he warns us as he goes. In this very unstraightforward poem, where irony rules and old hierarchies of meaning are destabilized, the importance of complexity and of multiple possibilities of interpretation is stressed. Moore again embraces the very danger she alerts us to. For this poet, abandonment of stable hierarchies of meaning is the only safety, and the danger such abandonment poses is the only grounds for hope.

Moore returns often to Milton, as a model both for her own wrestling with authority and for her ambivalence toward it, and also as an adversary in her working through of the relation of gender to poetry. Recalling the image of Mrs. Moore reading aloud to her children from *Paradise Lost*, we might understand Moore to attempt in her revisions of Milton an imagining of a maternal authority, which as I have outlined it would involve not necessarily a specific linking of authority with females but instead an undoing of strict gender role assignments. Milton offers the basis for this in his image at the start of *Paradise Lost* of the male bird that both makes pregnant the vast Abyss and broods upon it. Moore takes this image up in "He 'Digesteth Harde Yron,'" wherein the father ostrich "watches his chicks with / a maternal concentration — and he's / been mothering the eggs / at night six weeks — his legs / their only weapon of defense" (*CP*, 99).[73] Such a male nurturer (who is not excluded from poetry) is the necessary counterpart to a female poet (who is not excluded from nurturing). Moore, of course, though able to imagine a more flexible gender hierarchy, did not see it accomplished. But in raising questions about the structures of authority and in making her own authoritative mark, she worked toward realizing the changes she envisioned.

Having looked closely at Moore's method of quotation, we can appreciate its difference from the methods of Eliot and Williams, while recognizing that it operates in dialogue with their uses. As we saw in the last chapter, Williams's use of quotation responds to Eliot in ways that learn from Moore. And Moore's method also responds to and learns from Eliot; John Slatin has pointed to the relation between Eliot's use of quotation in *The Waste Land* and the explosion of quotation in Moore's poetry after *The Waste Land* appeared in 1922.[74] But the learning is not entirely one-sided, for Moore's poetry, already dotted with clearly marked borrowings, had been familiar to Eliot since at least 1915, when it began to appear in *The Egoist*.[75] In his 1918 review of Moore's work, Eliot compares her, following Pound's lead, to Laforgue, and he notes that "[e]ven in Laforgue there are unassimilated fragments of metaphysics and, on the other hand, of sentiment floating about."[76] Of course in Moore's work the unassimilated fragments are not metaphysical or not only metaphysical, and in this review we can observe Eliot assimilating this fact. His reference to her fragmentary metaphysics omits his equal or greater interest in her fragmentary technique.

Eliot also had a model for this fragmentary method in the early Pound, whose work was always pointedly allusive and sometimes involved quotations from the great poets of his peculiar canon. Pound's early quotations flesh out the sense of dialogue he establishes between his own poems and the work of earlier poets, which he invokes specifically. (See for instance his "Mesmerism," which addresses Browning and cites him to create a kind of conversation. Similarly his quotation from Bertran de Born in "Na Audiart" invokes that earlier poet.[77]) Pound's work also influenced Moore, though it is difficult to gauge whether he acted more in the role of teacher or more as a combined confidence builder and foil. He apparently did not introduce her to the use of poetic quotation, since her 1907 poem "Under a Patched Sail," written before she became familiar with Pound's work and published in Bryn Mawr's literary magazine, *Tipyn o'Bob*, begins with a two-line borrowing from a sea shanty. And her use of the device differs pointedly from his.

The pattern of Moore's transformation of Pound is demonstrated in her poem "Ezra Pound" (written in March 1915), a paean to Pound and to the journal *Blast*, in which Moore explores the relation of her method of quotation to his.[78] The poem takes as epigraph a line from a "Sonet" by the sixteenth-century Scots poet Mark Alexander Boyd, which Pound quotes in an essay called "The Palette" (published in *Poetry* in February 1915): "Fra bank to bank, fra wood to wood I rin."[79] This essay argues the importance to any new poet of a well-chosen "palette" of earlier poets (Pound chooses an eclectic set of "greats," including Homer, Sappho, Ibycus, Theocritus, Catullus, Dante, "one passage out of The Wanderer," and Villon), whose effects the new poet goes on to employ in his own work. Moore employs a double set of quotation marks in her epigraph, to indicate that her borrowing refers specifically to Pound's quotation of Boyd, not to Boyd per se. Pound does not recommend that new poets quote their predecessors (in fact, in the essay's third paragraph he warns against "cribbing, quoting or imitating"), rather that they learn from and adapt. And he does not recommend Boyd as a model—instead, Pound picks him out as an example of the kind of poet who may be enjoyed but not learned from: "Let anyone drink any sort of liqueur that suits him. . . . but let him not confuse enjoyment with criticism, constructive criticism, or preparation for writing."[80] While Moore's poem speaks glowingly of Pound, its epigraph flouts pointedly his rules for good poetry, managing at once to cite a proscribed poet, to point to its transgression, and to turn the quotation into a remark on this poet's own methods, all in the best of humor.[81]

The body of the poem includes two five-line stanzas, with one two-line quotation in the first stanza. This quotation continues the disobedience begun in the epigraph, coming as it does from the sort of lesser work—and prose at that—of which Pound disapproves as sources, in this case George Meredith's novel *Rhoda Fleming*. (Moore revises Meredith's line extensively, but she stresses the borrowing by setting it in quotation marks.) Moore's acknowledgment of the effect of Meredith's phrase on her own introduces a very different attitude toward poetry from that suggested by Pound's borrowings from "great" works: Moore's is an attitude of openness to a wide variety of influences, a pointed nonexclusivity.

Not only does Moore cite a different sort of source, her quotation also functions differently within the poem than do Pound's quotations in his early work. Thus, Moore's borrowing makes no attempt at dialogue with Meredith, whose particular presence it is not essential to the poem to recognize.[82] While, like Moore's, Pound's borrowings fail to digest the phrases that inspire them, they disguise this failure by constituting the alien text not as a sign of the present text's unintegral status, but as the voice of a partner in dialogue. The two interlocutors thus established appear then to be two self-limited entities. The dialogic effect counters the sense of the text's fragmentation that the presence of the borrowed lines would otherwise imply. Moore's texts, by including their quotations as part of the poem's fiber and not calling upon them to function also as dialogue at the level of the poem's conceit, stress the fragmentation. Moore's quotations may also introduce a dialogic effect (and such is clearly the case with the Pound/Boyd epigraph), but this is not their primary or ostensible product, since the dialogue is not performed directly or as part of the poem's specific premise. Instead, the dialogue Moore does set up is of an ironic, backhanded sort. This indirectness is especially noteworthy given the great proportion of Moore's early poems that are specifically addressed to others. While Moore uses quotations differently than Pound does in his early poems, changes in Pound's use of the device in *Hugh Selwyn Mauberly* (1920), where a fragmented effect is specifically sought and lamented (as it would be again in Eliot's *Waste Land* [1922]), may have been influenced by his reading of Moore, just as, earlier, Moore's own use of the device can be understood to have gained force from the example of Pound's (related but different) use. In *The Waste Land* Eliot takes over from Moore, along with the pointedly fragmentary effect, the device of sometimes citing less well-known works, along with the habit modeled by Pound of citing standard canonic works, or works that he meant to canonize. Later on Pound too would adopt the technique of noncanonic citation; Slatin for instance points to Moore's influence on the *Malatesta Cantos*.[83]

Clearly the pathways of influence overlap in the careers of these writers. But the understanding that Moore learned to quote at Eliot's knee will not stand up. While Eliot's adoption of the mode of quotation learned also from Pound and from the collage paintings of the cubists, and while he responds as the cubists do to the wide spread of mass cultural texts fashioned out of fragments, Moore's work in particular taught Eliot to build a poetry out of a refusal to digest the fragments of the texts that inspired it. And it is possible, despite his denials, that it is in recognition of this that Pound scrawled "Marianne?" on the *Waste Land* manuscript beside the first lines set off as quotations.[84] In employing quotation so complexly and effectively, Eliot returned Moore her own method with an endorsement that led her to take it up again with redoubled confidence. At the same time, his very different use of quotation provided her, as it did Williams, with a focus for her opposition.

Moore's quotations assist her work in its critique of the structures of authority—both literal and literary—and in its attempt to redress their ill effects. Supplying her with an avenue of entry into the modernist scene, which would not have received her without such indirection, they afforded her as well the means for ironic reflection, for deconstructing the myths of poetic self-reliance and of hierarchies of influence, and for embracing the difficult position of relativism. In all these respects, they function as revisions of the kinds of quotation associated with paternal authority, in both religious and literary contexts, and further the development of a more flexible hierarchy based in what I have called a maternal authority.

Moore's use of quotations extends their range much beyond that in which Eliot and Williams employ them, but the issues to which she responds via quotation are of the same order: all three poets concern themselves with issues of hierarchy. Where Eliot works to affirm the hierarchy that would rank him low as an American, and then to escape such ranking by denying his American associations, Williams brings such hierarchy into question. Both men employ femininity as an analogue for the secondary status of the American and of the modern in standard hierarchies that privilege the more "original" term (that is, the European and the antique). In Eliot's work, this implies the rejection of the feminine. In Williams's poems, it creates an ambivalence: the logic of undoing hierarchies to which his American identification commits him calls for an identifying embrace of the feminine and leads him to explore such possibilities, but his own investment in standard gender hierarchies turns that embrace into a much more standard kind. For Moore, the set of secondarinesses is expanded to include actual femininity along with the fact that she is a modern and an American. In her inquiries into the workings of hierarchy, gender is pivotal, while the related issues of Americanness and modernity also are explored. Because she is a woman she need not fear the consequences of analogizing those two forms of secondariness with femininity. This freedom enables her to press her questions further than do the other two poets and to develop alternatives to standard authority structures. At at the same time, however, it limits her audience and her public authority. In her later career Moore expanded her explorations of the workings of authority to new fields, creating a media persona that crossed the high/low culture line. In so doing she gave herself both new difficulties with and new opportunities for authority.[85] For Moore, femininity is exactly the element that hinders to succeed, though this kind of success involves no easy coming to rest on laurels. Instead it is a redefined success, paralleling Moore's redefinitions of authority and of genuine poetry. Such success accrues to a ceaseless process of recognizing authority in the unauthorized, acknowledging it, and moving on, in search of more of the genuine.

Appendix*

	number of poems including quotation marks, with or without corresponding notes	number of poems with notes but no quotation marks	number of poems in the volume
Poems (1921)	10	0	24
Observations (1924)	33	4	53
Selected Poems (1935)	34	3	48
The Pangolin (1936)	3	1	5
What Are Years (1941)	10	3	15
Nevertheless (1944)	2	0	6
Collected Poems (1951)	48	6	71
Like a Bulwark (1956)	8	2	11
O to Be a Dragon (1959)	9	3	15
The Arctic Ox (1964)	14	6	23
Tell Me, Tell Me (1966)	15	1	18
Complete Poems (1967; 1981)	88	16	125

* All figures in this chapter are of my tabulation.

Notes

Chapter 1

1. Eliot and Moore identify the sources of these borrowed lines in notes at the back, but some others they leave unidentified. Williams employs no notes.

2. I became aware of Leonard Diepeveen's work on modernist poetic quotation (*Changing Voices: The Modern Quoting Poem*) only after this text was completed. While we begin from the same phenomenon, our understandings of it differ radically. Where my reading of this kind of quotation takes history and issues of authority to be pivotal to its workings, Diepeveen concentrates on the structural effects of changing voices within individual texts.

3. For example, cf. Plato, *The Republic,* book 2, 363a & b and 364d & e, 40, 41. And books 2 and 3 both feature many citations offered as examples of what should *not* be repeated in the republic Socrates plans.

4. Antoine Compagnon, *La seconde main, ou le travail de la citation*, 201–2. My translation.

Exceptions to this characterization of classical quotation do appear in the Roman period. For instance, Catullus's "translation" of Sappho's "He seems to me to be a god" (to which he adds a line of his own) effectively quotes Sappho, but in the course of rendering it Catullus enters into debate with the earlier poem. The line he adds—"or more than a god"—can be read as a representation of his own attempt in this poem to overgo his predecessor, to argue his own case against the evidence of her skill represented in the quotation. This constitutes a use of the device analogous to that to which it is put by the modernists who are the subject of this study. And Catullus, of course, holds a position similar to that of the modernists—heir to a burden of great literature that can only make him fear that the best has already been said. Catullus's moment is a modern moment, in the general sense of that word. In a different vein, Ovid employs quotation not to contest the primacy of the earlier texts he borrows from (poems by Catullus and Ennius), but to create a past for the characters he writes about and to suggest the "reality" of the literary world. That is, he has his Ariadne refer to a statement made by Catullus's Ariadne, as though she were remembering her own past. (Cf. Gian Biagio Conti, *The Rhetoric of Imitation: Genre and Poetry Memory in Virgil and Other Latin Poets,* 57–63.)

5. Religious commentaries on passages of Scripture, which may seem at first to operate on an opposite, expansionary principle, operate instead with the understanding that the texts they explicate do have true, single meanings. These the commentators aim to pin down by setting limits on the welter of possible readings that their passages, like all passages scriptural or not, suggest. The commentaries expand on quotation on purpose finally to reinforce the scriptural text in its singularity, not to offer their commentaries as alternative texts or to suggest that alternative authorities might exist.

6. Compagnon, *La seconde main,* 230. My translation. By speaking the words of the prophet, of the apostle, or even of Christ, the commentator comes as near as is possible in a post-prophetic world to the state of inspiration, to being himself an embodiment of contact between the human and the divine. See Compagnon, *La seconde main,* 226–31.

7. The text Jesus cites here is the second of the Ten Commandments: Exod. 20 : 13.

8. John's quotation is from the Greek of the Septuagint, but the position of words in the Hebrew Bible makes the same point.

9. By the logic of this reading, Erasmus's translation (in his Latin version of the New Testament [Rotterdam, 1516]) of John's "Logos" as "Sermo" ("discourse") instead of as "Verbum" ("word"), which was Jerome's choice in the Vulgate, glosses John well. See Marjorie O'Rourke Boyle, *Erasmus on Language and Method in Theology*, chapter 1, for a discussion of the reasoning behind and the controversy surrounding this translation.

10. The phrases of scriptural text, surviving from ancient days, become in themselves icons, remnants of the forefathers whose contacts with divinity they record. Quotation serves thus as a mode of (almost) direct contact with that earlier world in which original authority was manifest.

11. For another, more critical discussion of the revisionary relation of John's text to that of the Hebrew Bible, see Harold Bloom, "Before Moses Was, I Am: The Original and the Belated Testaments."

12. G. R. Owst, *Preaching in Medieval England: An Introduction to Sermon Manuscripts of the Period c. 1350–1450;* and G. R. Owst, *Literature and Pulpit in Medieval England.*

13. Compagnon, *La seconde main,* 220–21.

14. E. E. Kellett, *Literary Quotation and Allusion*, 82.

15. Kellett, *Literary Quotation and Allusion*, 80.

16. Terence Cave, "The Mimesis of Reading in the Renaissance." See also Compagnon, *La seconde main*; and Marc Fumaroli, *L'Age de l'Eloquence: Rhétorique et "res literaria" de la Renaissance au seuil de l'époque classique*, 464–66, on the use of quotation rhetoric among seventeenth-century magistrates.

17. This habit developed alongside and in concert with the Renaissance mania for imitation of classical models in all spheres. The rage for imitation developed both as a means of compensating for the loss of direct connection with the sacred that accom-

panied the rise of humanism and as a result of the greater awareness of history (as process) that characterized that rise. Thomas Greene argues that imitation of the classics provided Renaissance writers with a means of coming to terms with their difference from the authors whose work they mime. (See "Petrarch and the Humanist Hermeneutic," in Greene, *The Light in Troy: Imitation and Discovery in Renaissance Poetry*, 81–103.) Renaissance imitation presupposed an awareness of the past as different from and more heroic than the present. Imitation is a form of emulation in this version, whereas in the Middle Ages, Greene suggests, borrowing from the classics involved little awareness of cultural difference and did not involve valuation of past over present. This new Renaissance sense of cultural loss was balanced, however, by the requirements of the effort of imitation, which called not for submission to the earlier text but for transformation of that text to reflect the interests of the new speaker, who was more sharply defined in the process of the comparison. Imitation operated thus as a species of allusion.

18. Quotation also appeared in at least one Renaissance play; cf. the discussion of Kyd's *The Spanish Tragedy* in chapter 2.

19. Many eighteenth-century novels, called "true histories" and such like, play on a confusion over whether they retell someone's real life experience (a form of quotation of that experience) or are fictional (that is, original with their novelist).

20. M. M. Bakhtin, *The Dialogic Imagination: Four Essays*, 49–50.

21. For discussion of the operation of quotation in these novels, cf. Herman Meyer, *The Poetics of Quotation in the European Novel.*

22. Cf. for instance Meyer's exploration of quotation's role in the European novel. He deals particularly with German humoristic novels, but examples are plentiful among novels from all cultures.

23. Wicke, *Advertising Fictions: Literature, Advertisement, & Social Reading*, 79–81. While literary quotation is no longer the predominant advertising technique, it is still with us. The 1989 campaign for Elizabeth Taylor's Passion perfume, for instance, involved her recitation of lines from Shakespeare to do with passion (though quotation's resonance there is not the same as in earlier campaigns, the Passion advertisements play on the outdatedness of the technique to create an image on the border between real nostalgia for the grand past that Taylor represents and the associations with camp that go along with the Taylor image generally). Similarly, the 1992 campaign for Obsession perfume (which may play on the Passion campaign) featured quotations from Flaubert and Lawrence that were particularly concerned with obsessional love.

24. Bella Landauer, "Literary Allusion in American Advertising as Sources of Social History."

25. Cf. Harold White, *Plagiarism and Imitation during the Renaissance: A Study in Critical Distinctions*.

26. Thomas MacFarland, *Originality and Imagination,* 6. The nature of the self whose worth was reasserted thus was presumably transformed in the process.

27. While *origin*, the word from which it derives, apparently an import from the French, occurs much earlier in English, and *original* in its first sense, "deriving from the origin" (the word is one of those with antithetical senses that Freud noted), occurs even earlier, *originality* makes its first appearance on record in 1776, meaning "authenticity." It does not appear with the sense "novelty or freshness of style or character"

and, as an attribute of persons, "the power of originating new or fresh ideas or methods" until 1787. (*Originality* in its nonderivative sense, meaning "having the quality of that which proceeds from oneself, or from the direct exercise of one's faculties, without imitation of or dependence on others," made its first recorded appearance in about 1756.) (*Oxford English Dictionary*, vol. 7, 202–3.) My earlier use of the word "original" in relation to Renaissance work was therefore anachronistic to the extent that it named a developing and not a fully developed idea.

28. Inquiring into the provenance of originality, MacFarland recognizes an originality paradox, consistent across history:

> The conception of originality is constantly and unavoidably involved in paradox. That involvement is essential, not accidental. It stems from the larger paradox of human existence, whereby we always hear and necessarily respond to the ineradicably conflicting claims of our social natures on the one hand and our individual natures on the other.
>
> The claims are rarely in equipoise. At times the social voice will historically become more insistent, as for instance in Marxist ideology, and at other times the call of the individual, as in Rousseau's *Confessions*, will seem of overwhelming importance. When one or the other gains the ascendance that defines a historical epoch, then cultural conceptions will veer toward the more clamorous summons and attempt to mute the voice of the conflicting reality. But the veering is necessarily temporary, and indeed its attendant conceivings will be necessarily characterized by half-truth, distortion, and illusion; and this effect will obtain no matter how absolute the good faith of those who formulate the conceivings. (MacFarland, *Originality and Imagination,* 31)

29. Cf. Gordon Williams, *Tradition and Originality in Roman Poetry*; Eric Havelock, *Preface to Plato,* 9–10; and MacFarland's discussion of Plato, *Originality and Imagination,* 18–22.

30. Perry Meisel's account of the difference between those moderns who invest in "the myth of the modern" (essentially a myth of the possibility of originality) and those who do not parallels my discussion here in some respects. (See Meisel, *The Myth of the Modern: A Study in British Literature and Criticism after 1850*.)

31. John Guillory, *Poetic Authority: Spenser, Milton, and Literary History*, 21, 22.

32. Gen. 10 : 8–9 reads:

> And Cush begat Nimrod: he began to be a mighty one in the earth.
>
> He was a mighty hunter before the Lord: wherefore it is said, even as Nimrod the mighty hunter before the Lord.

33. This comes from Gen. 9 : 25:

> And he said, Cursed be Canaan; a servant of servants shall he be unto his brethren.

34. Gen. 1 : 6–7 gives us:

> And God said, Let there be a firmament in the midst of the waters, and let it divide the waters from the waters.
>
> And God made the firmament, and divided the waters which were under the firmament from the waters which were above the firmament: and it was so.

35. Here Gen. 1:26 gives us:

> And God said, Let us make man in our image, after our likeness: and let them have dominion over the fish of the sea, and over the fowl of the air, and over the cattle, and over all the earth, and over every creeping thing that creepeth upon the earth.

36. Guillory, *Poetic Authority*, 176.

37. Guillory, *Poetic Authority*, 1–22.

38. Samuel Taylor Coleridge, *Poems*, 160. Further citations of this poem will be given in the text without note.

39. Coleridge suggests his closer tie to nature too in introducing his son as the inheritor of his learning, while Milton ("poor wretch") teaches only those with whom he has no natural bond.

40. William Wordsworth, *Poetical Works*, 590. Further citations of Wordworth's poems will refer to this edition and will be given in the text without note.

41. In his untitled poem to Dora, Wordsworth employs a structure very like that used by Coleridge in "The Nightingale." Beginning with an exact quotation of the first two lines of *Samson Agonistes*, Wordsworth then goes on to deny their applicability to his situation:

> *"A little onward lend thy guiding hand*
> *To these dark steps, a little further on!"*
> —What trick of memory to *my* voice hath brought
> This mournful iteration? For though Time
> The Conqueror, crowns the Conquered, on this brow
> Planting his favourite silver diadem,
> Nor he, nor minister of his—intent
> To run before him, hath enrolled me yet,
> Though not unmenaced, among those who lean
> Upon a living staff, with borrowed sight.
> (*Poetical Works*, 388–89)

The "borrowed sight" puns against the borrowing of vision at work in the citation from Milton to make the passage a repudiation of the form with which it begins, a rejection of any suggestion not that Wordsworth's eyes are failing but that he is not, or no longer, original. In the course of his reading of this poem, Geoffrey H. Hartman explores the ways in which the quotation from Milton not only works as an authority in itself here but mediates Wordsworth's contact with the different authority of the classics and of Scripture. (See Hartman, "Words, Wish, Worth: Wordsworth.")

42. Ralph Waldo Emerson, *Emerson's Complete Works*, 170. Further references to pages in this essay will be given in the text.

43. The case might be made that there is no such thing as simply a modernist writer, that every modernist adds to his or her sense of temporal secondariness another sort of secondariness, generally to do with nationality or gender. The cases of Yeats and Joyce (Irish modernists), Woolf (woman modernist), and Strachey and Forster (homosexual modernists) might all be offered as evidence that some combination of secondarinesses is necessary to expression of any. Without going on to speculate about why this might

be so, we can note that feminine gender, while one of many kinds of secondariness operating in this field, was particularly problematic.

44. Quite a few critics have pointed out that modernists and romantics have a great deal in common, and the suggestion has frequently been made that modernists are actually romantics in disguise or romantics manqué. Insofar as the romantics do occasionally quote, the reverse would seem to be just as true: romantic poets in these moments may be understood as modernists before the fact. Insofar as those quotations are rare and troubled, the romantics might be seen as modernists lacking some pivotal characteristic. Since the romantic notion of originality is set up to ward off the kind of anxiety about temporal lateness and loss of stable structure that manifests itself in the moderns, we can view the instances of romantic quotation as occasions in which that anxiety suggests itself in spite of the precautions taken against it. Rather than setting up one or the other as the true model for the group as a whole, it would seem finally more useful to understand modernists and romantics as representing related visions with opposite emphases.

45. Thus I will not devote a chapter to Pound, the most influential of those I have omitted. Though there are differences (and I will discuss some of those at relevant points in the chapters that follow), in the main I understand his use of quotation to work on principles similar to those that animate Eliot's.

46. That modernist responses tended to split along gender lines has been suggested by the recent spate of work on the gender of modernism. Cf., for example, Sandra M. Gilbert and Susan Gubar, *The War of the Words*, vol. 1, *No Man's Land: The Place of the Woman Writer in the Twentieth Century;* Shari Benstock, *Women of the Left Bank: Paris, 1900–1940;* and Bonnie Kime Scott, ed., *The Gender of Modernism: A Critical Anthology*.

47. Pound similarly identifies himself thoroughly with European culture (his traitorous behavior might be read as a particularly emphatic renunciation of Americanness).

48. Borges, "Pierre Menard, Author of the Quixote." And examples can be found in other disciplines as well. Aaron Copland's use of traditional tunes, for instance, fits the modernist mode at the same time that it continues a tradition of playful quotation that is harder to separate from allusion in music than it is in verbal art forms.

49. By the turn of the twentieth century, modern printing techniques—rotary presses and Linotype machines—had replaced handpresses and were printing most newspapers and periodicals. The possibilities of reproduction, which had grown greatly across the nineteenth century, reached new peaks at the start of the twentieth. In addition, posters were becoming more artful—using techniques learned, for example, from Japanese woodcuts. The advertising posters of Toulouse Lautrec, followed by the art nouveau group (including Beardsley and Klimt) and the expressionists (including Kokoschka and Schiele), all crossed boundaries between mass and high culture. See Carlo Arturo Quintavalle, "The Development of Poster Art"; and Max Gallo, *The Poster in History*, 48.

50. Benjamin, "The Work of Art in the Age of Mechanical Reproduction."

51. Christine Poggi, "Mallarmé, Picasso, and the Newspaper as Commodity." Poggi takes the increasing commodification of the stuff of private life as the source of a revision of the romantic notion of originality that occurred gradually over the course of

the nineteenth century and led at the start of the twentieth to a "new conception of the creative process" (141). "For Picasso," writes Poggi, " . . . the artist's use of newspaper and other mass-produced materials pointed toward the obsolescence of contemporary cultural hierarchies and theories of representation, in an age in which cultural artifacts had become commodities" (142). But the hierarchies brought into question by this simultaneous defamiliarization of mass-produced materials and familiarization of normally distanced works of art continue to operate in Picasso's works in the substantial degree to which cubist "unoriginality" also plays paradoxically on a claim to originality, even as it debunks originality as myth.

While Picasso assembled physical materials, such "cubist" poets as Apollinaire and Max Jacob were assembling disparate ready-made verbal materials, including phrases from advertisements, popular songs, and clichéd speech. They presented within single poems, or even within single lines, words taken from these disparate sources that continue to remind readers clearly of their earlier "unartistic" contexts. Cubist collage poetry thus continued the assault on standard distinctions between "high" art and nonartistic speech, "low" art, and mass-produced texts, while creating an awareness in its readers of the objective qualities of language, which itself operates as a drag on claims to poetic transcendence. The poems of Apollinaire's *Calligrams* (1913–16) stress the awareness of linguistic objectivity even more emphatically by taking the shapes of the objects they treat. This visual aspect to cubist collage poetry was matched by a strong verbal element in the painting. Printed words, generally from advertisements and newspapers, appeared frequently, various portions of the word *Journal* occurring, sometimes with punning implications, most often.

Such issues came into play in the realm of painting when the technology developed that made quotation possible. More recently, similar issues have begun to be raised in music (through sampling) and TV (through reruns and shows that use old clips in new stories). These differ from musical quotes of the old sort (where an old tune is included within a new score) because the quotation marks are visible to the auditor, where they cannot be in nonsampled music in the same way.

52. Marshall McLuhan, *The Mechanical Bride: Folklore of Industrial Man,* 3, 4.

53. In undergoing this transformation, quotation-filled poetry does not become a new form of novel. Though the term "novel" might in some vocabularies be extended after Bakhtin to include any dialogic text, the fact that these particular texts are principally in dialogue with the history of poetry marks them as distinct from other dialogic texts—and keeps them in the poetic camp.

Chapter 2

1. Cf., for instance, Louis Menand, *Discovering Modernism: T. S. Eliot and His Context*, 89–91.

2. Jay points out that in *From Ritual to Romance,* Jessie Weston notes and discounts this reading of the fisher king myth (Gregory S. Jay, *Eliot and the Poetics of Literary History,* 59–63; and Jessie Weston, *From Ritual to Romance,* 14–17).

3. Quotations are generally (though not always) signaled in *The Waste Land*'s notes by the use of "V". (for the Latin *vide*, "see"), while allusions are usually marked "Cf." (for the Latin *confer*, "compare").

4. These numbers (arrived at with help from the notes and a host of other researchers) involve some amount of interpretation, both of what constitutes an allusion or a quotation and of what exactly is referred to in the note, so other tabulators might come up with different figures. When the notes are understood to participate in the poem, twelve more quotations are added to the count—fifty-one in all. The number 444 includes 434 lines, 5 section headings, and 5 lines of epigraph.

5. Meisel has demonstrated the poem's similar repression of another, though nonpoetic parent—the aptly named Walter Pater, whose aesthetic of fragmentation and of recognition of the impossibility of originality Eliot draws on, represses acknowledgment of, and ultimately perverts. (Cf. Meisel, *The Myth of the Modern,* 71–108.) While I restrict this chapter's discussion to *The Waste Land*'s relation to its poetic fathers, Pater's presence in the poem has links to that of Whitman.

6. The poem's first title, *He Do the Police in Different Voices*, gave a much more emphatic announcement of its borrowedness—from Dickens's *Our Mutual Friend* (book 1, chapter 16)—at the same time that it declared its dependence on quotation as technique. Where Sloppy in *Our Mutual Friend*, reading the newspaper aloud to old Betty Higden, "do the Police" in a variety of vocal styles, changing his manner of enunciation for each character he reads, Eliot lets the words of others represent their various voices (here the nonstandard grammar marks the line as other than the speaker's). But, as with Sloppy, the differentiation of actor and role is never complete, and Eliot's use of borrowed words continues marked by his voice throughout. As was the case with his initial choice of the quotation from Conrad to serve as the first epigraph, Eliot seems to have chosen his first title for its "elucidative" qualities, and abandoned it when on second thought elucidation was no longer the central concern.

The draft Eliot sent Pound had as epigraph a few lines from Conrad's *Heart of Darkness*. In them Marlowe watches the dying Kurtz and hears him cry out, "The horror! The horror!" Eliot wrote to Pound of his choice of these lines: "It is much the most appropriate I can find, and somewhat elucidative" (Letter, Eliot to Pound, ? January 1922, in *The Letters of Ezra Pound*, 171). Pound had protested that the weight of Conrad's name was not great enough to open the poem, and Eliot made the change.

7. T. S. Eliot, *Collected Poems, 1909–1962*, 51. Further citations of this edition of *The Waste Land* will be given in the text without note.

In translation the first epigraph reads: "For I saw with my own eyes the Sibyl of Cumae hanging in a vial, and when the boys said to her: 'Sibyl, what do you want?' she answered: 'I want to die.'" The phrase in Italian in the second epigraph translates as "the better maker."

8. This passage from the *Purgatorio* is discussed in greater detail further on in the chapter, in relation to Eliot's second borrowing from it at the close of his poem.

9. The moment is further complicated by the fact that Dante does not have his character Dante speak the praise. Instead, it is assigned to the shade of the poet Guinizelli, whose mentor Arnaut was, though the line certainly belongs to Dante, author of

the *Commedia*. The effect here is that in addition to borrowing Dante's words, Eliot imitates Dante as well in citing the words of "another" to compliment Pound.

10. In equating Pound with Arnaut, Eliot sets him in the role of forerunner rather than that of collaborator, which, following Wayne Koestenbaum's reading of the homosexual dynamic implicit in this and other nineteenth- and twentieth-century male literary collaborations, may have been more comfortable for Eliot to deal with. (See Koestenbaum, *Double Talk: The Erotics of Male Literary Collaboration*, 112–39.) Collaboration raises issues of influence akin to those raised by quotation, but they differ in that no question of generational priority pertains. At any rate, casting Pound in the role of precursor provides Eliot, who in the course of the poem wrestles his precursors to the ground, with a means for both acknowledging Pound's assistance and asserting his own preeminence in the poem's power structure. (In keeping with the poem's suppression of feminine influence on the text, no acknowledgment is made of the collaborative contributions of Vivien Eliot, who also contributed to *The Waste Land*, though much less extensively than Pound. [Vivien Eliot's contributions in the facsimile edition of the manuscript include one deletion and one substitution that make it to the final poem.])

11. Eliot's choice of the Petronius as epigraph may be informed by Dante Gabriel Rossetti's earlier choice of the same fragment for translation in both prose and verse. Rossetti's translations were not published during his lifetime, but are among the notebook fragments preserved in his brother's 1911 edition of Rossetti's works. The fragment consists of the prose translation, with attribution to Petronius, which serves as epigraph to the verse translation that follows. The combination of the prose and verse translations might be read as a portrait of the process of poetic transformation, as Petronius's original provides the material for Rossetti's sing-songing new poem (which certainly moves toward parody): "'I saw the Sibyl of Cumae' / (One said) 'with mine own eye. / She hung in a cage, and read her rune / To all the passers-by. / Said the boys, "What wouldst thou, Sibyl?" / She answered, "I would die."'" The portrait is continued when, a few fragments later, the verse translation is itself transformed into a quite distinct poem, which nonetheless preserves two images from Rossetti's verse rendering: "If I could die like the British Queen / Who faced the Roman war, / Or hang in a cage for my country's sake / Like Black Ben of Dunbar!" (*The Works of Dante Gabriel Rossetti,* 240–41).

12. *The Complete Poetry and Prose of Geoffrey Chaucer*, 9, lines 1–4.

13. Charles-Louis Phillippe, *Bubu de Montparnasse* (1932), 25–26. "Notre chair a gardé tous nos souvenirs, nous les melons à nos desirs" (*Bubu de Montparnasse* [1901], 53).

14. James Thomson ("B. V."), *The City of Dreadful Night and Other Poems,* 141–49. Further citations of Thomson's poems will refer to this edition and will be given in the text without note.

15. George L. K. Morris, the discoverer of Eliot's borrowing from Larisch, points out that her family had a house by the Starnbergersee, that she had several archduke cousins, and that she usually went south in the winter. He points also to more general resemblances between episodes in her story and later scenes in *The Waste Land*. (Morris, "Marie, Marie, Hold on Tight.")

Larisch also contributes a sequence of events: she describes a ride she took as a young girl with her aunt the Empress Elizabeth to see the mad king Ludwig. Their return ride was interrrupted by a sudden "downpour of tropical rain." The women take refuge not in a colonnade, but in a cottage occupied by the widow of a fisherman, who mysteriously announces that she awaits the return of her son who drowned in the Starnbergersee seven years before. Lightning flashes and thunder rolls as the woman insists that "He will return. . . . When God wills." Larisch relates this to the later drowning of Ludwig in the same lake, the widow having predicted as well that when her son returned another would take his place. As the rain clears the women ride off and a rainbow appears. (Marie Larisch, *My Past: Reminiscences of the Courts of Austria and Bavaria; Together with the True Story of the Events Leading up to the Tragic Death of Rudolph, Crown Prince of Austria*, 66–68.) The encounter with the widow, omitted in Eliot's reworking, is part of the context invoked by the borrowing, perhaps more important for its being left *unsaid*, a stress through elision. Though Eliot could not have expected that his allusion would be recognized, his choice of this imagery here at the poem's start is made in part for the proleptic suggestion of the poem's close made through the joining of the storm imagery with the imagery of Christ's resurrection.

The note on Larisch in the facsimile edition of *The Waste Land* tells us that Eliot met her (where and when are not known, but a meeting might have taken place in Germany in 1914), and that he takes the description of the sledding verbatim from their conversation (Eliot, *The Waste Land: A Facsimile*, 125–26). The note suggests that he did not read her book, but if he did not, she clearly told him the story of her visit to King Ludwig and of the stop in the cottage.

16. Preface to *Bubu of Montparnasse* (1932), x.

17. Thomson, *The City of Dreadful Night*, 1–48.

18. William S. Peterson, *Interrogating the Oracle: A History of the London Browning Society*, 55.

19. Thomson's other pseudonyms, much less used, included "Crepusculus" (twilight), suggesting further his sense of belatedness, "X," "Sigvat," "T. J.," and "J. S. T."

20. One critic argues that this poem and Edward Fitzgerald's *Rubá'iyát of Omar Khayyám* are the major sources of "themes, symbols, characters, setting and form," in short of everything that matters, in *The Waste Land* (A. F. Beringause, "Journey through *The Waste Land*"). The connection with Khayyám, like Thomson an emphatic atheist, is general, not a question of borrowing specific phrases but of a gathering together of like concerns and related images.

21. Thomson's explication of the relation of belated poet to his predecessors is much less overt than that of Eliot, whose theoretical and critical essays bring these issues under direct scrutiny and so aid our recognition of the explanation of poetic relations presented in *The Waste Land*. Thomson's treatment of poetic relations is self-consciously oblique:

> O sad Fraternity, do I unfold
> Your dolorous mysteries shrouded from of yore?
> Nay, be assured; no secret can be told
> To any who divined it not before:

None uninitiate by many a presage
Will comprehend the language of the message,
Although proclaimed aloud for evermore.
("The City of Dreadful Night," proem, lines 36–41)

Eliot is much less secretive.

22. Cf. particularly Calvin Bedient, *He Do the Police in Different Voices*.

23. A posture, he notes, "which both contains and expresses quite a violent revisionist impulse" (Guillory, "The Ideology of Canon-Formation: T. S. Eliot and Cleanth Brooks," 176).

24. John Hollander, *The Figure of Echo: A Mode of Allusion in Milton and After,* ix.

25. Hollander, *The Figure of Echo*, 103.

26. William Arrowsmith, "Daedal Harmonies: A Dialogue of Eliot and the Classics."

27. Peter Ackroyd, *T. S. Eliot: A Life*, 120.

28. Eliot, "Philip Massinger," 182.

29. Bloom, *The Breaking of the Vessels*, 21. Hart Crane's *The Bridge* gives a poetic correction of Eliot's claims to freedom from Whitman's influence.

30. Jay, *Eliot and the Poetics of Literary History*, chapter 10, 156–71.

31. Eliot, "American Literature and the American Language," 52–54.

32. Cleo McNelly Kearns's summary of Eliot's transformations of "When Lilacs Last in the Dooryard Bloom'd" is very complete. She cites, among other shared images and motifs, the lilacs, the song of the hermit thrush, and the presence of a second self, as well as a shared "assertion of the identity of the deep self with the divine, fully realized only in and through both a literal and a metaphorical death" (Kearns, "Eliot, Russell, and Whitman: Realism, Politics, and Literary Persona in *The Waste Land*," 150–51). For further discussion of Eliot's relation to Whitman, see Jay, *Eliot and the Poetics of Literary History*, 168–71; Hollander, *The Figure of Echo*, 104–5; and S. Musgrove, *T. S. Eliot and Walt Whitman*.

33. Cf. "Out of the Cradle Endlessly Rocking."

34. Whitman, *Leaves of Grass*, 89. Further citations of Whitman's poems will refer to this edition and will be given in the text without note.

35. Thomson published two essays on Whitman's work.

36. See chapter 1 for discussion.

37. Guillory, "The Ideology of Canon-Formation," 180.

38. Eliot, "Milton I," 157.

39. W. K. Wimsatt remarked this similarity distinguished by irony in "Prufrock and Maud: From Plot to Symbol." Carol Christ demonstrates the close relation of the work of the Victorians to that of the moderns in *Victorian and Modern Poetics*.

40. The notes themselves expand the number of texts quoted, including various references to nonliterary sources for background (often spurious) on concepts rather than phrases.

41. Marvell is a special case. Eliot in his essay on Marvell argues that he is in the standard canon for the wrong reasons, and so claims him, for the right reasons, for the alternative, minor canon as well.

42. Eliot, "Milton I," 156.

43. Eliot, "Milton I," 157.

44. Guillory, "The Ideology of Canon-Formation," 176.

45. In a number of instances phrases can be attributed to more than one source, as with line 30, which is from both Donne and Tennyson. Grover Smith argues that the phrase attributed to Milton in line 98 comes as well from Virgil. Such evidence of the intertwinedness of the tradition is further proof for Eliot's case that all poems are transformations of their predecessors. The large number of quotations—as well as the heavy determination—serves Eliot by stirring up a sense of the vastness of the cultural past and the complex interconnectedness of the culture as a whole, in comparatively short order, and then bringing that immense weight to bear on the poem. The heaviness of the burden enforces the great sense of difficulty on which the poem builds. At the same time, the intricacy of the interweavings of allusions and quotations speaks eloquently of Eliot's skill.

46. My point here is not to account for all the quotations and allusions Eliot makes, but to suggest the general outline of his pattern of borrowing. Another reader might expand upon these numbers.

47. This count includes the title, as well as the first and last lines.

48. An account of the dialogue of the original context of each of these borrowings with its role within *The Waste Land* would get tedious quickly. I offer a representative example instead:

Section 3 opens with an evocation of Spenser's *Prothalamion*, signaled most clearly in the quotation of a line from the refrain in line 176 and then again in lines 183–84, and supported in the surrounding lines (173–84). In taking this line from Spenser, Eliot situates his poem emphatically in the midst of concerns with time's swift flow in general and with the greater concern with influence of the belated poet in particular. Spenser's refrain figures Eliot's burden in two respects. In the general sense implicit in Spenser's argument, the river represents time, which disinherits everyone eventually. *Prothalamion*, like *The Waste Land*, begins by mourning an ideal world past—not a specific past, but a past qua past. (This is represented in three particular manifestations: the restricted past of the poet's own youth, spent happy in London, where now he struggles to find an audience for his "freendless case"; the more distant historical past of an earlier London in which the Knights Templar still lived in the quarters that bear their name in Spenser's day, before they "decayd through pride"; and a mythical past, when nymphs haunted the banks of the Thames and allegory tied symbols directly to meaning, [almost] without gap.) By the poem's close, however, Spenser suggests that while, inevitably, "the brydale day, which is not long," and every day, must end, the poem itself can work nonetheless to confound time's murderous progress; that indeed Sweet Time can be made to run more slowly by means of the emblematizing properties of song. In this respect, Eliot's use of this line here puts it to work in his defense. It serves as demonstration of the place of his poem's argument within the tradition, and of his success at stemming time's tide, on a historical rather than a personal scale, and at undoing the decline in value that would seem to be the necessary result of greater temporal distance from the point of origin.

In the particular sense, figured in the unabsorbedness of this quotation that refuses to be transformed into an allusion, the refrain is made to make the opposite case, against Eliot's place within the tradition; the refrain per se represents the enormous inheritance of the modern poet, which leaves him nothing new to supply. This is very like what each of the unabsorbed quotations in *The Waste Land* does, but here the point is made with particular complexity (and each convolution works in Eliot's defense, demonstrating his transformative skill), for the line has a history, having been echoed through English poetry since Spenser and coming thus in itself to represent the river of poetic tradition. (John Hollander traces the history of the echoing of this refrain from Spenser through Denham, Collins, and Wordsworth; *The Figure of Echo*, 71n, 76–77.) In failing to incorporate *this* phrase, Eliot claims to belong to a truly diminished poetic world.

49. This poem had been published (in *Poems, 1920*), unlike the earlier "Death of Narcissus," a few echoes of which, much fainter than the borrowing in section 4, play in the red rock passage in section 1.

50. Eliot, *Collected Poems, 1909–1962*, 43–44.

51. Translation by William Arrowsmith, in "Daedal Harmonies," 4.

52. And "Dans le Restaurant" gains entrance to this new canon on grounds of its foreignness as well as its (claimed) minority, since Eliot actually went to the extraordinary length of constituting himself as foreign to his own language, as well as to his native culture, writing four poems in French, as an indication of the context in which he preferred to be considered. The earlier poem enters *The Waste Land* as a translation from its original French version, and so is linked by association with the other works translated here, of Dante, Baudelaire, and so forth.

53. The note to line 307 gives more of the sentence from which this phrase was taken: "'to Carthage then I came, where a cauldron of unholy loves sang all about mine ears.'" In this passage, Augustine describes youthful temptations to sensuality. The note to line 308 refers us to a translation of the Fire Sermon, in which Buddha characterizes all sensual impressions as fire ("whatever sensation, pleasant, unpleasant, or indifferent, originates in dependence on impressions received by the eye, that also is on fire. And with what are these on fire? With the fire of passion, say I, with the fire of hatred, with the fire of infatuation . . . "). These two warnings against sensuality are followed by a remark from further on in Augustine's history ("I entangle my steps with these outward beauties, but Thou pluckest me out, O Lord, Thou pluckest me out!") that suggests the overcoming of sensual dangers, and then by a final "burning."

54. Eliot's doctrine of impersonality is a version of the concept of the poet's personal self-sacrifice for immortality in art, moved from the temporal and physical realm into the realm of metaphor.

55. Eliot, "Tradition and the Individual Talent," 40.

56. Eliot specifies pointedly that he means here generally communicable feelings, feelings learned through reading, not personal passions.

57. Eliot, "Tradition and the Individual Talent," 41.

58. Eliot, "Tradition and the Individual Talent," 38.

59. Eliot, "Tradition and the Individual Talent," 39. The word *current* is wrought upon further, playfully, in the explicatory note to line 210, which tells us that "*The currants were quoted* at a price 'cost insurance and freight to London'" [my italics]. Next to the local pun of the quotation of the phrase abbreviated "c.i.f." in the line this note

explains beside the different use of the word *quoted*, the italicized phrase remarks fondly on the technique of the poem as a whole.

60. Arrowsmith traces references through the Homeric Hymn to Demeter, through Plato, Lucretius, Virgil, and Ovid, to Dante and Shakespeare, and even as far forward as Gide's *Le Promethee mal enchainé*.

61. *Philebus* 48e, translated by Hackforth, quoted in Arrowsmith, "Daedal Harmonies," 28.

62. Arrowsmith, "Daedal Harmonies," 27–28, 31.

63. Arrowsmith, "Daedal Harmonies," 37, 38, 40.

64. For a full account of these echoes, see Jay, *Eliot and the Poetics of Literary History*, chapter 10.

65. The difference between Eliot's view of the relation of tradition and the individual talent and Emerson's view of the same issue, which he names the relation of quotation and originality [see the discussion of that essay in chapter 1] is one of emphasis. Where Emerson acknowledges that only the smallest possible portion of any new work is really new but holds nonetheless that even this small bit is enough to make the necessary difference, Eliot stresses the importance of adherence to tradition to effecting anything original (though Eliot uses the word *individual* rather than *original* to mark his different emphasis). This difference in emphasis is another way of stating the basis of Eliot's claim to a transformed kind of originality, a claim that builds upon both Emerson's and Eliot's definitions of the workings of originality.

66. Like the grail story to which Eliot refers his readers in the first of his endnotes, *The Waste Land* is a quest romance. In constructing his poem thus, Eliot signals its relation to a set of romantic and Victorian quest poems and through them to concerns with the processes of writing poetry. In the quest poems of Eliot's nineteenth-century predecessors, heroes in pursuit of elusive objects fail over and over to achieve them. When these heroes are seen as figures for their poets and the heroes' adventures along the way as figures for their poems, we recognize an outline of the poetic process, wherein the *pursuit* of contact with a muse or an originary experience is discovered to be the fount of their work, while the contact itself would leave them happy but mute. Shelley's *Alastor* offers a prime romantic example, as does the Simplon pass episode in book 6 of Wordsworth's *Prelude*. When Wordsworth discovers he has crossed the Alps unknowingly and has missed what was to have been the climax of his trip, he quickly translates his disappointment into a celebration of the powers of imagination, which are imaged as the process of seeking rather than finding:

> Our destiny, our being's heart and home,
> Is with infinitude, and only there;
> With hope it is, hope that can never die,
> Effort, and expectation, and desire,
> And something evermore about to be.
> (book 6, lines 604–8)

A similarly Faustian destiny of eternal striving is vaunted in Browning's "'Childe Roland to the Dark Tower Came,'" which introduces as its Victorian difference an emphatic lugubriousness that still does not manage to undo the fact that out of the much-mourned failure of its speaker's quest has come a poem.

Eliot in his turn maintains the pattern while introducing a modern difference by building in a second quest, parallel to the rather sketchy quest narrative that readers under pressure from Eliot's reference to the grail legend have discovered (a narrative much complicated by the fact that no clear quester figure appears). This second quest is structural in nature and is also indicated by the notes: the very fact that notes are necessary tells us that readers of this poem are being sent on a quest of their own—to figure out not just what the poem means (as can be the case with every poem), but what it says. The quotations play an important part in motivating this quest, raising such questions as How do all the borrowed phrases work together? Where are they from? Do they bring their first context with them into the new poem? And how does the fact of the borrowing per se add to the poem's point? The notes begin to answer these questions, but many remain unresolved.

67. In a note to the section as a whole, Eliot outlines themes employed. A note on the hermit thrush of line 357 gives species name and a description of habitat, an emphatic evasion of the clear source in Whitman for the bird's presence here. A note to line 360 suggests that the sense that there is one more present than can be accounted for comes from a description of an Antarctic expedition. A fourth note, to lines 367–77, refers us to Hermann Hesse's description of the descent into chaos of Eastern Europe.

68. It has been suggested that the fifty-seventh line in section 5, "A woman drew her long black hair out tight" (line 378), may be read as overt allusion to Tennyson's Princess "combing her long black hair" (*The Princess*, 4, line 257), but in this quotationless context the allusion means quite differently than did its earlier counterparts, and its status as allusion is debatable at any rate.

69. Webster's "they'll remarry / Ere the worm pierce your winding-sheet, ere the spider / Make a thin curtain for your epitaphs" is the source, we are told in the note to line 408, for "memories draped by the beneficent spider."

70. Dante's "ed io sentii chiavar l'uscio di sotto / all'orrible torre" becomes, according to the note to line 412, "I have heard the key / Turn in the door once and turn once only."

71. Letters to Ford Madox Ford: [14 August 1923] "There are *I* think about 30 *good* lines in *The Waste Land*. Can you find them? The rest is ephemeral." . . . [4 October 1923] "As for the lines I mention, you need not scratch your head over them. They are the 29 lines of the water-dripping song in the last part" (quoted in Eliot, *The Waste Land: A Facsimile and Transcript of the Original Drafts Including the Annotations of Ezra Pound*, 129).

72. Bedient, *He Do the Police*, 203–4.

73. Allen Mandelbaum, *The Divine Comedy of Dante Alighieri: Purgatorio*, 246–47.

74. Mandelbaum, trans., *The Divine Comedy*, 386.

75. Ver novum, ver iam canorum, vere natus orbis est;
Vere concordant amores, vere nubunt alites,
Et nemus comam resolvit de maritis imbribus. (lines 1–4)

[The spring is new, the spring is now full of song, the spring of the world is reborn. In spring the loves come together, in spring the birds mate, and the wood shakes her hair free under the marriage showers.] Latin from Sir Cecil Clementi, trans., *Pervigilium*

Veneris, 192; English from *The Penguin Book of Latin Verse*, 72. Further citations will be from these editions and will be given in the text without note.

76. Bedient supports his reading of the poem's will to succumb to silence by referring us to the refrain (Cras amet . . .) and equating divine love with silence, but he fails to mention the tenor of the stanza from which the phrase itself comes, which with its reference to the unpunctual coming of spring would seem to be pertinent to this poem.

77. Cf. explanatory notes in Clementi, *Pervigilium Veneris*.

78. Alfred, Lord Tennyson, *The Poems of Tennyson*, 234–35.

79. Though the Prince's song overtly concerns the winning of a new love, and might seem to conform to the Princess's demand for a song about the future, it is essentially a plea that the Princess abandon her brave new world and return with the Prince to the traditional society outside:

> "O, tell her, Swallow, thou that knowest each,
> That bright and fierce and fickle is the South,
> And dark and true and tender is the North.
>
> "Why lingereth she to clothe her heart with love,
> Delaying as the tender ash delays
> To clothe herself, when all the woods are green?
>
> "O, tell her, Swallow, that thy brood is flown;
> Say to her, I do but wanton in the South,
> But in the North long since my nest is made."

The Princess cannot read the specifically nostalgic character of the Prince's song, as she does not know that this is he, but she does recognize in love songs generally a threat to her project.

80. Cf. in particular John Churton Collins, *Illustrations of Tennyson;* and A. C. Bradley, *A Commentary of Tennyson's In Memoriam*.

81. Gérard de Nerval, *Poésies*. Translation, *The Penguin Book of French Verse*, vol. 3, *The Nineteenth Century*, 96. Posilipo, a mountain near Naples, was known in classical times as Pausilypus Mons, a name taken from the Greek *pauson lupen*, literally pain-stopping, care-dispelling. The tomb of Virgil is said to be nearby, and we can perceive a link here between the loss of a personal Eden and the loss of a world in which poetry was made with less (apparent) effort. Jacques Dhaenens hints at this in *Le destin d'Orphée: étude sur "El Desdichado" de Nerval*, 42–43.

82. Nerval, translation, *Penguin Book of French Verse*, 97.

The identities of Lusignan and Biron are debated. Lusignan is generally taken for the first Lusignan du Poitou, married in legend to the fairy Melusine and then effectively widowed when he discovered her serpent nature and was compelled to banish her from his house. Lusignan d'Agenais may play in here as well, since Nerval believed there was a connection between his family and that of the Agenais (cf. Dhaenens, *Le destin d'Orphée*, 49). Several medieval figures held the name Biron. Although little is known that would connect any of them with this poem, by reason of the joining of the definitely medieval Lusignan it has generally been assumed that Nerval had one of these Birons in mind. But it seems equally likely that Nerval intended Lord Byron here, either solely or in conflation with the shadowy medieval Birons. Dhaenens points out that

Nerval sometimes spelled Byron with an "i" and on one occasion called him "un fils de soleil." Whether or not these evidences are deemed in themselves sufficient, Nerval's association of himself with Byron, whom he revered, makes great psychological sense here.

83. Cf. Dhaenens, *Le destin d'Orphée*, 87.

84. Kyd's confusion is mirrored in the confusion Hieronymo pointedly creates by having the actors in his final production all speak their parts in different foreign languages. Their failure to understand each other and the audience's failure to understand any of them increases the likelihood that no one will see his intent in time to stop the murders. Eliot's conclusion in lines in various languages plays on Hieronymo's.

85. Cf. Jonathan Freedman, "Autocanonization: Tropes of Self-Legitimation in Popular Culture"; and Meisel, *The Myth of the Modern*, 93.

86. The editors of *The Norton Anthology of Modern Poetry* attribute identification of the "Shakespearian Rag" as "an actual ragtime song which was a hit of Ziegfield's follies of 1912" to Bruce R. McElderry (*The Norton Anthology of Modern Poetry,* 463; cited in Bedient, *He Do the Police*, 97).

87. Andreas Huyssen notes in a related context that attempts to blur the boundary between high and low culture have tended rather to enforce the dichotomy (Huyssen, *After the Great Divide: Modernism, Mass Culture, Postmodernism,* vii).

88. Eliot, *The Waste Land: A Facsimile,* 127.

89. Both Peter Ackroyd and Grover Smith take this attribution for granted. "Accepting [section 2's] portrayal of herself and its mimicry of her mannerisms and nervous *staccato* outbursts, [Vivien Eliot] called the effect 'wonderful' in the comments she jotted on the [manuscript]" (Smith, *The Waste Land*, 69). Ackroyd explains what might seem to be Vivien Eliot's oddly friendly response to her husband's characterization of her as the result of the couple's self-acceptance: "No nervous, anxious woman who saw herself mirrored in such a passage would write in this manner, and it is more likely to be the case that Eliot and Vivien were quite aware of their nervous predicament, recognizing the effect which it had upon themselves and others, and were at this stage inclined to make a kind of game out of it. They both possessed a strong theatrical streak and the element of willed drama in their relationship was not entirely negligible" (Ackroyd, *T. S. Eliot: A Life*, 115).

90. Eliot, *The Waste Land: A Facsimile*, 125–26.

91. Eliot, *The Waste Land: A Facsimile*, 27. Gilbert explores Eliot's portrayal of women in the early version of *The Waste Land* in her "Costumes of the Mind: Transvestism as Metaphor in Modern Literature," 202–6.

92. For further exploration of this creative dichotomy, see my discussion of *Paradise Lost* in chapter 4.

93. Cf. Gilbert and Gubar, *The War of the Words,* and Gilbert, "Costumes of the Mind."

94. Ackroyd, *T. S. Eliot: A Life*, 19–20.

95. Headnote to *The Waste Land.*

96. Hugh Kenner, *The Pound Era*, 59.

97. This is not to say that the story might not be told otherwise; only that however it works out, the characters are defined in their relation to one another.

Chapter 3

1. Cf., for example, J. Hillis Miller, *Poets of Reality;* Joseph Riddel, *The Inverted Bell: Modernism and the Counterpoetics of William Carlos Williams;* Vera M. Kutzinsky, *Against the American Grain: Myth and History in William Carlos Williams, Jay Wright, and Nicolás Guillén;* Terence Diggory, *William Carlos Williams and the Ethics of Painting;* and Brian Bremen, *William Carlos Williams and the Diagnostics of Culture.*

2. Jessica Benjamin, *The Bonds of Love: Psychoanalysis, Feminism, and the Problems of Domination.*

3. Bremen, *William Carlos Williams and the Diagnostics of Culture.* I am indebted to Bremen's work for aligning Williams and Benjamin. Before reading his book, I had developed an understanding of Williams's work as involving a revision of the oedipal pattern, but I had not connected it with Benjamin.

4. That volume collects accounts of moments and characters from New World history (including Eric the Red, Cortéz and Montezuma, de Soto, Washington, frontierswomen, the advent of slavery, Poe, and Lincoln) to reflect the complexity of the history-writing process. Not only did Williams's stress on things American in *In the American Grain* speak against the explicitly nostalgic Eurocentrism of *The Waste Land*, but his selection of a nonstandard set of American forefathers (and a few foremothers) challenged the notion of canon and its exclusionary assumptions much more insistently than did Eliot's introduction of an alternative literary canon. Williams's quotations further complicated the issues raised by his challenge to canon by suggesting a breakdown in the distinction between literary and nonliterary works and by bringing into question the notion of authority per se, since control of the words belonged much less clearly than with *The Waste Land* to the man whose name appeared on the cover.

5. Meryl Altman explores another dimension of Williams's ambivalence—this time toward Europe—in "The Clean and the Unclean: William Carlos Williams, Europe, Sex and Ambivalence."

6. Williams, *Kora in Hell*, 26–27.

7. Williams, *The Autobiography of William Carlos Williams*, 174.

8. Williams, *In the American Grain*, 226.

9. As Hugh Kenner points out, Williams began responding to *The Waste Land* in his writing within weeks of its publication. His manifesto "The Traditionalists of Plagiarism" (a very Poe-like title) responds condemningly (though elliptically) to Eliot's use of quotation, which suggested to Williams a rejection of the "New World's immediacies, the real language of men, audible in Rutherford," for a recovery of the European past (Kenner, *A Homemade World: The American Modernist Writers*, 61–67).

10. Williams, *Paterson*, 3. All further references to this edition *(P)* will appear in the text.

11. This lameness reappears in the closing passage of book 1, where a paragraph from John Addington Symonds's *Studies of the Greek Poets* expounds on choliambics ("lame or limping iambics"), which were by doing "the utmost violence to the rhythmical structure" meant "to bring the meter still more within the sphere of prose and common speech" (*P*, 40).

12. Further on, in book 1 of *Paterson,* the choices of "the rest" are contrasted again with Williams's own:

> Moveless
> he envies the men that ran
> and could run off
> toward the peripheries —
> to other centers, direct —
> for clarity (if
> they found it)
>   loveliness and
> authority in the world —
> a sort of springtime
> toward which their minds aspired
> but which he saw,
> within himself — ice bound
> (*P*, 36)

13. Kutzinski, *Against the American Grain,* 3–46.
14. Kutzinski, *Against the American Grain,* 18.
15. Kutzinski, *Against the American Grain,* 18.
16. Kutzinski, *Against the American Grain,* 46.
17. Kutzinski too suggests that *Paterson* is less avant garde than *In the American Grain* (Kutzinski, *Against the American Grain,* 26).
18. Williams describes his first book of poems, a pamphlet printed up by a friend in 1909, as "bad Keats, nothing else — oh well, bad Whitman too" (*Autobiography*, 107).
19. Williams, *Autobiography*, 60.
20. In reading this passage, J. Hillis Miller emphasizes the "seeking a home that was his own" element of this search. He understands Williams to describe a search for a truly American place, and the barbarous land to be the Europeanized America (Miller, *Poets of Reality*, 286). I do not contest this reading. Miller's reading describes a vision Williams is moving toward, mine the ground he moves from, and they both may be understood to operate here.
21. *The Wanderer* is, as others have noted, also a rewriting of *Hyperion* and *The Fall of Hyperion*, poems in which Keats too rewrote *Endymion*. See, for instance, Carl Rapp, *William Carlos Williams and Romantic Idealism*.
22. In a letter to Marianne Moore that suggests similarly the process of coming to terms with his American "exile," Williams describes a kind of conversion experience to an "inner security," made at about the time of the destruction of his pseudo-*Endymion:* "[This security] is something which occurred once when I was about twenty, a sudden resignation to existence, a despair — if you wish to call it that, but a despair which made everything a unit and at the same time a part of myself. I suppose it might be called a sort of nameless religious experience. I resigned, I gave up" (Williams, *Selected Letters*, 147).

23. Williams, *The Wanderer*, in *The Collected Poems of William Carlos Williams,* vol. 1, 27–28.

24. Williams, *In the American Grain*, 216.

25. That it is nonetheless present as an underlying concern is suggested a little later in the same essay, when mention of this third sense of originality—as primacy—emerges in rather obscure form:

> On [Poe] is FOUNDED A LITERATURE—typical; an anger to sweep out the unoriginal, that became ill-tempered, a monomaniacal driving to destroy, to annihilate the copied, the slavish, the FALSE literature about him: this is the major impulse in his notes . . . He declares, maintains himself, presupposes himself and IS first rate. FIRST!—madly, valiantly battling for the right to be first—to hold up his ORIGINALITY—(Williams, *In the American Grain*, 223)

The brief modulation from "first rate" into "first" and then back into the severally defined "originality" suggests that in spite of the many statements of the importance of local origins, a desire to obliterate the past and to claim a temporal primacy still operates in Williams, who attributes to Poe all that he desires for and believes of himself.

26. Williams, *In the American Grain*, 231.

27. Williams, *In the American Grain*, 225, 230–31.

28. Barbara Johnson, "The Frame of Reference: Poe, Lacan, Derrida," 110.

29. Williams, *In the American Grain*, 225.

30. E. P. Bollier, "Against the American Grain: William Carlos Williams between Whitman and Poe," 133.

31. The block of text describing a doctor more concerned with the label on a mayonnaise jar than with his patients (*P*, 33) would seem to be such an instance.

32. These falls into the falls, in their punning excess of signification, literalize the perversion of language—the movement from direct, single meanings to ambiguous, double meanings—that follows from the fall in Eden, at least as Milton represents it. Williams carries the point even further when he tells us that he means us to pay special attention to the pun here by punning again, and pointedly, in the first line of his commentary on the Cumming quotation: "A false language. A true. A false language pouring—a language (misunderstood) pouring (misinterpreted) without dignity, without minister, crashing upon a stone ear." But he tells us as well here that his judgment of the value of this false/falls language differs from the standard (he calls it "A true" language on second thought), suggesting that reinterpretation of the fall, not condemnation, is the appropriate response. Thomas R. Whitaker notes that *Paterson*'s "vital complexity . . . might be called Williams's version of the 'fortunate fall'" (Whitaker, *William Carlos Williams*, 133).

33. Here is an example to demonstrate the general style of Williams's redoings of historical texts:

Original: "It took the dean but a moment to evolve a plan which promised success to his endeavors to restore peace. Taking Dalzell by the arm, in full view of the infuriated mob, he led the man to the hack and, seating himself by his side, ordered the driver to proceed. The crowd hesitated, bewildered between the bravery of the dean and his display of Christian charity . . ." (William Nelson and Charles A. Shriner, *History of Paterson and Its Environs [The Silk City]*, 501).

On page 46 of *Paterson*, Williams redoes sentence one, adds a sentence two to give facts, then keeps the rest verbatim: "In a moment the Dean set on a plan. He proceeded to the scene in a hack. Taking Dalzell by the arm, in full view of the infuriated mob, he led the man to the hack and seating himself by his side, ordered the driver to proceed. The crowd hesitated, bewildered between the bravery of the Dean and ."

The several paragraphs that precede this one are taken from an essay in the *Prospector* describing the same event (*Prospector* 2, 33 [12 November 1936]: 5).

34. Williams had initially planned to include material from the prodigious letters of David Lyle—a self-appointed distiller of the flow of mass-media information—as a masculine counterpart to the Nardi letters.

35. Williams, *Paterson* Manuscript, 187, p. 106; further citations from this collection will be indicated (Yale) in the text.

36. That Williams's poetry reflects his contact in the teens and twenties with avant-garde artists of a number of schools, including dadaists and surrealists as well as cubists, has been argued by several critics, who generally understand that his radicalness inheres in his reflection of that influence. Cf. Bram Dijkstra, *the hieroglyphics of a new speech: Cubism, Stieglitz, and the Early Poetry of William Carlos Williams;* James E. B. Breslin, *William Carlos Williams: An American Artist;* Dickran Tashjian, *William Carlos Williams and the American Scene, 1920–1940;* William Marling, *William Carlos Williams and the Painters, 1909–1923;* and Peter Schmidt, *William Carlos Williams, the Arts, and Literary Tradition*.

37. These lines come (slightly rearranged) from a poem within Aragon's novel *Le Paysan de Paris*, 68–69.

Les Réalités
Fable

Il y avait une fois une réalité
Avec ses moutons en laine réelle
Le fils du roi vint à passer
Les moutons bêlent Qu'elle est belle
La ré la ré la réalité

Il y avait une fois dans la nuit
Une réalité qui ne parvenait pas à dormir
Alors la fée sa marraine
La prit réellement par la main
La ré la ré la réalité

Il y avait une fois sur son trône
Un vieux roi qui s'ennuyait
Son manteau dans le soir glissait
Alors on lui donna pour reine
La ré la ré la réalité .

CODA: Ité ité la réa

Ité ité la réalité
La réa la réa
Té té La réa .
Li
Té La réalité
Il y avait une fois LA RÉALITÉ .

38. Peter Schmidt distinguishes between Williams's cubist and dadaist influences along lines similar to those I have employed here in distinguishing between Williams's hierarchic and antihierarchic impulses. Where both cubists and dadaists employ collage, Schmidt sees the cubists' use as defined by careful composition, on principles similar to those Williams outlines in his note to himself on how to present his quotations, cited above. Dada, on the other hand, is dedicated to decomposition, and he finds its influence on Williams expressed in the poem's insistence on burning down the library (all art of the past is dead art and must be destroyed) and in its refusals to impose harmonies on its diverse and divergent materials. See Schmidt, *William Carlos Williams, the Arts, and Literary Tradition*.

Williams points to his dadaist connections specifically in invoking Antonin Artaud in the collection of phrases, some borrowed some not, set slantwise on a page to evoke the look of ads and notices pasted beside and across each other on a billboard or in a collage painting (an effect that the cubist Apollinaire had achieved several decades earlier in his poem "SP"): "Salut à Antonin Artaud pour les / lignes, trés pures" (*P*, 137). In book 5, Williams rejects the dadaist connection with its predictions of the end of art: "What has happened / since Soupault gave him the novel / the Dadaist novel / to translate—/ *The Last Nights of Paris*. / 'What has happened to Paris / since that time? / and to myself'? // A WORLD OF ART / THAT THROUGH THE YEARS HAS // *SURVIVED*!" (*P*, 209). Cf. Philippe Soupault, *Last Night of Paris*.

39. The term is Henry Sayre's. See Sayre, *The Visual Text of William Carlos Williams*.

40. This reading seems first to have been offered by James E. B. Breslin in *William Carlos Williams: An American Artist*.

41. Perloff, *The Poetics of Indeterminacy: Rimbaud to Cage*, 151.

42. Chaucer appears again, much further on (*P*, 177), when he is made (via a rather confusing analogy, based on a misidentification of the speaker—the lines quoted are spoken by the Host to Sir Thopas) to condemn his own poetry:

Sir Thopas (The Canterbury Pilgrims) says (to Chaucer)
Namoor—
Thy drasty rymyng is not
worth a toord
—and Chaucer seemed to think so too for he stopped and went .
on in prose . .

Chaucer's lines are made here to authorize Williams's own "inelegant" style as well as his combinings of poetry and prose.

43. Gale C. Schricker, "The Case of 'Cress': Implications of Allusion in *Paterson*," 27.

44. Joseph G. Kronick, *American Poetics of History: From Emerson to the Moderns*, 222.

45. This name is mentioned earlier in *Paterson*, in the historical summary on page 13.

46. John Slatin has pointed to the way in which Williams's uses of quotation in *In the American Grain* respond to Eliot in a manner borrowed from Moore. Slatin argues that Williams learns from Moore the value of quoting from earlier texts as a way of contacting the past in its pastness, and that he then goes on to seek out a specifically American past, where Moore sought to contact a more general religious tradition. While I will argue for a different understanding of Moore's purposes in employing quotation, the relation of influence does seem clear. See John M. Slatin, "American Beauty: William Carlos Williams and Marianne Moore," 63–66.

47. Mourning the old order that clearly separated rich and poor, Gray's poet looks back fondly on the poor's illiteracy as one of the marks of that separation (the names and dates on their headstones are misspelled). The account of the poet's death is set in the mouth of an old rustic of the sort admired here, who distinguishes between himself and the poem's reader at the close when he points out the poet's grave, saying "'Approach and read (for thou can'st read) the lay, / 'Graved on the stone beneath yon aged thorn.'" But the problem is exactly that the group invoked in the word "thou" is no longer so limited as the swain's distinction suggests; it includes not only the privileged few but, more and more frequently, the children of even such rustics as this speaker.

48. The passage plays on the alteration undergone by the word *nostalgia* on its entrance into English to make again the point of the inadequacy, even unavailability, of the past to the present. The Greek word *nostos*, which names Odysseus's journey home, resurfaces in modern English usage in the word *nostalgia* (excruciating desire or painful longing for home, from the Greek *nostos* + *algos*, desire, though the word was not coined until later, out of the Greek roots), whose operative sense Williams suggests here constitutes a perversion of etymological integrity, naming no longer a desire for a return to an actual home but, instead, a harking after a return to a world that is not and never has been our home. *Nostalgia* in English is, in this view, falsely defined and so, by definition, false. The mistransmission figures for Williams the very disappearance of the possibility of a return to a place of origin (a "place" which comes into existence specifically as a useful fiction, not at the point of leaving it, since its existence cannot be assumed ever to have obtained, but upon entrance into historical consciousness), the very fall into time and difference that modern nostalgia laments and that it is Williams's purpose to teach us to celebrate.

In setting the argument specifically in terms of Odysseus's nostos (a journey which the term describes quite properly), Williams makes the passage respond directly to what he perceives as Pound's nostalgia (and here the word *nostalgia* is invoked in all its inappropriate modernity), especially as communicated through his use of a long quotation from the *Odyssey* in the *Cantos*. Like Eliot, Pound is accused in *Paterson* of a nostalgic overvaluation of the past and a concomitant undervaluation of the present, though in Pound's case the accusation is made much more fondly.

49. Letter to Viola Baxter (later Viola Baxter Jordan), 6 January 1911, cited in Mike Weaver, *William Carlos Williams: The American Background*, 22.

50. Williams, *The Collected Poems of William Carlos Williams*, 40.

51. Williams, *In the American Grain*, 234.

52. Kutzinski too reads Williams's image of Lincoln as woman as a trope of his

(Williams's) own marginality and of that marginality as saving difference (see Kutzinski, *Against the American Grain,* 45).

53. By rewriting Whitman's portrait, Williams claims to reject Whitman's influence. But at the same time that it corrects Whitman, this portrait pays him tribute in the merger of the character Lincoln with suggestions of Whitman, in his role as Civil War nurse. (Cf. Bollier, "Against the American Grain," 136–40, and Kutzinski, *Against the American Grain,* 46.) Williams's page-long chapter on Lincoln, inserted at the request of his publisher after the manuscript had been submitted, builds on the similarly active suppression of reference to Whitman at work in the original closing chapter, which discusses Poe as the sole American writer of note.

54. Sandra M. Gilbert, "Purloined Letters: William Carlos Williams and 'Cress,'" 10–11.

55. Such endorsement of secondariness per se can only serve as a stage in the process of reinterpretation, however. If it becomes a goal in itself, the larger purpose of eliminating such categories is lost.

56. Huyssen, *After the Great Divide: Modernism, Mass Culture, Postmodernism,* 44–62.

57. Williams's biographer Paul Mariani treats the issue without much reflection (*William Carlos Williams: A New World Naked*). Henry Sayre speaks more provocatively, but imprecisely. Referring to Mariani's reading of Williams's decision to substitute a letter from Edward Dahlberg for one from Cid Corman in the final-letter position, Sayre writes:

> Mariani argues [that] "Williams moved the poem away from the subject of the transmission of the craft to one's sons to the more fundamental issue of the Woman: the hidden core of his poem finally revealing itself." But I think it is fair to argue that the so-called issue of the Woman and the subject of the transmission of the craft are really one and the same. The poem, Williams says, is no more than a "'passionate letter' / to a woman" (*P*, 230)—no more, that is, and no less. It is an opening out to "the Woman" and to poetic sons equally. The woman in the Dahlberg letter is meant to recall and echo Marcia Nardi's predicament and the risk she had taken in addressing Williams so intimately. (Sayre, *The Visual Text of William Carlos Williams,* 141–42)

But while he points to a linkage between "the Woman" and poetic sons, Sayre does not explore the nature of their connection.

58. "I don't need the *publication* of my poetry with your name lent to it," writes "Cress" (*P,* 88); "A. G." writes: "Dear Dr. Williams: Thanks for your introduction. The book is over in England being printed, and will be out in July sometime. Your foreword is personal and compassionate and you get the point of what has happened" (*P*, 212). Williams's essay accompanied a selection of Nardi's poems published in *New Directions* (7 [1942]: 413–14), under the title "A Group of Poems by Marcia Nardi: Introduction by William Carlos Williams, who discovered her." For Ginsberg he wrote two introductions, to *Howl* (San Francisco: City Lights Books, 1956) and *Empty Mirror* (New York: Totem, 1961).

59. This version of the sequence of events comes from Theodora R. Graham, "'Her

Heigh Compleynte': The Cress Letters of William Carlos Williams' *Paterson*"; and Elizabeth M. O'Neil, "Marcia Nardi: Woman of Letters."

60. Laughlin did not take Williams's suggestion, however. Nardi's first and only book, *Poems*, was published in 1956 by Alan Swallow (Denver) as part of his New Poetry Series (number 16).

61. Cited in O'Neil, "Marcia Nardi: Woman of Letters," 90.

62. Cf. Graham, "'Her Heigh Compleynte.'"

63. Mariani, *William Carlos Williams*, 463.

64. Cited in Weaver, *William Carlos Williams: The American Background*, 209.

65. Book 3 includes no such letters and book 4 introduces the very deferential A. G. (Allen Ginsberg), two of whose letters appear therein. In book 5 Ginsberg reappears, along with a letter from the novelist Josephine Herbst, a bit of a story presented as a letter from G. S. (Gilbert Sorrentino), and a final letter from Dahlberg.

66. Chaucer, "Wife of Bath's Tale," *Canterbury Tales*, in *The Complete Poetry and Prose of Geoffrey Chaucer*, 114, line 447.

67. In book 3, section 3, Williams quotes his mother, speaking of her home: "Let me see, Puerto Plata is / the port of Santo Domingo" (*P*, 136). Toward the end of book 5, in section 3, he quotes his grandmother Emily Dickenson Wellcome: "She was old when she saw her grandson: / You young people / think you know everything. / She spoke in her Cockney accent / and paused / looking at me hard: / The past is for those that lived in the past. Cessa!" (*P*, 238–39). He refers to this same phrase earlier, in book 4, section 3, as well: "'The past is for those who / lived in the past,' is all she told me" (*P*, 187). In book 4, section 2, Williams addresses his son, quoting his wife, Flossie: "(What I miss, said your mother, is the poetry, the pure poem / of the first parts .)" (*P*, 171).

68. Bremen, *William Carlos Williams and the Diagnostics of Culture*, 46, 170–77, 195.

69. Though Ginsberg seems to have felt that his homosexuality was an issue to avoid with Williams (Mariani points out that in "To WCW" [in *Indian Journal*] Ginsberg suggests that he lied to Williams and "told you I was never a fairy / when I was—didn't want to / shock yr palsied hand. . . ." [cited in Mariani, *William Carlos Williams*, 730]), my sense is that Williams was much more aware and less shockable than Ginsberg allowed. At any rate, within the poem the association of homosexuality with feminization of the male has clear parallels with the issues of gender realignment Williams explores in a less physical sphere, while the fact that the poet in question is in fact male makes the challenge to the system less radical and so less threatening.

70. Williams, *Autobiography*, 270.

71. This section is modeled in shape though not in theme on Edna St. Vincent Millay's play *Aria da Capo*, in favor of which Alfred Kreymbourg decided against mounting Williams's play *The Apple Tree* in 1917 (Gilbert, "Purloined Letters," 10; Mariani, *William Carlos Williams*, 154–55).

72. John Hollander points out that, in casting Corydon as a homosexual lover burning for an unresponsive beauty, Williams follows Virgil's lead. In *Eclogue II*, Corydon (the name is always masculine, and in adopting it here Williams's character indulges in a bit of linguistic cross-dressing) sings of his love for another male shepherd, Alexis,

knowing that he has no chance of success. While Corydon is often employed for heterosexual shepherds, it has a history of use as a name for homosexual pursuers.

73. Quoted in Mariani, *William Carlos Williams*, 616.

74. Fragment 31 in Sappho, *Poems*.

75. Catullus (in his "Ille mi paresse deo videtur") acknowledges his Sapphic source when he cloaks his lover Clodia Pulcher in the name Lesbia, a clear reference to Sappho's home. But any sense of respect this gesture might suggest is undermined by its second effect, for with it he also effectively erases Sappho's role as speaker of her own poem. The name Lesbia makes the beloved a figure for Sappho, transformed from lover (and speaker) to love object, while Catullus takes over the role she leaves. The turnaround figures powerfully the appropriation of the poetry involved here. Where Catullus substantially alters the poem's gender dynamic, Williams (whose poem no less than Catullus's employs Sappho's words, but in setting them off as a quotation makes it clear that they continue to be hers) sets up a comparison of his situation to hers without denying her the speaking place in her own work.

76. Eliot in *The Waste Land* also refers to Sappho, though in a deeply buried allusion brought to light through a note, rather than through a direct quotation (Eliot, *The Waste Land*, in *Collected Poems 1909–1962*, 61, 73, line 221 and note).

77. Sappho's name also appears at another point: "Woman is the weaker vessel, but the mind is neutral, a bead linking / continents, brow to toe / and will at best take out / its spate in mathematics / replacing murder / Sappho vs. Elektra" (*P*, 179–80). She seems to be cited here as example of a reasonable, thinking woman, and set in contrast to Elektra, a woman defined as dangerous because she puts her mind to work for emotional (or unreasonable) ends.

78. The passage goes on:

> for they were
> unwrapped, fragment by fragment, from
> outer mummy cases of papier mâché inside
> Egyptian sarcophagi
> flying papers
> from old conflagrations, picked up
> haphazard by the undertakers to make
> moulds, layer after layer
> for the dead
> (*P*, 119).

Chapter 4

1. See Appendix.

2. Marie Borroff, *Language and the Poet: Verbal Artistry in Frost, Stevens, and Moore,* 80.

3. Notes to "Sojourn in the Whale," in *The Complete Poems of Marianne Moore,* 276. Further references to this book will be abbreviated *CP* and noted in the text.

4. John M. Slatin's *The Savage's Romance: The Poetry of Marianne Moore* is the most important and extensive study of the role of Moore's nationality in her work.

5. The particularly relevant studies here are Sandra M. Gilbert and Susan Gubar, *The Madwoman in the Attic: The Woman Writer and the Nineteenth-Century Literary Imagination;* Margaret Homans, *Women Writers and Poetic Identity: Dorothy Wordsworth, Emily Brontë and Emily Dickinson;* and Alicia Ostriker, *Stealing the Language: The Emergence of Women's Poetry in America.*

6. The groundwork for this argument is laid in Andreas Huyssen, "Mass Culture as Woman: Modernism's Other," in *After the Great Divide: Modernism, Mass Culture, Postmodernism.*

7. Jessica Benjamin, *The Bonds of Love: Psychoanalysis, Feminism, and the Problem of Domination,* 112.

8. Margaret Holley, *The Poetry of Marianne Moore: A Study in Voice and Value,* 2.

9. The pun is also present in the Hebrew. The word *shmat* in Genesis 2 : 7, translatable as "soul," "breath," or "spirit," is also the root of the words meaning inspiration and aspiration. I am grateful to Charlotte Berkowitz for her etymological help as well as for her discussions of the ways in which issues of female creativity are treated in Genesis.

10. Harold Bloom, *The Anxiety of Influence: A Theory of Poetry,* 19–25.

11. Cf. my discussion of Milton in the chapter 1.

12. The problem with this dichotomy, of course, is that by the poem's own logic it cannot stand: a clear distinction between pre- and post-fall worlds works within the terms of stable meaning, terms which the poem denies as a possibility in the world in which it exists. And we do see this contradiction acknowledged and represented in the poem. Though we are told that meaning in Eden is stable and clear, Eve is able to interpret the prohibition in more than one way and imagines biting the apple. This suggests that she is fallen before the fall itself takes place, and so that meaning was open to deconstruction all along.

13. Charles Molesworth, *Marianne Moore: A Literary Life,* 229.

14. For instance, Mrs. Moore advised Marianne against publishing her first book of poems, saying it was not yet ready—advice which may have led to Moore's allowing the book to seem to have been published without her knowledge, by her friends Bryher and H. D. This kind of duplicity, which honors the authority of the prohibitor while going around it, puts Moore in the role of Satan or Eve in relation to her mother's rendition of God the Father.

15. Elizabeth Bishop, *The Collected Prose,* 129.

16. Holley, *The Poetry of Marianne Moore,* 77.

17. Holley, *The Poetry of Marianne Moore*, 76.

18. Bishop, *Collected Prose*, 129.

19. Moore, *Selected Poems by Marianne Moore,* 108.

20. Laurence Stapleton, *Marianne Moore: The Poet's Advance,* 129–41. Moore's borrowings from her mother include the following:

Line 3, "They're fighting, fighting, fighting," was "We are fighting, fighting, fighting" in the notebook;

Lines 3–4, "the blind / man who thinks he sees," and lines 33–34, "nothing can be so defeating / as a blind man who / can see," come from Mrs. Moore's "None are so frightening as the blind who can see";

Lines 36–37, "O small dust of the earth / that walks so arrogantly," were "The dust of the earth that walks so arrogantly";

Lines 38–39, "faith is / an affectionate thing," were cited verbatim; and

Lines 73–74, "There never was a war that was not inward," evolved out of "War—there is one answer—the warfare within."

21. According to Moore, line 3 in "A Grave" ("it is human nature to stand in the middle of a thing") comes from Mary Warner Moore: "As for 'A Grave,' it has a significance apart from the literal origin, which was a man who placed himself between my mother and me, and surf we were watching from a middle ledge of rocks on Monhegan Island after a storm. ('Don't be annoyed,' my mother said. 'It is human nature to stand in the middle of a thing.')." (Cited in Bonnie Costello, *Marianne Moore: Imaginary Possessions*, 62.) Likewise, Moore's notebooks indicate that Mrs. Moore is the source of the line "like Henry James 'damned by the public for decorum'; / not decorum, but restraint" in "An Octopus" (*CP*, 76). Mrs. Moore, commenting on Carl Van Doren's *The American Novel*, said:

> He says what damns James w[ith] the public is his decorum—It isn't his decorum it's his self control, his restraint[,] his ability to do hard things w[ith] suavity. It wears them out. (Cited in Patricia C. Willis, "The Road to Paradise: First Notes on Marianne Moore's 'An Octopus,'" 259.)

In the same notebook, Moore quotes Mrs. Moore saying "The deepest feeling ought to show itself in restraint." This line reappears, slightly revised, in "Silence" as "The deepest feeling always shows itself in silence; / not in silence, but restraint." Holley attributes the title "The Mind Is an Enchanting Thing" to Mrs. Moore (Holley, *The Poetry of Marianne Moore,* 78); and Molesworth credits her as first speaker of the phrase "The power of the visible is the invisible" in "He 'Digesteth Harde Yron'" (Molesworth, *Marianne Moore: A Literary Life*, 307–8, 401). In a letter to Hildegarde Watson, Moore credits her mother with a phrase from "What Are Years": "'Satisfaction is a lowly thing how pure a thing is joy.' (I got the idea from Mole.) Am worse than a rodent about appropriating,—as you know" (cited in Jeredith Merrin, *An Enabling Humility: Marianne Moore, Elizabeth Bishop, and the Uses of Tradition,* 135).

22. Holley, *The Poetry of Marianne Moore*, 156. Other evidence of their bond and of the profound loss Moore suffered upon her mother's death comes in Bryher's descriptions of visits to Moore in letters to H. D. When Mary Warner Moore became ill in the 1940s, Moore ate only what her mother could. Bryher found this most upsetting:

> She terrified me, she was so very queer about her mother. The mother was thought to be dying of cancer and in such agony Marianne wanted the Dr. to do something, as the mother could neither eat nor speak, and could eat nothing, because she could not eat if Mother could not eat, and thus got rashes and kidney trouble and pains. Now she will only eat her mother's diet—raw vegetable juice. Really I was frightened about Marianne. (Cited in Molesworth, *Marianne Moore: A Literary Life*, 323.)

Molesworth reports that "[a]fter her mother's death, Moore experienced some troubled days. She mentioned to Bryher in January, 1948, that she had recently spent fifteen days in bed, and that she felt an attack of pneumonia a year or two previous had made her very susceptible to temperature. Though the time spent with friends . . . was restorative, Moore wrote to her brother about her feelings of grief and weakness" (Molesworth, *Marianne Moore: A Literary Life*, 337).

23. Holley suggests that Mary Warner Moore made sure that Moore sent out only polished poems, and that after her mother's death Moore's work suffered from the lack of censorship (Holley, *The Poetry of Marianne Moore*, 156).

24. Holley writes of Mary Warner Moore that "[s]he was always supportive of Marianne's literary ambitions, even when she was severe about individual poems. She had strong personal and literary tastes, the core of which might be understood as a disdain for the facile" (Holley, *The Poetry of Marianne Moore*, 76).

25. Slatin accounts for Moore's expanded use of quotation after 1922 with two arguments. He reads it as a response to Eliot's modeling of the device in *The Waste Land*, and suggests as well that the lesson came fortuitously at the point at which Moore began trying to accommodate readers by abandoning syllabic verse, a characteristic of her work that had provided her with both a distinctive voice and the protection from the public eye that she now sought to circumvent. Extensive quotation gave her a new distinction, while making her text more approachable. (See Slatin, *The Savage's Romance*, 99–103.) This reading is helpful, but it fails to account for the fact that quotation was a feature of her work from the beginning.

26. In fact, Moore's restraint is doubled, for she, characteristically, takes her quotations not directly from their first speaker, but from secondary sources. Cf. the specific discussion of mediation in the notes, further on.

27. Bonnie Costello discusses these issues at length in *Marianne Moore: Imaginary Possessions*.

28. In *Stealing the Language*, Alicia Ostriker discusses similar transformations of existing structures in the works of more recent women poets.

29. Moore's poems having to do with armored or otherwise well-protected animals include "Black Earth," "The Plumet Basilisk," "The Fish," "In the Days of Prismatic Color," "An Octopus," "Sea Unicorns and Land Unicorns," "He 'Digesteth Harde Yron,'" "The Pangolin," "The Paper Nautilus," "Elephants," "The Icosasphere," "His Shield," "Armor's Undermining Modesty," "Like a Bulwark," "O to Be a Dragon," "To a Chameleon," and "A Jelly-Fish."

30. Women poets before Moore had remarked on the obstacles the quest myth put in their path. Christina Rossetti's *The Prince's Progress,* for example, provides a particularly clear statement of the problem.

31. While the Burke line too was initially a remark and not part of a literary text, it has since acquired a literary pedigree in having been cited in Prior's biography of Burke, which is then cited in the note.

32. An early version of "Silence" includes after the three lines of the sentence about superior people the remark: "You are not then so grateful to them / when they go away" (Moore, "Silence" Manuscript).

33. John Slatin makes similar points about the poem's structure, though he does not discuss the poem as emblematic of Moore's use of quotation in general. See Slatin, *The Savage's Romance*, 150–55.

34. Henry Wadsworth Longfellow, *The Complete Poetical Works*, 108.

35. The two phrases share a structure of opposition: where Longfellow's line works with the pattern "X, not Y," Moore's runs it backwards as "not Y, X." The structure of Moore's sentence as a whole, "Y, not Y, X," where "X" qualifies "Y" slightly but importantly, rather than opposing it directly, evidently pleased her, for she employs it in at least two other poems of the period as well: "with its silence—not its silence but its silences" ("Marriage," *CP*, 64); and "like Henry James, 'damned by the public for decorum'; / not decorum, but restraint" ("An Octopus," *CP*, 76).

36. Emerson, "Nature," in *Selections from Ralph Waldo Emerson*, 21.

37. Emerson, *Selections from Emerson*, 271.

38. Emerson, "Quotation and Originality," in *Complete Works of Ralph Waldo Emerson*, 190.

39. Emerson, "Quotation and Originality," 170.

40. Cf. discussion in chapter 1.

41. Of the 170 pairings of quotation marks and notes in *The Complete Poems of Marianne Moore*, there are 26 in which the line borrowed is reprinted in the note and corresponds exactly to the set-off phrase within the poem. Forty-five notes to set-off phrases give evidence of some reworking. Eleven phrases include the original exactly but add to that something of Moore's own, which is also set within the marks. Eighty-eight notes give attribution but do not cite the original. Research into the sources of these lines suggests that many of the 88 also have been reworked.

The examples that follow are representative of Moore's reworkings of quotations:

> *Quotation* as given in "Novices": "The smell of the cypress strengthens the nerves of the brain" (*CP*, 60, line 13);
>
> *Original* of quotation, as given in note: "The cypress too seems to strengthen the nerves of the brain." Landor, "Petrarca," in *Imaginary Conversations* (*CP*, 270).
>
> *Quotation* as given in "Camellia Sabina": "born / of nature and of art" (*CP*, 17, lines 35–37);
>
> *Original* of quotation, as given in note: " . . . In France you eat grapes which have ripened for the table. They are a product at once of nature and of art" (*CP*, 263).
>
> *Quotation* from "Light Is Speech": "The word France means / enfranchisement; means one who can / animate whoever thinks of her" (*CP*, 98, lines 34–38);
>
> *Original* of quotation, from source cited in note ("Janet Flanner, 'Paradise Lost,' *Decision*, January 1941" [*CP*, 277]): "As a matter of fact, so salubrious was the pulse of France that she could still animate anyone who so much as thought of her, in a particular way, even at a nostalgic distance."

42. Moore's association of Emerson and Burke continues in "The Student," a poem which builds on Emerson's "American Scholar" essay. Three borrowings of (altered) Emersonian phrases are noted, and a modification of a line from Burke, noted but not

set in quotes, follows soon after. A third quotation from Burke cited in Moore's notes comes in "Marriage."

43. Willis, "The Road to Paradise," 259.

44. Joanne Feit Diehl, *Women Poets and the American Sublime,* 82.

45. Slatin, *The Savage's Romance*, 46.

46. In addition to these attributions, the notes include 36 statements of fact and 3 authorial comments on the poems, for a total of 317 notes.

47. Moore did not set the line in quotes until the *Collected Poems* (1951) version, but she did add marks by hand to her copies of *Poems* (1921) and *Selected Poems* (1935) (at what point is not clear), suggesting that she felt they should have been there all along. See *Marianne Moore Newsletter* 1.1 (spring 1977): 21.

48. Moore's appeal to Blake's model here follows up on a more explicit acknowledgment of influence in an early, uncollected poem called "Blake" (*Others* 1.6 [December 1915]: 105).

49. Personal communication, recorded in Holley, *The Poetry of Marianne Moore*, 63.

50. Moore, *Observations,* 24; further references to this volume will be indicated with *Obs.* and given in the text.

51. Bishop, *Collected Prose*, 129.

52. Elizabeth Bishop describes how Moore's conversation with her mother was marked by quotations: "Marianne once gave me her practical rules for the use of indecent language. She said, 'Ordinarily, I would never use the word *rump*. But I can perfectly well say to Mother, "Mother, there's a thread on your *rump*," because *she* knows that I'm referring to Cowper's pet hare, "Old Tiney," who liked to play on the carpet and "swing his rump around!"'" (Bishop, *Collected Prose*, 129).

53. Antoine Compagnon, *La seconde main, ou le travail de la citation,* 230.

54. Holley, *The Poetry of Marianne Moore*, 69.

55. *Marianne Moore Newsletter* 1.1 (spring 1977): 20.

56. The extent of alterations seems to have no bearing on whether Moore sets a phrase in quotation marks or not. Moore's notes in *The Complete Poems* inform us that (approximately) 78 additional phrases, which are not set in quotation marks, are also taken from other sources. Most of these unmarked quotes are rephrased when they are taken into a poem. In the notes to "The Student," we are told that the lines "Wolf's wool is the best of wool, / but it cannot be sheared, because / the wolf will not comply . . ." (*CP*, 102, lines 37–39) are a reworking of Edmund Burke's comment, "There is excellent wool on the back of a wolf and therefore he must be sheared. . . . But will he comply?" (*CP*, 278). In "Marriage," the passage

> able to write simultaneously
> in three languages—
> English, German and French—
> and talk in the meantime
> (*CP*, 62, lines 25–28)

is taken, according to the notes, from an article in *Scientific American* that describes a "Miss A— [who] will write simultaneously in three languages, English, German, and French, talking in the meantime" (*CP*, 271). The variation between original and "quotation" is no greater in these examples than in many of the instances where quotation marks do set off the borrowed lines in the poem. In at least one instance a direct quotation is unmarked. The note to "Four Quartz Crystal Clocks" tells us that the title is taken directly from a leaflet published by the Bell Telephone Company (*CP*, 280). Though eleven of the poem titles in *Complete Poems* are set in quotation marks, this one is not.

57. The work of Moore's archivists has revealed many instances of phrases taken from other sources but not noted or set in quotes. For example, the passage

> His sweet face and powerful feet go about
> in chieftain's coat of Chilcat cloth.
> He is his own protection from the moth . . .
> (*CP*, 127, lines 9–11)

in "The Wood-Weasel," which goes unannotated in all versions, derives from an article by S. Hall Young on Chilcat blankets. One paragraph in particular serves as basis for Moore's lines:

> The splendid chieftain's robe shown in the picture could not be obtained now for less than three or four hundred dollars. These robes were handed down from uncle to nephew, and were packed in yellow cedar boxes, with great care to protect them from the moths. ("The Wood-Weasel," *Marianne Moore Newsletter* 4.1 [spring 1980]: 6)

Moore recorded the reference in a diary, "material for wood-weasel! S. Hall Young on the famous Chilcat blanket" (ibid., 5). While the phrasing is certainly altered, it is no more changed than many of the examples to which she did give references.

This same sort of discovery has been made about the passage

> if you demand on the one hand,
> the raw material of poetry in
> all its rawness . . .
> (*CP*, 267, lines 25–27)

from the "longer version" of "Poetry." The editors of the *Marianne Moore Newsletter* tell us that Moore saved a clipping of a *Spectator* review, written by "C," of *Ancient Gems in Modern Settings* by G. B. Grundy. Discussing the continuing charm of the Greek Anthology, "C" writes "All [of the poems] appeal to emotions which endure for all time, and which, it has been aptly said, are the raw material of poetry" ("On Raw Material," *Marianne Moore Newsletter* 1.2 [fall 1977]: 10–11). Though "C" does not say where he found the phrase, Moore surely knew where she did. Yet the phrase stands unmarked and without note.

58. Hugh Kenner, *A Homemade World: The American Modernist Writers*, 98–99.

59. Costello, *Marianne Moore: Imaginary Possessions*, 185. Eliot and Moore are alike, however, along with Williams, in employing quotations and notes, in one respect at least, to stake their own claims to particular kinds of authority through reference to particular kinds of texts. Within the frame of that claim process, none of the texts quoted by any of these poets are important in themselves; instead they are invoked for their cultural penumbra. While Eliot's borrowings refer us to a world of literature we may have read and which we can infer he wants us to believe we should read (or should have read), Moore's borrowings refer us to texts we are unlikely to know individually but likely are familiar with in a general way. And in these she too asks us to recognize value.

60. Holley, *The Poetry of Marianne Moore*, 72.

61. Moore remarks on this unwillingness in "Saint Nicholas," a wish-list poem, in which each item named is desired only insofar as it seems unlikely that it can be obtained. The final item is a painting by Hans von Marées, of Saint Hubert kneeling beside his horse and before an apparition of Christ in the horns of a stag he had been hunting. The story interests Moore for the transformation of Hubert from a killer of animals into a respecter of animals who leaves them alone. And she rejoices not only in his abandonment of his intent to kill the stag, in whose tines the image of Christ appears, but in the fact that he has got down from his horse, freeing this second animal from cruel rule as well. Moore admires the painting but requests "Not the original, of course. Give me / a postcard of the scene" (*CP*, 197). This mediated desire plays on a fact from the real world—a friend had sent her just such a postcard and pleased her greatly. But it points as well to her preference for respectful distance in all contacts with things other—texts and images among them.

62. Cited in "New York: 'Accessibility to Experience,'" *Marianne Moore Newsletter* 4.1 (spring 1980): 13.

63. Dixon Scott, *Men of Letters* (London: Hodder and Stoughton, 1917), 96.

64. And the history of Moore's borrowing of the phrase may be even further mediated. She takes it from a letter written by her mother to her brother, in which Mrs. Moore cites Dixon Scott's use of James's phrase. See "New York: 'Accessibility to Experience,'" *Marianne Moore Newsletter* 4.1 (spring 1980): 14.

65. Nestor, "Fragment 129," *Greek Anthology*, vol. 3, 67.

66. Slatin, *The Savage's Romance*, 94–96, 265. I have argued elsewhere that the older Moore has been too often condescended to as a poet of diminished ironic capacity. See my "Stamps, Money, Pop Culture and Marianne Moore."

67. Willis, "The Road to Paradise," 261–62.

68. In the America of this poem even the trees (perhaps particularly as they represent knowledge of good and evil) are "more eloquent than elsewhere" (*CP*, 75, line 137).

69. So saying, her rash hand in evil hour
Forth reaching to the Fruit, she pluck'd, she eat;
Earth felt the wound, and Nature from her seat
Sighing through all her Works gave signs of woe,
That all was lost.
(*PL*, book 9, lines 780–84)

70. Diehl, *Women Poets and the American Sublime*, 71–85.

71. Randall Jarrell, "Her Shield."

72. Lynn Keller reads "Marriage" in ways sympathetic to this reading in "'For inferior who is free?': Liberating the Woman Writer in Marianne Moore's 'Marriage.'" I was introduced to Keller's essay as this book went to press.

73. In this he is very like the mother mollusc in "The Paper Nautilus," who "guards [the shell] / day and night; she scarcely eats until the eggs are hatched" (*CP*, 121).

74. Slatin, *The Savage's Romance*, 136–40.

75. Six of Moore's poems appeared in *The Egoist* in 1915, three of which included quotations ("To the Soul of 'Progress,'" "To a Steam Roller," and "Diligence Is to Magic as Progress Is to Flight") and three of which did not. Three more appeared in

1916, two with quotations ("'He Wrote the History Book,' It Said" and "Pedantic Literalist") and one without. Three more appeared in 1918, all without quotations. And in the same year, Eliot reviewed an anthology of poems published in *Others*, in which his own "Portrait of a Lady" had appeared, and spoke particularly of Moore. Three of the five poems representing her work in the *Others Anthology* included quotations ("To Statecraft Embalmed," "George Moore," and *"So far as the future is concerned, / 'Shall not one say, with the Russian philosopher, / "How is one to know what one doesn't know?"' / So far as the present is concerned. . . ."* [later retitled "The Past Is the Present"]).

76. Eliot, "Observations," *The Egoist* 5 (May 1918): 69.

77. "Na Audiart" responds to de Born's poem about his desire to make an ideal girl from a collection of physical parts taken from a set of ladies not perfect in themselves but each perfect in one aspect. The poem consists in a series of pleas to the various ladies. Pound's poem includes only Bertran's address to Audiart, the woman whose scorn of him set him on his quest and from whom he asks "the lineaments of the torse" for his patchwork ideal girl. The poem closes with a citation from de Born's poem ("Audiart / Que be-m vols mal" [Audiart who wishes me ill]), a displacement of a fragment of a beloved original that mimicks the speaker's expropriatory quest. Pound's poetic realization of de Born's attempt turns his poem into an address to de Born (Pound is to de Born as de Born was to Audiart), and the final citation again suggests a dialogue.

78. This poem was not published in Moore's lifetime, and for that reason the estate withholds permission to reprint. It can be found, however, in the *Marianne Moore Newsletter* 3.2 (fall 1979): 5.

79. "The Palette," though published on its own in *Poetry*, is the first section of the essay called "The Renaissance" (*Literary Essays of Ezra Pound,* 214–26).

80. Pound, *Literary Essays*, 216.

81. This reading of the effect of the Boyd line in Moore's poem differs from that of Slatin (27), who holds that the context in which Pound cites Boyd is not significant, except insofar as "The Palette" involves mention of Pound's interest in Chinese literature. Because his point is to emphasize Moore's desire to establish connections between her work and Pound's at a point in her career when she was almost entirely isolated from sympathetic readers, Slatin's account of this poem strains. While the whole premise of the poem obviously does work to mark a sympathy with Pound, Moore does not abandon an equally strong sense of her own difference.

82. Knowledge of *Rhoda Fleming* may add fruit, however: for instance, in the fact that the line Moore cites comes from a description of a sparring match between two friends (an analogy that would suggest that this is not an attempt at hagiography on Moore's part).

83. Slatin, *The Savage's Romance*, 10.

84. Eliot, *The Waste Land: A Facsimile and Transcript,* 7. The notes to this edition, written by Eliot's widow, tell us that though Pound does not remember definitely what he meant by this note, he is clear that he did not mean to refer to Marianne Moore. He suggests that he may have been invoking Tennyson's *Mariana*.

85. Cf. my "Stamps, Money, Pop Culture and Marianne Moore."

Bibliography

Ackroyd, Peter. *T. S. Eliot: A Life*. New York: Simon and Schuster, 1984.

Altman, Meryl. "The Clean and the Unclean: William Carlos Williams, Europe, Sex and Ambivalence." *The William Carlos Williams Review* 18.1 (spring 1992): 10–20.

Aragon, Louis. *Le Paysan de Paris*. Paris: Gallimard, 1926.

Arrowsmith, William. "Daedal Harmonies: A Dialogue of Eliot and the Classics." *Southern Review* 13 (1977): 1–47.

Bakhtin, M. M. *The Dialogic Imagination: Four Essays*. Austin: University of Texas Press, 1981.

Bedient, Calvin. *He Do the Police in Different Voices*. Chicago: University of Chicago Press, 1986.

Benjamin, Jessica. *The Bonds of Love: Psychoanalysis, Feminism, and the Problems of Domination*. New York: Pantheon Books, 1988.

Benjamin, Walter. "The Work of Art in the Age of Mechanical Reproduction." In *Illuminations*, 217–51. New York: Schocken, 1977.

Benstock, Shari. *Women of the Left Bank: Paris, 1900–1940*. Austin: University of Texas Press, 1986.

Beringause, A. F. "Journey through *The Waste Land*." *South Atlantic Quarterly* 50 (1957): 79–90.

Bishop, Elizabeth. *The Collected Prose*. New York: Farrar, Straus & Giroux, 1984.

Bloom, Harold. *The Anxiety of Influence: A Theory of Poetry*. New York: Oxford, 1973.

———. "Before Moses Was, I Am: The Original and the Belated Testaments." In *Modern Critical Views: The Bible*, 291–304. New Haven: Chelsea House, 1987.

———. *The Breaking of the Vessels*. Chicago: University of Chicago Press, 1982.

Bollier, E. P. "Against the American Grain: William Carlos Williams between Whitman and Poe." *Tulane Studies in English* 23 (1978): 123–42.

Borges, Jorge Luis. "Pierre Menard, Author of the *Quixote*." In *Labyrinths: Selected Stories and Other Writings*. New York: New Directions Books, 1964.

Borroff, Marie. *Language and the Poet: Verbal Artistry in Frost, Stevens, and Moore*. Chicago: University of Chicago Press, 1979.

Boyle, Marjorie O'Rourke. *Erasmus on Language and Method in Theology*. Toronto: University of Toronto Press, 1977.

Bradley, A. C. *A Commentary of Tennyson's In Memoriam*. London: Macmillan and Co., 1901.

Bremen, Brian. *William Carlos Williams and the Diagnostics of Culture*. New York: Oxford University Press, 1993.

Breslin, James E. B. *William Carlos Williams: An American Artist*. 1970; Chicago: University of Chicago Press, 1985.

Cave, Terence. "The Mimesis of Reading in the Renaissance." In *Mimesis: From Mirror to Method, Augustine to Descartes*, edited and with an introduction by John D. Lyons and Stephen G. Nichols, Jr., 155–59. Hanover, New Hampshire: University Press of New England for Dartmouth College, 1982.

Chaucer, Geoffrey. *The Complete Poetry and Prose of Geoffrey Chaucer*. Edited by John H. Fisher. New York: Holt, Rinehart and Winston, 1977.

Christ, Carol. *Victorian and Modern Poetics*. Chicago: University of Chicago Press, 1984.

Clementi, Sir Cecil, translator. *Pervigilium Veneris*. 3rd ed. Oxford: Basil Blackwell, 1936.

Coleridge, Samuel Taylor. *Poems*. Edited by John Beer. London: J. M. Dent & Sons Ltd, Everyman's Library, 1974.

Collins, John Churton. *Illustrations of Tennyson*. London: Chatto & Windus, 1891.

Compagnon, Antoine. *La seconde main, ou le travail de la citation*. Paris: Editions du Seuil, 1979.

Conrad, Bryce. "William Carlos Williams and Europe: The Trans-Atlantic Construction of America." *William Carlos Williams Review* 18.1 (spring 1992): 1–9.

Conti, Gian Biagio. *The Rhetoric of Imitation: Genre and Poetry Memory in Virgil and Other Latin Poets*. Ithaca: Cornell University Press, 1986.

Costello, Bonnie. *Marianne Moore: Imaginary Possessions*. Cambridge: Harvard University Press, 1981.

Dhaenens, Jacques. *Le destin d'Orphée: étude sur "El Desdichado" de Nerval*. Paris: Minard/Lettres Modernes, 1972.

Diehl, Joanne Feit. *Women Poets and the American Sublime*. Bloomington: Indiana University Press, 1990.

Diepeveen, Leonard. *Changing Voices: The Modern Quoting Poem*. Ann Arbor: University of Michigan Press, 1993.

Diggory, Terence. *William Carlos Williams and the Ethics of Painting*. Princeton: Princeton University Press, 1991.

Dijkstra, Bram. *the hieroglyphics of a new speech: Cubism, Stieglitz, and the Early Poetry of William Carlos Williams*. Princeton: Princeton University Press, 1969.

Driscoll, Kerry. *William Carlos Williams and the Maternal Muse*. Ann Arbor: UMI Research Press, 1987.

Eliot, T. S. "American Literature and the American Language." In *To Criticize the Critic and Other Writings*. New York: Farrar, Straus & Giroux, 1965.

———. *Collected Poems, 1909–1962*. New York: Harcourt, Brace & World, 1970.

———. "Milton I." In *On Poetry and Poets*. New York: Noonday/Farrar, Straus & Giroux, 1976. (First published as "A Note on the Verse of John Milton." In *Essays and Studies by the Members of the English Association*, vol. 21. Oxford: Clarendon, 1936.)

———. "Observations." *The Egoist* 5 (May 1918): 69.

———. "Philip Massinger." In *Selected Essays, 1917–1932*, revised edition. New York: Harcourt Brace Jovanovich, 1950.

———. *Poems, 1920*. New York: Knopf, 1920.

———. "Tradition and the Individual Talent." In *Selected Prose of T. S. Eliot*, edited and with an introduction by Frank Kermode, 37–44. New York: Harcourt Brace Jovanovich/Farrar, Straus & Giroux, 1975.

———. *The Waste Land: A Facsimile and Transcript of the Original Drafts Including the Annotations of Ezra Pound*. Edited by Valerie Eliot. New York: Harcourt Brace Jovanovich, 1971.

Emerson, Ralph Waldo. *Emerson's Complete Works*. Riverside edition. Vol. 7, *Letters and Social Aims*. Boston: Houghton Mifflin, 1899.

———. *Selections from Ralph Waldo Emerson*. Edited by Stephen E. Whicher. Boston: Houghton Mifflin, 1960.

Freedman, Jonathan. "Autocanonization: Tropes of Self-Legitimation in Popular Culture." *Yale Journal of Criticism* 1.1 (fall 1987): 203–17.

Fumaroli, Marc. *L'Age de l'Eloquence: Rhétorique et "res literaria" de la Renaissance au seuil de l'époque classique*. Geneva: Droz, 1980.

Gallo, Max. *The Poster in History*. New York: New American Library/Times Mirror, 1975.

Gilbert, Sandra M. "Costumes of the Mind: Transvestism as Metaphor in Modern Literature." In *Writing and Sexual Difference,* edited by Elizabeth Abel, 193–219. Chicago: University of Chicago Press, 1982.

———. "Purloined Letters: William Carlos Williams and 'Cress.'" *William Carlos Williams Review* 11.2 (fall 1985): 5–15.

Gilbert, Sandra M., and Susan Gubar. *The Madwoman in the Attic: The Woman Writer and the Nineteenth-Century Literary Imagination*. New Haven: Yale University Press, 1979.

———. *The War of the Words*. Vol. 1, *No Man's Land: The Place of the Woman Writer in the Twentieth Century*. New Haven: Yale University Press, 1988.

Graham, Theodora R. "'Her Heigh Compleynte': The Cress Letters of William Carlos Williams' *Paterson*." In *Ezra Pound & William Carlos Williams: The University of Pennsylvania Conference Papers*, edited by Daniel Hoffman, 164–93. Philadelphia: University of Pennsylvania Press, 1983.

Greek Anthology. Translated by W. R. Paton. London and New York: Heinemann and Putnam's, 1925.

Greene, Thomas. *The Light in Troy: Imitation and Discovery in Renaissance Poetry*. New Haven: Yale University Press, 1982.

Gregory, Elizabeth. "Stamps, Money, Pop Culture and Marianne Moore." *Discourse* 17.1 (fall 1994): 123–46.

Guillory, John. "The Ideology of Canon-Formation: T. S. Eliot and Cleanth Brooks." *Critical Inquiry* 10 (September 1983): 173–98.

———. *Poetic Authority: Spenser, Milton, and Literary History*. New York: Columbia University Press, 1983.

Guimond, James. *The Art of William Carlos Williams: A Discovery and Possession of America*. Urbana: University of Illinois Press, 1968.

Hartman, Geoffrey H. "Words, Wish, Worth: Wordsworth." In *Deconstruction and Criticism*, edited by Harold Bloom, et al., 177–216. New York: Seabury, 1979.

Havelock, Eric. *Preface to Plato*. Cambridge: Harvard University Press, 1963.

Heinzelman, Kurt. *The Economics of the Imagination*. Amherst: University of Massachusetts Press, 1980.

Hollander, John. *The Figure of Echo: A Mode of Allusion in Milton and After*. Berkeley: University of California Press, 1981.

Holley, Margaret. *The Poetry of Marianne Moore: A Study in Voice and Value*. New York: Cambridge University Press, 1987.

Homans, Margaret. *Women Writers and Poetic Identity: Dorothy Wordsworth, Emily Brontë, and Emily Dickinson*. Princeton: Princeton University Press, 1980.

Huyssen, Andreas. *After the Great Divide: Modernism, Mass Culture, Postmodernism*. Bloomington: Indiana University Press, 1986.

Jarrell, Randall. "Her Shield." In *Poetry and the Age*. New York: Knopf, 1953. Reprinted in *Marianne Moore: A Collection of Critical Essays*, edited by Charles Tomlinson. Englewood Cliffs, New Jersey: Prentice-Hall, 1969.

Jay, Gregory S. *Eliot and the Poetics of Literary History*. Baton Rouge: Louisiana State University Press, 1983.

Johnson, Barbara. "The Frame of Reference: Poe, Lacan, Derrida." In *The Critical Difference: Essays in the Contemporary Rhetoric of Reading*, 110–46. Baltimore: Johns Hopkins University Press, 1980.

Kearns, Cleo McNelly. "Eliot, Russell, and Whitman: Realism, Politics, and Literary Persona in *The Waste Land*." In *Modern Critical Interpretations: T. S. Eliot's "The Waste Land,"* 137–52. New Haven: Chelsea House, 1986.

Keller, Lynn. "'For inferior who is free?': Liberating the Woman Writer in Marianne Moore's 'Marriage.'" In *Influence and Intertextuality in Literary History*, edited by Jay Clayton and Eric Rothstein, 219–42. Madison: University of Wisconsin Press, 1991.

Kellett, E. E. *Literary Quotation and Allusion*. 1933; Port Washington, New York: Kennikat Press, 1969.

Kenner, Hugh. *A Homemade World: The American Modernist Writers*. New York: Knopf, 1975.

———. *The Pound Era*. Berkeley: University of California Press, 1971.

Koestenbaum, Wayne. *Double Talk: The Erotics of Male Literary Collaboration*. New York: Routledge, 1989.

Kronick, Joseph G. *American Poetics of History: From Emerson to the Moderns*. Baton Rouge: Louisiana State University Press, 1984.

Kutzinski, Vera M. *Against the American Grain: Myth and History in William Carlos Williams, Jay Wright, and Nicolás Guillén*. Baltimore: Johns Hopkins University Press, 1987.

Landauer, Bella. "Literary Allusion in American Advertising as Sources of Social History." *New York Historical Society Quarterly* 31.3 (July 1947): 148–59.

Larisch, Marie. *My Past: Reminiscences of the Courts of Austria and Bavaria; Together with the True Story of the Events Leading up to the Tragic Death of Rudolph, Crown Prince of Austria*. New York: G. P. Putnam's Sons, 1913.

Longfellow, Henry Wadsworth. *The Complete Poetical Works*. Boston: Houghton Mifflin, 1893.

MacFarland, Thomas. *Originality and Imagination*. Baltimore: Johns Hopkins University Press, 1985.

Mandelbaum, Allen, translator, *The Divine Comedy of Dante Alighieri: Purgatorio*. With notes by Laury Magnus, Allen Mandelbaum, and Anthony Oldcorn, with Daniel Feldman. New York: Bantam, 1984.

Mariani, Paul. *William Carlos Williams: A New World Naked*. New York: McGraw-Hill, 1981.

Marianne Moore: Woman and Poet. Edited by Patricia C. Willis. Orono: National Poetry Foundation, University of Maine Press, 1991.

Marianne Moore Newsletter, vols. 1–7 (1977–83).

Marling, William. *William Carlos Williams and the Painters, 1909–1923*. Athens: Ohio University Press, 1982.

McLuhan, Marshall. *The Mechanical Bride: Folklore of Industrial Man*. New York: Vanguard Press, 1951.

Meisel, Perry. *The Myth of the Modern: A Study in British Literature and Criticism after 1850*. New Haven: Yale University Press, 1987.

Menand, Louis. *Discovering Modernism: T. S. Eliot and His Context*. New York: Oxford University Press, 1986.

Merrin, Jeredith. *An Enabling Humility: Marianne Moore, Elizabeth Bishop, and the Uses of Tradition*. New Brunswick, New Jersey: Rutgers University Press, 1990.

Meyer, Herman. *The Poetics of Quotation in the European Novel*. Princeton: Princeton University Press, 1968.

Miller, J. Hillis. *Poets of Reality*. Cambridge: Harvard/Belknap, 1965.

Molesworth, Charles. *Marianne Moore: A Literary Life*. New York: Atheneum, 1990.

Moore, Marianne. *The Arctic Ox*. London: Faber and Faber, 1964.

———. *Collected Poems of Marianne Moore*. New York: Macmillan, 1951.

———. *The Complete Poems of Marianne Moore*. New York: Macmillan/Viking, 1981.

———. *Like a Bulwark*. New York: Viking, 1956.

———. *Nevertheless*. New York: Macmillan, 1944.

———. *O to Be a Dragon*. New York: Viking, 1959.

———. *Observations*. New York: Dial Press, 1924.

———. *The Pangolin and Other Verse*. London: Brendin, 1936.

———. *Poems*. London: Egoist Press, 1921.

———. *Selected Poems by Marianne Moore*. New York: Macmillan, 1935.

———. "Silence" Manuscript. (1:04:17). The Rosenbach Museum and Library, Philadelphia.

———. *Tell Me, Tell Me: Granite, Steel, and Other Topics*. New York: Viking, 1966.

———. *What Are Years*. New York: Macmillan, 1941.

Morris, George L. K. "Marie, Marie, Hold on Tight." *Partisan Review* 21 (March-April 1954): 231–33.

Musgrove, S. *T. S. Eliot and Walt Whitman*. Wellington: New Zealand University Press, 1952.

Nardi, Marcia. *Poems*. New Poetry Series (number 16). Denver: Alan Swallow, 1956.

Nash, Ralph. "The Use of Prose in 'Paterson.'" In *Perspective* 6.4 (autumn-winter 1953): 191–99.

Nelson, William, and Charles A. Shriner. *History of Paterson and Its Environs (The Silk City)*. Vol. 1 of 3. New York: Lewis Historical Publishing Co., 1920.

Nerval, Gérard de. *Poésies*, 7. Paris: Gallimard, 1964. Translation: *The Penguin Book of French Verse*. Vol. 3, *The Nineteenth Century*, edited by A. Hartly, 96. Baltimore: Penguin Books, 1967.

The Norton Anthology of Modern Poetry. Edited by Richard Ellmann and Robert O'Clair. New York: W. W. Norton, 1973.

O'Neil, Elizabeth M. "Marcia Nardi: Woman of Letters." In *Rossetti to Sexton: Six Women Poets at Texas*, 73–111. Austin: University of Texas/Harry Ransom Humanities Research Center, 1992.

Ostriker, Alicia. *Stealing the Language: The Emergence of Women's Poetry in America*. Boston: Beacon Press, 1986.

Owst, G. R. *Literature and Pulpit in Medieval England*. 2nd edition. New York: Barnes & Noble, 1966.

———. *Preaching in Medieval England: An Introduction to Sermon Manuscripts of the Period c. 1350–1450*. New York: Russell & Russell, 1965.

Oxford English Dictionary. 12 vols. Oxford: Clarendon, 1933.

The Penguin Book of Latin Verse. Edited by Frederick Brittain. Baltimore: Penguin, 1964.

Perloff, Marjorie. *The Poetics of Indeterminacy: Rimbaud to Cage*. Princeton: Princeton University Press, 1981.

Peterson, William S. *Interrogating the Oracle: A History of the London Browning Society*. Athens: Ohio University Press, 1969.

Phillippe, Charles-Louis. *Bubu de Montparnasse*. 1901; Paris: Garnier-Flammarion, 1978.

———. *Bubu de Montparnasse*. Translated by Laurence Vail. Paris: Crosby Continental Editions, 1932.

Plato. *The Republic*. Edited by Allan Bloom. New York: Basic Books, 1991.

Poggi, Christine. "Mallarmé, Picasso, and the Newspaper as Commodity." *Yale Journal of Criticism* 1.1 (fall 1987): 133–51.

Pound, Ezra. *The Letters of Ezra Pound*. Edited by D. D. Paige. New York: Harcourt, Brace, 1950.

———. *Literary Essays of Ezra Pound*. New York: New Directions, 1968.

Quintavalle, Carlo Arturo. "The Development of Poster Art." In *The Poster in History*, by Max Gallo, 217–24. New York: New American Library/Times Mirror, 1975.

Rapp, Carl. *William Carlos Williams and Romantic Idealism*. Hanover, New

Hampshire: Brown University Press/University Press of New England, 1984.

Riddel, Joseph. *The Inverted Bell: Modernism and the Counterpoetics of William Carlos Williams*. Baton Rouge: Louisiana State University Press, 1974.

Rieke, Alison. "'Quotation and Originality': Notes and Manuscripts to Louis Zukofsky's 'A.'" In *Lawrence, Jarry, Zukofsky: A Triptych,* edited by Dave Oliphant and Gena Dagel, 76–105. Austin: University of Texas Press, 1987.

Rossetti, Christina. *The Prince's Progress*. In *The Complete Poems of Christina Rossetti,* edited by R. W. Crump, vol. 1. Baton Rouge: Louisiana State University Press, 1979.

Rossetti, Dante Gabriel. *The Works of Dante Gabriel Rossetti*. Edited with preface and notes by William M. Rossetti. 1911; Reprint, Hildesheim and New York: Georg Olms Verlag, 1972.

Sappho. *Poems*. In *Poetarum Lesbiorum Fragmenta,* by Edgar Lobel and Denys Page. Oxford: Oxford University Press, 1963.

Sayre, Henry. *The Visual Text of William Carlos Williams*. Urbana: University of Illinois Press, 1983.

Schmidt, Peter. *William Carlos Williams, the Arts, and Literary Tradition*. Baton Rouge: Louisiana State University Press, 1988.

Schricker, Gale C. "The Case of 'Cress': Implications of Allusion in *Paterson*." *William Carlos Williams Review* 11.2 (fall 1985): 16–29.

Scott, Bonnie Kime, editor. *The Gender of Modernism: A Critical Anthology*. Bloomington: Indiana University Press, 1990.

Slatin, John M. "American Beauty: William Carlos Williams and Marianne Moore." In *WCW & Others,* edited by Dave Oliphant and Thomas Zigal, 49–73. Austin: Harry Ransom Humanities Research Center at the University of Texas, 1985.

———. *The Savage's Romance: The Poetry of Marianne Moore*. University Park: Pennsylvania State University Press, 1986.

Smith, Grover. *The Waste Land*. London: George Allen and Unwin, 1983.

Soupault, Philippe. *Last Night of Paris*. Translated by William Carlos Williams. Originally published in French, 1928; New York: Full Court, 1982.

Stapleton, Laurence. *Marianne Moore: The Poet's Advance*. Princeton: Princeton University Press, 1978.

Tashjian, Dickran. *William Carlos Williams and the American Scene, 1920–1940*. Berkeley: University of California Press, 1978.

Tennyson, Alfred, Lord. *The Poems of Tennyson*. Edited by Christopher Ricks. 2nd ed. London: Longman, 1987.

Thomson, James ("B. V."). *The City of Dreadful Night and Other Poems*. London: Bertram Dobell, 1910.

Weaver, Mike. *William Carlos Williams: The American Background*. Cambridge: Cambridge University Press, 1971.

Weston, Jessie. *From Ritual to Romance*. 1920; Garden City, New York: Doubleday, 1957.

Whitaker, Thomas R. *William Carlos Williams*. New York: Twayne Publishers, 1968.

White, Harold. *Plagiarism and Imitation during the Renaissance: A Study in Critical Distinctions*. Cambridge: Harvard University Press, 1935.

Whitman, Walt. *Leaves of Grass*. Edited by Harold W. Blodgett and Sculley Bradley. New York: Norton, 1965.

Wicke, Jennifer. *Advertising Fictions: Literature, Advertisement, & Social Reading*. New York: Columbia University Press, 1988.

Williams, Gordon. *Tradition and Originality in Roman Poetry*. Oxford: Clarendon, 1968.

Williams, William Carlos. *The Autobiography of William Carlos Williams*. 1951; New York: New Directions, 1967.

———. *The Collected Poems of William Carlos Williams*. Vol. 1. Edited by A. Walton Litz and Christopher MacGowan. New York: New Directions, 1986.

———. *In the American Grain*. 1925; New York: New Directions, 1967.

———. *Kora in Hell*. 1918; reprinted in *Imaginations*. New York: New Directions, 1970.

———. *Paterson*. New York: New Directions, 1963.

———. *Paterson* Manuscript. Collection of American Literature, Beinecke Rare Book and Manuscript Library, Yale University.

———. *Selected Letters*. Edited by John Thirlwall. 1957; New York: New Directions, 1984.

Willis, Patricia C. "The Road to Paradise: First Notes on Marianne Moore's 'An Octopus.'" *Twentieth-Century Literature* 30.2/3 (summer/fall 1984): 242–72.

Wimsatt, W. K. "Prufrock and Maud: From Plot to Symbol." *Yale French Studies* 9 (1952): 90–91.

Wordsworth, William. *Poetical Works*. Edited by Thomas Hutchinson and revised by Ernest de Selincourt. Oxford: Oxford University Press, 1981.

Index